THE
SACRED BOOKS OF THE EAST

Translated by
VARIOUS ORIENTAL SCHOLARS

Edited by
F. MAX MÜLLER

VOLUME 7

SACRED BOOKS OF THE EAST

(50 VOLUMES)

Series Editor : *F. Max-Müller*

ISBN: 978-81-208-0101-1 (Set)

These volumes of the Sacred Books of the East series include translations of all the most important works of the seven non-Christian religions that have exercised a profound influence on the civilisations of the continent of Asia. The Vedic Brahmanic system claims 21 volumes, Buddhism 10, and Jainism 2; 8 volumes comprise Sacred Books of the Parsis; 2 volumes represent Islam; and 6 the two main indigenous systems of China. Translated by twenty leading authorities in their respective fields, the volumes have been edited by the late F. Max Müller. The inception, publication and the compilation of these books cover almost 34 years.

I. BUDDHISM

Vol. 49: Buddhist Mahayana Texts (2 Parts)
Vol. 11: Buddhist Suttas
Vol. 10: The Dhammapada and Sutta Nipata
Vols. 35 & 36: The Questions of King Milinda (2 Parts)
Vol. 21: The Saddharma Pundarika or the Lotus of the True Law
Vols. 13, 17 & 20: Vinaya Texts (3 Parts)

II. CHINESE

Vol. 19: The Fo-Sho-Hing-Tsan-King
Vols. 3, 16, 27, 28, 39 & 40: The Sacred Books of China (6 Parts)

III. A GENERAL INDEX

Vol. 50: A General Index to the Names and Subject-matter of the Sacred Books of the East

IV. ISLAM

Vols. 6 & 9: The Qur'an (2 Parts)

V. JAINISM

Vols. 22 & 45: The Jaina Sutras (2 Parts)

VI. PARSIS

Vols. 5, 18, 24, 37 & 47: Pahlavi Texts (5 Parts)
Vols. 4, 23 & 31: The Zend-Avesta (3 Parts)

VII. VEDIC-BRAHMANIC SYSTEM

Vol. 8: The Bhagavadgita with the Sanatsujatiya and the Anugita
Vols. 29 & 30: The Grihya-Sutras: Rules of Vedic Domestic Ceremonies (2 Parts)
Vol. 42: Hymns of the Atharva Veda together with Extracts from the Ritual Books and the Commentaries
Vol. 7: The Institutes of Vishnu
Vol. 25: The Laws of Manu
Vol. 33: The Minor Law Books
Vols. 2 & 14: The Sacred Laws of the Aryas as Taught in the Schools of Apastamba, Gautama, Vasishtha and Baudhayana (2 Parts)
Vols. 12, 26, 41, 43 & 44: The Satapatha Brahmana According to the Text of the Madhyandina School (5 Parts)
Vols. 1 & 15: The Upanishads (2 Parts)
Vols. 34 & 38: The Vedanta Sutras (2 Parts)
Vol. 48: The Vedanta-Sutras (with the commentary by Ramanuja)
Vols. 32 & 46: Vedic Hymns (2 Parts)

THE
INSTITUTES OF VISHNU

Translated by

JULIUS JOLLY

MOTILAL BANARSIDASS PUBLISHERS
PRIVATE LIMITED • DELHI

*Reprint: Delhi, 1970, 1977, 1986, 1992, 2002, **2008***
First Indian Edition: 1965
First Published by the Clarendon Press, 1880

ISBN: 978-81-208-0108-0

MOTILAL BANARSIDASS

41 U.A. Bungalow Road, Jawahar Nagar, Delhi 110 007
8 Mahalaxmi Chamber, 22 Bhulabhai Desai Road, Mumbai 400 026
203 Royapettah High Road, Mylapore, Chennai 600 004
236, 9th Main III Block, Jayanagar, Bangalore 560 011
Sanas Plaza, 1302 Baji Rao Road, Pune 411 002
8 Camac Street, Kolkata 700 017
Ashok Rajpath, Patna 800 004
Chowk, Varanasi 221 001

UNESCO COLECTION OF REPRESENTATIVE WORKS— Indian Series
*This book has been accepted in the Indian Translation Series of the
UNESCO Collection of Representative Works, jointly sponsored
by the United Nations Educational Scientific and Cultural
Organization (UNESCO) and the Government of India*

PRINTED IN INDIA

BY JAINENDRA PRAKASH JAIN AT SHRI JAINENDRA PRESS,
A-45 NARAINA, PHASE-I, NEW DELHI 110 028
AND PUBLISHED BY NARENDRA PRAKASH JAIN FOR
MOTILAL BANARSIDASS PUBLISHERS PRIVATE LIMITED,
BUNGALOW ROAD, DELHI 110 007

Rashtrapati Bhavan,
New Delhi-4
June 10, 1962

I am very glad to know that the Sacred Books of the East, published years ago by the Clarendon Press, Oxford, which have been out-of-print for a number of years, will now be available to all students of religion and philosophy. The enterprise of the publishers is commendable and I hope the books will be widely read.

S. Radhakrishnan

PUBLISHER'S NOTE

First, the man distinguished between eternal and perishable. Later he discovered within himself the germ of the Eternal. This discovery was an epoch in the history of the human mind and the *East was the first to discover it.*

To watch in the Sacred Books of the East the dawn of this religious consciousness of man, must always remain one of the most inspiring and hallowing sights in the whole history of the world. In order to have a solid foundation for a comparative study of the Religions of the East, we must have before all things, complete and thoroughly faithful translation of their Sacred Books in which some of the ancient sayings were preserved because they were so true and so striking that they could not be forgotten. They contained eternal truths, expressed for the first time in human language.

With profoundest reverence for Dr. S. Radhakrishnan, President of India, who inspired us for the task; our deep sense of gratitude for Dr. C. D. Deshmukh & Dr. D. S. Kothari, for encouraging assistance; esteemed appreciation of UNESCO for the warm endorsement of the cause; and finally with indebtedness to **Dr. H. Rau, Director, Max Müller Bhawan, New Delhi,** in procuring us the texts of the Series for reprint, we humbly conclude.

PREFATORY NOTE TO THE NEW EDITION

Since 1948 the United Nations Educational, Scientific and Cultural Organisation (UNESCO), upon the recommendation of the General Assembly of the United Nations, has been concerned with facilitating the translation of the works most representative of the culture of certain of its Member States, and, in particular, those of Asia.

One of the major difficulties confronting this programme is the lack of translators having both the qualifications and the time to undertake translations of the many outstanding books meriting publication. To help overcome this difficulty in part, UNESCO's advisers in this field (a panel of experts convened every other year by the International Council for Philosophy and Humanistic Studies), have recommended that many worthwhile translations published during the 19th century, and now impossible to find except in a limited number of libraries, should be brought back into print in low-priced editions, for the use of students and of the general public. The experts also pointed out that in certain cases, even though there might be in existence more recent and more accurate translations endowed with a more modern apparatus of scholarship, a number of pioneer works of the greatest value and interest to students of Eastern religions also merited republication.

This point of view was warmly endorsed by the Indian National Academy of Letters (Sahitya Akademi), and the Indian National Commission for UNESCO.

It is in the spirit of these recommendations that this work from the famous series "Sacred Books of the East" is now once again being made available to the general public as part of the UNESCO Collection of Representative Works.

CONTENTS.

LIST OF THE MORE IMPORTANT ABBREVIATIONS.

Âpast. — Âpastamba's Dharma-sûtra, ed. Bühler.

Âsv. — Âsvalâyana's Gri*hya-sûtra, ed. Stenzler.

Gaut. — Gautama's Dharmasâstra, ed. Stenzler.

Gobh. — Gobhila's Gri*hya-sûtra, in the Bibl. Ind.

M. — Mânava Dharmasâstra, Calcutta edition, with the Commentary of Kullûka.

Nand. — Nandapan*d*ita, the commentator of the Vish*n*u-sûtra.

Pâr. — Pâraskara's Gri*hya-sûtra, ed. Stenzler.

Sâṅkh. — Sâṅkhâyana's Gri*hya-sûtra, ed. Oldenberg, in the fifteenth volume of the Indische Studien.

Y. — Yâgñavalkya's Dharmasâstra, ed. Stenzler.

Âpast. and Gaut. refer also to Dr. Bühler's translation of these two works in the second volume of the Sacred Books of the East.

INTRODUCTION.

THE Vish*n*u-sm*r*iti or Vaish*n*ava Dharma*s*âstra or Vish*n*u-sûtra is in the main a collection of ancient aphorisms on the sacred laws of India, and as such it ranks with the other ancient works of this class which have come down to our time[1]. It may be styled a Dharma-sûtra, though this ancient title of the Sûtra works on law has been preserved in the MSS. of those Sm*r*itis only, which have been handed down, like the Dharma-sûtras of Âpastamba, Baudhâyana, and Hira*n*yake*s*in, as parts of the respective Kalpa-sûtras, to which they belong. The size of the Vish*n*u-sûtra, and the great variety of the subjects treated in it, would suffice to entitle it to a conspicuous place among the five or six existing Dharma-sûtras; but it possesses a peculiar claim to interest, which is founded on its close connection with one of the oldest Vedic schools, the Ka*th*as, on the one hand, and with the famous code of Manu and some other ancient law-codes, on the other hand. To discuss these two principal points, and some minor points connected with them, as fully as the limits of an introduction admit of, will be the more necessary, because such a discussion can afford the only safe basis for a conjecture not altogether unsupported regarding the time and place of the original composition of this work, and may even tend to throw some new light on the vexed question as to the origin of the code of Manu. Further on I shall have to speak of the numerous interpolations traceable in the Vish*n*u-sûtra, and a few remarks regarding the materials

---

[1] This was first pointed out by Professor Max Müller, History of Ancient Sanskrit Literature, p. 134. His results were confirmed and expanded by the subsequent researches of Dr. Bühler, Introduction to Bombay Digest, I, p. xxii; Indian Antiquary, V, p. 30; Ka*s*mîr Report, p. 36.

used for this translation, and the principles of interpretation that have been followed in it, may be fitly reserved
for the last.

There is no surer way for ascertaining the particular
Vedic school by which an ancient Sanskrit law-book of
unknown or uncertain origin was composed, than by examining the quotations from, and analogies with, Vedic
works which it contains. Thus the Gautama Dharmasâstra might have originated in any one among the divers
Gautama *Kara*nas with which Indian tradition acquaints
us. But the comparatively numerous passages which its
author has borrowed from the Sa*m*hitâ and from one Brâhma*n*a of the Sâma-veda prove that it must belong to one
of those Gautama *Kara*nas who studied the Sâma-veda[1].
Regarding the code of Yâ*g*ñavalkya we learn from tradition that a Vedic teacher of that name was the reputed
author of the White Ya*g*ur-veda. But this coincidence
might be looked upon as casual, if the Yâ*g*ñavalkya-sm*ri*ti
did not contain a number of Mantras from that Vedic
Sa*m*hitâ, and a number of very striking analogies, in the
section on funeral ceremonies particularly, with the Gr*i*hya-
sûtra of the Vâ*g*asaneyins, the Kâtîya Gr*i*hya-sûtra of Pâraskara[2]. In the case of the Vish*n*u-sûtra an enquiry of this
kind is specially called for, because tradition leaves us
entirely in the dark as to its real author. The fiction
that the laws promulgated in Chapters II–XCVII were
communicated by the god Vish*n*u to the goddess of the
earth, is of course utterly worthless for historical purposes;
and all that it can be made to show is that those parts
of this work in which it is started or kept up cannot rival
the laws themselves in antiquity.

Now as regards, first, the Vedic Mantras and Pratîkas
(beginnings of Mantras) quoted in this work, it is necessary to leave aside, as being of no moment for the present
purpose, 1. very well-known Mantras, or, speaking more

---

[1] See Bühler, Introduction to Gautama (Vol. II of the Sacred Books of the
East), pp. xlv–xlviii.

[2] Bühler, Introduction to Digest, p. xxxii ; Stenzler, on Pâraskara's Gr*i*hya-
sûtra, in the Journal of the German Oriental Society, VII, p. 527 seq.

precisely, all such Mantras as are frequently quoted in Vedic works of divers Sâkhâs ; 2. the purificatory texts enumerated under the title of Sarva-veda-pavitrâni in LVI. The latter can afford us no help in determining the particular Sâkhâ to which this work belongs, because they are actually taken, as they profess to be, from all the Vedas indiscriminately, and because nearly the whole of Chapter LVI is found in the Vâsishtha-smriti as well (see further on), which probably does not belong to the same Veda as this work. Among the former class of Mantras may be included, particularly, the Gâyatrî, the Purushasûkta, the Aghamarshana, the Kûshmândîs, the Vyâhritis, the Gyeshtha Sâmans, the Rudras, the Trinâkiketa, the Trisuparna, the Vaishnava, Sâkra, and Bârhaspatya Mantras mentioned in XC, 3, and the Mantra quoted in XXVIII, 51 (= Gautama's 'Retasya'). Among the twenty-two Mantras quoted in Chapters XLVIII, LXIV, LXV (including repetitions, but excluding the Purushasûkta, Gâyatrî, Aghamarshana) there are also some which may be referred to this class, and the great majority of them occur in more than one Veda at the same time. But it is worthy of note that no less than twelve, besides occurring in at least one other Sâkhâ, are either actually found in the Samhitâ of the Kârâyanîya-kathas, the Kâthaka [1] (or Karaka-sâkhâ?), or stated to belong to it in the Commentary, while one is found in the Kâthaka alone, a second in the Atharva-veda alone, a third in the Taittirîya Brâhmana alone, and a fourth does not occur in any Vedic work hitherto known [2]. A far greater number of Mantras occurs in Chapters XXI, LXVII, LXXIII, LXXIV, LXXXVI, which treat of daily oblations, Srâddhas, and the ceremony of setting a bull at liberty. Of all these Mantras, which,—including the Purushasûkta and other such well-known Mantras as well as the short invocations addressed to Soma, Agni, and other deities, but excluding the invocations addressed to Vishnu in the spurious Sûtra, LXVII, 2,—are more than a hundred in number, no more than forty or so are found in Vedic

---

[1] In speaking of this work I always refer to the Berlin MS.
[2] XLVIII, 10. Cf., however, Vâgas. Samh. IV, 12.

works hitherto printed, and in the law-books of Manu, Yâgñavalkya, and others; but nearly all are quoted, exactly in the same order as in this work, in the *Kârâyanîya-kâthaka Grihya-sûtra*, while some of them have been traced in the Kâthaka as well. And what is even more important, the Kâthaka Grihya does not contain those Mantras alone, but nearly all the Sûtras in which they occur; and it may be stated therefore, secondly, that the Vishnu-sûtra has four long sections, viz. Chapter LXXIII, and Chapters XXI, LXVII, LXXXVI, excepting the final parts, in common with that work, while the substance of Chapter LXXIV may also be traced in it. The agreement between both works is very close, and where they differ it is generally due to false readings or to enlargements on the part of the Vishnu-sûtra. However, there are a few cases, in which the version of the latter work is evidently more genuine than that of the former, and it follows, therefore, that the author of the Vishnu-sûtra cannot have borrowed his rules for the performance of *Srâddhas* &c. from the Kâthaka Grihya-sûtra, but that both must have drawn from a common source, i. e. no doubt from the traditions current in the Katha school, to which this work is indebted for so many of its Mantras as well.

For these reasons[1] I fully concur in the view advanced by Dr. Bühler, that the bulk of the so-called Vishnu-smriti is really the ancient Dharma-sûtra of the *Kârâyanîya-kâthaka Sâkhâ* of the Black Yagur-veda. It ranks, like other Dharma-sûtras, with the *Grihya* and *Srauta*-sûtras of its school; the latter of which, though apparently lost now, is distinctly referred to in the Grihya-sûtra in several places, and must have been in existence at the time when the Commentaries on Kâtyâyana's *Srauta*-sûtras were composed, in which it is frequently quoted by the name

---

[1] For details I may refer the reader to my German paper, Das Dharmasûtra des Vishnu und das Kâthakagrihyasûtra, in the Transactions of the Royal Bavarian Academy of Science for 1879, where the sections corresponding in both works have been printed in parallel columns, the texts from the Kâthaka Grihya-sûtra having been prepared from two of the MSS. of Devapâla's Commentary discovered by Dr. Bühler (Kasmîr Report, Nos. 11, 12), one in Devanâgarî, and the other in Sâradâ characters.

of Ka*th*a-sûtra on divers questions concerning *S*rauta offerings, and at the time, when the Ka*s*mîrian Devapâla wrote his Commentary on the Kâ*th*aka G*ri*hya-sûtra, which was, according to the Ka*s*mîrian tradition, as explored by Dr. Bühler, before the conquest of Ka*s*mîr by the Mahommedans. Devapâla, in the Introduction to his work, refers to 'thirty-nine Adhyâyas treating of the Vaitânika (= *S*rauta) ceremonies,' by which the G*ri*hya-sûtra was preceded, from which statement it may be inferred that the Kâ*th*aka *S*rauta-sûtras must have been a very voluminous work indeed, as the G*ri*hya-sûtra, which is at least equal if not superior in extent to other works of the same class, forms but one Adhyâya, the fortieth, of the whole Kalpa-sûtra, which, according to Devapâla, was composed by one author. It does not seem likely that the Vish*n*u-sûtra was composed by the same man, or that it ever formed part of the Kâ*th*aka Kalpa-sûtra, as the Dharma-sûtras of Baudhâyana, Âpastamba, and Hira*n*yake*s*in form part of the Kalpa-sûtras of the respective schools to which they belong. If that were the case, it would agree with the G*ri*hya-sûtra on all those points which are treated in both works, such as e. g. the terms for the performance of the Sa*m*skâras or sacraments, the rules for a student and for a Snâtaka, the enumeration and definition of the K*rikkh*ras or 'hard penances,' the forms of marriage, &c. Now though the two works have on those subjects a number of such rules in common as occur in other works also, they disagree for the most part in the choice of expressions, and on a few points lay down exactly opposite rules, such as the Vish*n*u-sûtra (XXVIII, 28) giving permission to a student to ascend his spiritual teacher's carriage after him, whereas the other work prescribes, that he shall do so on no account. Moreover, if both works had been destined from the first to supplement one another, they would, instead of having several entire sections in common, exhibit such cross-references as are found e. g. between the Âpastamba G*ri*hya and Dharma-sûtras[1]; though the absence of such

---

[1] Bühler, Introduction to Âpastamba, Sacred Books, II, pp. xi–xiv.

references might be explained, in the case of the Vishnu-sûtra, by the activity of those who brought it into its present shape, and who seem to have carefully removed all such references to other works as the original Dharma-sûtra may have contained. Whatever the precise nature of the relations between this work and the other Sûtra works of the Kârâyanîya-kâthaka school may have been, there is no reason for assigning to it a later date than to the Kâthaka Srauta and Grihya-sûtras, with the latter of which it has so much in common, and it may therefore claim a considerable antiquity, especially if it is assumed, with Dr. Bühler, that the beginning of the Sûtra period differed for each Veda. The Veda of the Kathas, the Kâthaka, is not separated from the Sûtra literature of this school by an intermediate Brâhmana stage; yet its high antiquity is testified by several of the most eminent grammarians of India from Yâska down to Kaiyata[1]. Thus the Kâthaka is the only existing work of its kind, which is quoted by the former grammarian (Nirukta X, 5; another clear quotation from the Kâthaka, XXVII, 9, though not by name, may be found, Nirukta III, 4), and the latter places the Kathas at the head of all Vedic schools, while Patañgali, the author of the Mahâbhâshya, assigns to the ancient sage Katha, the reputed founder of the Katha or Kâthaka school of the Black Yagur-veda, the dignified position of an immediate pupil of Vaisampâyana, the fountain-head of all schools of the older or Black Yagur-veda, and mentions, in accordance with a similar statement preserved in the Râmâyana (II, 32, 18, 19 ed. Schlegel), that in his own time the 'Kâlâpaka and the Kâthaka' were 'proclaimed in every village[2].' The priority of the Kathas before all other existing schools of the Yagur-veda may be deduced from the statements of the Karanavyûha[3], which work assigns to them one of the first places among the divers branches of

---

‒‒‒‒

[1] See Weber, Indische Studien XIII, p. 437 seq.

[2] Mahâbhâshya, Benares edition, IV, fols. 82 b, 75 b.

[3] See Weber, Ind. Stud. III, p. 256 seq.; Max Müller, Hist. Anc. Sansk. Lit., p. 369. I have consulted, besides, two Munich MSS. of the Karanavyûha (cod. Haug 45).

the *K*arakas, whom it places at the head of all schools of
the Ya*g*ur-veda. Another argument in favour of the high
antiquity of the Ka*th*as may be derived from their geographical position [1]. Though the statements of the Mahâ-
bhâshya and Râmâya*n*a regarding the wide-spread and
influential position of the Ka*th*as in ancient times are borne
out by the fact that the *K*ara*n*avyûha mentions three subdivisions of the Ka*th*as, viz. the Ka*th*as proper, the Prâ*k*ya
Ka*th*as, and the Kapish*th*ala Ka*th*as, to which the *K*ârâya*n*îyas may be added as a fourth, and by the seeming
identity of their name with the name of the Ka*θ*αῖοι in the
Pañ*g*âb on the one hand, and with the first part of the
name of the peninsula of Kattivar on the other hand, it
seems very likely nevertheless that the original home of the
Ka*th*as was situated in the north-west, i. e. in those regions
where the earliest parts of the Vedas were composed. Not
only the Kαθαῖοι, but the Καμβίσθολοι as well, who have
been identified with the Kapish*th*ala Ka*th*as [2], are mentioned by Greek writers as a nation living in the Pañ*g*âb;
and while the Prâ*k*ya Ka*th*as are shown by their name
('Eastern Ka*th*as') to have lived to the east of the two
other branches of the Ka*th*as, it is a significant fact that
adherents of the *K*ârâya*n*îya-kâ*th*aka school survive nowhere but in Ka*s*mîr, where all Brâhma*n*as perform their
domestic rites according to the rules laid down in the
Gr*i*hya-sûtra of this school [3]. Ka*s*mîr is moreover the
country where nearly all the yet existing works of the
Kâ*th*aka school have turned up, including the Berlin MS.
of the Kâ*th*aka, which was probably written by a Kas-
mîrian [4]. It is true that some of the geographical and
historical data contained in that work, especially the way
in which it mentions the Pañ*k*âlas, whose ancient name, as
shown by the *S*atapatha Brâhma*n*a (XIII, 5, 4, 7) and Rig-

---

[1] See Weber, Über das Râmâya*n*a, p. 9; Ind. Stud. I, p. 189 seq.; III, p 469
seq.; XIII, pp. 375, 439; Ind. Litteraturgeschichte, pp. 99, 332; Zimmer,
Altindisches Leben, p. 102 seq.

[2] See, however, Max Müller, Hist. Anc. Sansk. Lit., p. 333.

[3] Bühler, Ka*s*mîr Report, p. 20 seq.

[4] This was pointed out to me by Dr. Bühler.

veda (VIII, 20, 24 ; VIII, 22, 12), was Krivi, take us far off
from the north-west, the earliest seat of Âryan civilization,
into the country of the Kuru-Pañ*k*âlas in Hindostân proper.
But it must be borne in mind that the Kâ*th*aka, if it may
be identified with the '*K*araka-*s*âkhâ,' must have been
the Veda of all the *K*arakas except perhaps the Maitrâya-
*n*îyas and Kapish*th*alas, and may have been altered and
enlarged, after the Ka*th*as and *K*arakas had spread themselves across Hindostân. The Sûtras of a *S*âkhâ which
appears to have sprung up near the primitive home of Âryan
civilization in India, which was probably the original home
of the Ka*th*as at the same time, may be far older than
those of mere Sûtra schools of the Black Ya*g*ur-veda, which
have sprung up, like the Âpastamba school, in South India,
i. e. far older than the fourth or fifth century B. C. [1]

But sufficient space has been assigned to these attempts
at fixing the age of the Kâ*th*aka-sûtras which, besides remaining only too uncertain in themselves, can apply with
their full force to those parts of the Vish*n*u-sûtra only,
which have been traced in the Kâ*th*aka G*ri*hya-sûtra. It
will be seen afterwards that even these sections, however
closely connected with the sacred literature of the Ka*th*as,
have been tampered with in several places, and it might be
argued, therefore, that the whole remainder of the Vish*n*u-
sûtra, to which the Kâ*th*aka literature offers no parallel,
may be a subsequent addition. But the antiquity of the
great majority of its laws can be proved by independent
arguments, which are furnished by a comparison of the
Vish*n*u-sûtra with other works of the same class, whose
antiquity is not doubted.

In the foot-notes to my translation I have endeavoured
to give as complete references as possible to the analogous passages in the Sm*ri*tis of Manu, Yâ*g*ñavalkya,
Âpastamba, and Gautama, and in the four G*ri*hya-sûtras
hitherto printed. A large number of analogous passages
might have been traced in the Dharma-sûtras of Vâsish*th*a [2]

---

[1] See Bühler, Introd. to Âpastamba, p. xliii.

[2] See the Benares edition (1878), which is accompanied with a Commentary
by K*ri*sh*n*apa*nd*ita Dharmâdhikârin. I should have given references to this

and Baudhâyana as well, not to mention Hira*n*yakesin's
Dharma-sûtra, which, according to Dr. Bühler, is nearly identical with the Dharma-sûtra of Âpastamba. Two facts may
be established at once by glancing at these analogies, viz.
the close agreement of this work with the other Sûtra works
in point of form, and with all the above-mentioned works in
point of contents. As regards the first point, the Sûtras or
prose rules of which the bulk of the Vish*n*u-sûtra is composed, show throughout that characteristic laconism of the
Sûtra style, which renders it impossible in many cases to
make out the real meaning of a Sûtra without the help of a
Commentary ; and in the choice of terms they agree as
closely as possible with the other ancient law-books, and in
some cases with the G*ri*hya-sûtras as well. Numerous
verses, generally in the *S*loka metre, and occasionally de-
signed as 'Gâthâs,' are added at the end of most chapters,
and interspersed between the Sûtras in some ; but in this
particular also the Vish*n*u-sûtra agrees with at least
one other Dharma-sûtra, the Vâsish*th*a-sm*ri*ti, and it contains in its law part, like the latter work, a number of
verses in the ancient Trish*t*ubh metre[1]. Four of these
Trish*t*ubhs are found in the Vâsish*th*a-sm*ri*ti, and three in
Yâska's Nirukta as well, and the majority of the *S*lokas has
been traced in the former work and the other above-mentioned law-books, and in other Sm*ri*tis. In point of contents
the great majority both of the metrical and prose rules of
the Vish*n*u-sûtra agrees with one, or some, or all of the
works named above. The G*ri*hya-sûtras, excepting the Kâ-
*th*aka G*ri*hya-sûtra, naturally offer a far smaller number of
analogies with it than the Sm*ri*tis, still they exhibit several
rules, in the Snâtaka-dharmas and otherwise, that have not
been traced in any other Sm*ri*ti except the work here translated. Among the Sm*ri*tis again, each single one may be seen

---

work, the first complete and reliable edition of the Vâsish*th*a-sm*ri*ti, in the foot-
notes to my translation, but for the fact that it did not come into my hands
till the former had gone to the press. For Baudhâyana I have consulted a
Munich MS. containing the text only of his Sûtras (cod. Haug 163).

[1] XIX, 23, 24; XXIII, 61; XXIX, 9, 10; XXX, 47 (see Nirukta II, 4;
Vâsish*th*a II, 8–10); LVI, 27 (see Vâsish*th*a XXVIII, 15); LIX, 30; LXXII, 7;
LXXXVI, 16.

from the references to contain a number of such rules, as are only met with in this work, which is a very important fact because, if the laws of the Vish*n*u-sûtra were found either in all other Sm*r*itis, or in one of them only, its author might be suspected of having borrowed them from one of those works. As it is, meeting with analogous passages now in one work, and then in another, one cannot but suppose that the author of this work has everywhere drawn from the same source as the other Sûtrakâras, viz. from ancient traditions that were common to all Vedic schools.

There are, moreover, a number of cases in which this work, instead of having borrowed from other works of the same class, can be shown to have been, directly or indirectly, the source from which they drew, and this fact constitutes a third reason in favour of the high antiquity of its laws. The clearest case of this kind is furnished by the Vâsish*tha*-sm*r*iti, with which this work has two entire chapters in common, which are not found elsewhere. I subjoin in a note the text of Vâsish*tha* XXVIII, 10–15, with an asterisk to those words which contain palpable mistakes (not including blunders in point of metre), for comparison with Chapter LVI of this work in the Calcutta edition, which is exceptionally correct in this chapter and in Chapter LXXXVII, which latter corresponds to Vâsish*tha* XXVIII, 18–22[1]. In both

---

[1] सर्ववेदपवित्राणि वक्ष्याम्यहमतः परम् ।
येषां जपैश्च होमैश्च पूयन्ते नात्र संशयः ॥१०॥
अघमर्षणां देवकृतं शुद्धवत्य*स्तरत्समाः ।
कूष्माण्डानि पावमान्यो दुर्गासावित्रिरेव (?) च ॥११॥
*अभिपङ्गाः पदस्तोभाः सामानि व्याहृतीस्तथा (?) ।
*भारदण्डानि सामानि गायत्रं रैवतं तथा ॥१२॥
पुरुषव्रतं च भासं च तथा देवव्रतानि च ।
आर्त्विगं (?) बार्हस्पत्यं वाक्सूक्तं मध्वृचस्तथा ॥१३॥
शतरुद्रियमथर्वशिरस्त्रिसुपर्णं महाव्रतम् ।
गोसूक्तं चाश्वसूक्तं च इन्द्रशुद्धे (?) च सामनी ॥१४॥
वीर्याज्यदोहानि रथन्तरं च
अग्नेर्व्रतं वामदेव्यं बृहच्च ।

chapters Vish*n*u has mainly prose Sûtras and throughout a perfectly correct text, whereas Vâsish*th*a has bad *S*lokas which, supported as they are by the Commentary or by the metre or by both, can only be accounted for by carelessness or clerical mistakes in some cases, and by a clumsy versification of the original prose version preserved in this work in others. Another chapter of the Vish*n*u-sûtra, the forty-eighth, nowhere meets with a parallel except in the third Pra*s*na of the Dharma-sûtra of Baudhâyana, where it recurs almost word for word. An examination of the various readings in both works shows that in some of the *S*lokas Baudhâyana has better readings, while in one or two others the readings of Vish*n*u seem preferable, though the unsatisfactory condition of the MS. consulted renders it unsafe to pronounce a definitive judgment on the character of Baudhâyana's readings. At all events he has a few Vedic Mantras more than Vish*n*u, which however seem to be very well-known Mantras and are quoted by their Pratîkas only. But he omits the two important Sûtras 9 and 10 of Vish*n*u, the latter of which contains a Mantra quoted at full, which, although corrupted (see Vâ*g*as. Sa*m*h. IV, 12) and hardly intelligible, is truly Vedic in point of language; and he adds on his part a clause at the end of the whole chapter[1], which inculcates the worship of Ga*n*e*s*a or *S*iva or both, and would be quite sufficient in itself to cast a doubt on the genuineness and originality of his version. It is far from improbable that both Vâsish*th*a and Baudhâyana may have borrowed

---

एतानि * जप्रानि (= गीतानि Vish*n*u LVI, 27) पुनन्ति जन्तून् जातिस्मरत्वं लभते यदीच्छेत् ॥१५॥

Vish*n*u LVI, 15, 16, the best MSS. read पुरुषव्रते सामनी ।१५। अबिलङ्गम् ।१६। but the Calc. ed. and one London MS. have पुरुषव्रते । भासम् । like Vâsish*th*a. Of Vish*n*u LXXXVII the latter has an abridged version, which contains the faulty readings कृष्णामागेजम् ('the skin of a black antelope,' Comm.) and चतुर्वेक्त्रा (as an epithet of the earth = चतुरत्ना Vish*n*u LXXXVII, 9).

[1] गणान्पश्यति गणाधिपतिं पश्यति विद्यां पश्यति विद्याधिपतिं पश्यति । इत्याह भगवान्बौधायनः ।

the sections referred to directly from an old recension of this work, as Baudhâyana has borrowed another chapter of his work from Gautama, while Vâsish*th*a in his turn has borrowed the same chapter from Baudhâyana[1]. It may be added in confirmation of this view, that as far as Vâsish*th*a is concerned, his work is the only Sm*ri*ti, as far as I know, which contains a quotation from the 'Kâ*th*aka' (in XXIX, 18). The Dharma-sûtras of Âpastamba and Gautama have nowhere a large number of consecutive Sûtras in common with the Vish*n*u-sûtra, but it is curious to note that the rule, which the latter (X, 45) quotes as the opinion of 'some' (eke), that a non-Brahmanical finder of a treasure, who announces his find to the king, shall obtain one-sixth of the value, is found in no other law-book except in this, which states (III, 61) that a *S*ûdra shall divide a treasure-trove into twelve parts, two of which he may keep for himself. Of the metrical law-books, one, the Yâ*gñ*avalkya-sm*ri*ti, has been shown by Professor Max Müller[2] to have borrowed the whole anatomical section (III, 84–104), including the simile of the soul which dwells in the heart like a lamp (III, 109, 111, 201), from this work (XCVI, 43–96; XCVII, 9); and it has been pointed out by the same scholar, that the verse in which the author of the former work speaks of the Âra*n*yaka and of the Yoga-*s*âstra as of his own works (III, 110) does not occur in the Vish*n*u-sûtra, and must have been added by the versificator, who brought the Yâ*gñ*avalkya-sm*ri*ti into its present metrical form. Several other *S*lokas in Yâ*gñ*avalkya's description of the human body (III, 99, 105–108), and nearly the whole section on Yoga (Y. III, 111–203, excepting those *S*lokas, the substance of which is found in this work and in the code of Manu, viz. 131–140, 177–182, 190, 198–201) may be traced to the same source, as may be also the omission of Vish*n*u's enumeration of the 'six limbs' (XCVI, 90) in the Yâ*gñ*avalkya-sm*ri*ti, and probably all the minor points on which it differs from this work. Generally speaking, those

---

[1] See Bühler, Introduction to Gautama, pp. l–liv.
[2] Hist. Anc. Sansk. Lit., p. 331.

passages which have been justly noticed as marking the comparatively late period in which that law-book must have been composed[1]: such as the allusions to the astrology and astronomy of the Greeks (Y. I, 80, 295), which render it necessary to refer the metrical redaction of the Yâgñavalkya-smriti to a later time than the second century A. D.; the whole passage on the worship of Ganesa and of the planets (I, 270–307), in which, moreover, a heterodox sect is mentioned, that has been identified with the Buddhists; the philosophical doctrines propounded in I, 349, 350; the injunctions regarding the foundation and endowment of monasteries (II, 185 seq.)—all these passages have no parallel in this work, while it is not overstating the case to say that nearly all the other subjects mentioned in the Yâgñavalkya-smriti are treated in a similar way, and very often in the same terms, in the Vishnu-sûtra as well. Some of those rules, in which the posteriority of the Yâgña-valkya-smriti to other law-books exhibits itself, do occur in the Vishnu-sûtra, but without the same marks of modern age. Thus the former has two Slokas concerning the punishment of forgery (II, 240, 241), in which coined money is referred to by the term nânaka; the Vishnu-sûtra has the identical rule (V, 122, 123; cf. V, 9), but the word nânaka does not occur in it. Yâgñavalkya, in speaking of the number of wives which a member of the three higher castes may marry (I, 57), advocates the Puritan view, that no Sûdra wife must be among these; this work has analogous rules (XXIV, 1–4), in which, however, such marriages are expressly allowed. The comparative priority of all those Sûtras of Vishnu, to which similar Slokas of Yâgñavalkya correspond, appears probable on general grounds, which are furnished by the course of development in this as in other branches of Indian literature; and to this it may be added,

---

[1] See Stenzler, in the Preface to his edition of Yâgñavalkya; Jacobi, on Indian Chronology, in the Journal of the German Oriental Society, XXX, 305 seq., &c. Vishnu's rules (III, 82) concerning the wording &c. of royal grants, which agree with the rules of Yâgñavalkya and other authors, must be allowed a considerable antiquity, as the very oldest grants found in South India conform to those rules. See Burnell, South Indian Palæography, 2nd ed., p. 95.

as far as the civil and criminal laws are concerned, that the former enumerates them quite promiscuously, just like the other Dharma-sûtras, with which he agrees besides in separating the law of inheritance from the body of the laws, whereas Yâgñavalkya enumerates all the laws in the order of the eighteen 'titles of law' of Manu and the more recent law-books, though he does not mention the titles of law by name.

However much the Vishnu-sûtra may have in common with the Yâgñavalkya-smriti, there is no other law-book with which it agrees so closely as with the code of Manu. This fact may be established by a mere glance at the references in the foot-notes to this translation, in which Manu makes his appearance far more frequently and constantly than any other author, and the case becomes the stronger, the more the nature of these analogies is inquired into. Of Slokas alone Vishnu has upwards of 160 in common with Manu, and in a far greater number of cases still his Sûtras agree nearly word for word with the corresponding rules of Manu. The latter also, though he concurs in a very great number of points with the other law authors as well, agrees with none of them so thoroughly as with Vishnu. All the Smritis of Âpastamba, Baudhâyana, Vâsishtha, Yâgñavalkya, and Nârada contain, according to an approximate calculation, no more than about 130 Slokas, that are found in the code of Manu as well. The latter author and Vishnu differ of course on a great many minor points, and an exhaustive discussion of this subject would fill a treatise; I must therefore confine myself to notice some of those differences, which are particularly important for deciding the relative priority of the one work before the other. In a number of Slokas Manu's readings are decidedly older and better than Vishnu's. Thus the latter (XXX, 7) compares the three 'Atigurus' to the 'three gods,' i. e. to the post-Vedic Trimûrti of 'Brahman, Vishnu, and Siva,' as the commentator expressly states, whereas Manu in an analogous Sloka (II, 230) refers to the 'three orders' instead. At the end of the section on inheritance (XVIII, 44) Vishnu mentions among other indivisible objects 'a book,' pustakam; Manu (IX, 219) has the same *S*loka, but for pustakam he reads pra*k*akshate. Now pustaka is a modern word[1], and Varâhamihira, who lived in the sixth century A.D., appears to be the first author, with a known date, by whom it is used. It occurs again, Vish*n*u-sûtra XXIII, 56 (proksha*n*ena *k*a pustakam), and here also Manu (V, 122) has a different reading (puna*h*pâkena m*r*inmayam). The only difference between Vish*n*u-sûtra XXII, 93 and Manu V, 110 consists in the use of singular forms (te, *sri*n*u) in the former work, and of plural forms (va*h*, *sri*nuta) in the latter. Now there are a great many other Sm*r*itis besides the Manu-sm*r*iti, such as e. g. the Yâg*ñ*avalkya and Parâsara Sm*r*itis, in which the fiction is kept up, that the laws contained in them are promulgated to an assembly of *R*ishis; but there are very few Sm*r*itis of the least notoriety or importance besides the Vish*n*u-sûtra, in which they are proclaimed to a single person. Other instances in which Manu's readings appear preferable to Vish*n*u's may be found, LI, 60 (pretya *k*eha *k*a nishk*r*itim) = Manu V, 38 (pretya *g*anmani *g*anmani); LI, 64 (iti katha*ñk*ana) = M. V, 41 (ity abravînmanu*h*); LI, 76 (tasya) = M. V, 53 (tayo*h*); LIV, 27 (brâhma*n*yât) = M. XI, 193 (brahma*n*â); LVII, 11 (purastâd anu*k*oditâm) = M. IV, 248; Vâsish*th*a XIV, 16; Âpastamba I, 6, 19, 14 (purastâd apra*k*oditâm); LXVII, 45 (sâyamprâtas tvatithaye) = M. III, 99 (samprâptâya tvatithaye), &c. But these instances do not prove much, as all the passages in question may have been tampered with by the Vish*n*uitic editor, and as in some other cases the version of Vish*n*u seems preferable. Thus 'practised by the virtuous' (sâdhubhi*sk*a nishevitam, LXXI, 90) is a very common epithet of '*âk*âra,' and reads better than Manu's nibaddha*m* sveshu karmasu (IV, 155); and k*rikkh*râtik*rikkh*ram (LIV, 30) seems preferable to Baudhâyana's and Manu's k*rikkh*râtik*rikkh*rau (XI, 209). What is more important, the Vish*n*u-sûtra does not only contain a number of verses in the ancient Trish*t*ubh metre, whereas Manu has none, but it shows those identical three Trish*t*ubhs of Vâsish*th*a and Yâska, which Dr. Bühler

---

[1] See Max Müller, Hist. Anc. Sansk. Lit., p. 512.

has proved to have been converted into Anush*t*ubh *S*lokas by Manu (II, 114, 115, 144)[1]; and Manu seems to have taken the substance of his three *S*lokas from this work more immediately, because both he (II, 144) and Vish*n*u (XXX, 47) have the reading âv*r*inoti for ât*r*inatti, which truly Vedic form is employed both by Vâsish*th*a and Yâska. The relative antiquity of Vish*n*u's prose rules, as compared to the numerous corresponding *S*lokas of Manu, may be proved by arguments precisely similar to those which I have adduced above in speaking of the Yâg*ñ*avalkya-sm*r*iti. As regards those points in the code of Manu, which are usually considered as marks of the comparatively late date of its composition, it will suffice to mention, that the Vish*n*u-sûtra nowhere refers to South Indian nations such as the Dravi*d*as and Andhras, or to the Yavanas; that it shows no distinct traces of an acquaintance with the tenets of any other school of philosophy except the Yoga and Sânkhya systems; that it does not mention female ascetics disparagingly, and in particular does not contain Manu's rule (VIII, 363) regarding the comparatively light punishment to be inflicted for violation of (Buddhist and other) female ascetics; and that it does not inveigh (see XV, 3), like Manu (IX, 64–68), against the custom of Niyoga or appointment of a widow to raise offspring to her deceased husband. It is true, on the other hand, that in many cases Vish*n*u's rules have a less archaic character than the corresponding precepts of Manu, not only in the *S*lokas, but in the Sûtra part as well. Thus written documents and ordeals are barely mentioned in the code of Manu (VIII, 114, 115, 168; IX, 232); Vish*n*u on the other hand, besides referring in divers places to royal grants and edicts, to written receipts and other private documents, and to books, devotes to writings (lekhya) an entire chapter, in which he makes mention of the caste of Kâyasthas, 'scribes,' and he lays down elaborate rules for the performance of five species of ordeals, to which recourse should be had, according to him, in all suits of some importance. But in nearly all such cases the antiquity of Vish*n*u's

---

[1] Introduction to Bombay Digest, I, p. xxviii seq.

rules is warranted to a certain extent by corresponding rules occurring in the Sm*ri*tis of Yâg̃navalkya and Nârada; and the evidence for the modifications and entire transformations, which the code of Manu must have undergone in a number of successive periods, is so abundant, that the archaic character of many of its rules cannot be considered to constitute a sufficient proof of the priority of the whole code before other codes which contain some rules of a comparatively modern character. To this it must be added that the Nârada-sm*ri*ti, though taken as a whole it is decidedly posterior to the code of Manu[1], is designated by tradition as an epitome from another and more bulky recension of the code of Manu than the one which we now possess; and if this statement may be credited, which is indeed rather doubtful, the very particular resemblance between both works in the law of evidence and in the rules regarding property (see LVIII) can only tend to corroborate the assumption that the Vish*nu*-sûtra and the Manu-sm*ri*ti must have been closely connected from the first.

This view is capable of further confirmation still by a different set of arguments. The so-called code of Manu is universally assumed now to be an improved metrical edition of the ancient Dharma-sûtra of the (Maitrâya*nî*ya-) Mânavas, a school studying the Black Ya*g*ur-veda; and it has been shown above that the ancient stock of the Vish*nu*-sûtra, in which all the parts hitherto discussed may be included, represents in the main the Dharma-sûtra of the *K*ârâya*nî*ya-ka*th*as, another school studying the Black Ya*g*ur-veda. Now these two schools do not only belong both to that Veda, but to the same branch of it, as may be seen from the *K*ara*n*avyûha, which work classes both the Ka*th*as and *K*ârâya*n*îyas on the one hand, and the Mânavas

---

[1] See the evidence collected in the Preface to my Institutes of Nârada (London, 1876), to which the important fact may be added that Nârada uses the word dînâra, the Roman denarius. It occurs in a large fragment discovered by Dr. Bühler of a more bulky and apparently older recension of that work than the one which I have translated; and I may be allowed to mention, incidentally, that this discovery has caused me to abandon my design of publishing the Sanskrit text of the shorter recension, as it may be hoped that the whole text of the original work will soon come to light.

together with the six or five other sections of the Maitrâ-yaṇîyas on the other hand, as subdivisions of the *K*araka *S*akhâ of the Black Ya*g*ur-veda. What is more, there exists a thorough-going parallelism between the literature of those two schools, as far as it is known. To begin with their respective Sa*m*hitâs, it has been shown by L. Schröder[1] that the Maitrâyaṇî Sa*m*hitâ has more in common with the Kâ*th*aka, the Sa*m*hitâ of the Ka*th*as, than with any other Veda. As the Ka*th*as are constantly named, in the Mahâ-bhâshya and other old works, by the side of the Kâlâpas, whereas the name of the Maitrâya*n*îyas does not occur in any Sanskrit work of uncontested antiquity, it has been suggested by the same scholar that the Maitrâya*n*îyas may be the Kâlâpas of old, and may not have assumed the former name till Buddhism began to prevail in India. However this may be, the principal Sûtra works of both schools stand in a similar relation to one another as their Sa*m*hitâs. Some of those Mantras, which have been stated above to be common to the Vish*n*u-sûtra and Kâ*th*aka G*ri*hya only, and to occur in no other Vedic work hitherto printed, have been traced in the Mânava *S*rauta-sûtra, in the chapter on Pi*nd*a-pit*ri*ya*g*ña (I, 2 of the section on Prâk-soma)[2], and the conclusion is, that if the *S*rauta-sûtra of the Kâ*th*aka school were still in existence, it would be found to exhibit a far greater number of analogies with the *S*rauta-sûtra of the Mânavas. The G*ri*hya-sûtra of this school[3] agrees with the Kâ*th*aka G*ri*hya-sûtra even more closely than the latter agrees with the Vish*n*u-sûtra, as both works have not only several entire chapters in common (the chapter on the Vai*s*vadeva sacrifice among others, which is found in the Vish*n*u-sûtra also), but concur every-where in the arrangement of the subject-matter and in the choice of expressions and Mantras. The Brâhma*n*a stage of Vedic literature is not represented by a separate work in either of the two schools, but a further argument in

---

[1] On the Maitrâya*n*î Sa*m*hitâ, Journal of the German Oriental Society, XXXIII, 177 seq.

[2] Cod. Haug 53 of the Munich Library.

[3] Codd. Haug 55 and 56 of the Munich Library. For details, see my German paper above referred to.

favour of their alleged historical connection may be derived
from their respective geographical position. If it has been
rightly conjectured above, that the original seats of the
Ka*th*as were in the north-west, whence they spread themselves over Hindostân, the Maitrâya*n*îyas, though now
surviving nowhere except in some villages 'near the Sât-
pu*d*a mountain, which is included in the Vindhyas[1],' must
have been anciently their neighbours, as the territory occu-
pied by them extended 'from the Mayûra mountain into
Gu*g*arât,' and reached 'as far as the north-western country'
(vâyavyade*s*a)[2]. Considering all this evidence regarding
the original connection between the Ka*th*as and Mânavas,
it may be said without exaggeration, that it would be far
more surprising to find no traces of resemblance between
their respective Dharma-sûtras, such as we possess them,
than to find, as is actually the case, the contrary; and it
may be argued, vice versâ, that the supposed connection
of the two works with the Vedic schools of the Ka*th*as and
Mânavas[3] respectively, is confirmed by the kinship existing
between these two schools.

In turning now from the ancient parts of the Vish*n*u-
sûtra to its more recent ingredients, I may again begin by
quoting Professor Max Müller's remarks on this work,
which contain the statement, that it is 'enlarged by modern
additions written in *S*lokas[4].' After him, Dr. Bühler pointed
out[5] that the whole work appears to have been recast by an
adherent of Vish*n*u, and that the final and introductory
chapters in particular are shown by their very style to have
been composed by another author than the body of the

---

[1] Bhâû Dâjî, Journal of the Bombay Branch of the Royal Asiatic Society,
X, 40.

[2] See a passage from the Mahâr*n*ava, as quoted by Dr. Bühler, Introduction
to Âpastamba, p. xxx seq. The same readings are found in a Munich MS. of
the Kara*n*avyûha-vyâkhyâ (cod. Haug 45). With the above somewhat unclear
statement Manu's definition of the limits of Brahmâvarta (II, 17) may not un-
reasonably be compared.

[3] The code of Manu has very little in common with the Mânava G*ri*hya-
sûtra, both in the Mantras and otherwise. Both Vish*n*u and Manu agree with
the Kâ*th*aka in the use of the curious term abhinimrukta or abhinirmukta; but
the same term is used by Âpastamba, Vâsish*th*a, and others.

[4] Hist. Anc. Sansk. Lit., p. 134.

[5] Introduction to Bombay Digest. p. xxii.

work. If the latter remark were in need of further confirmation, it might be urged that the description of Vishnu as 'the boar of the sacrifice' (yagñavarâha) in the first chapter is bodily taken from the Harivamsa (2226–2237), while most of the epithets given to Vishnu in I, 49–61 and XCVIII, 7–100 may be found in another section of the Mahâbhârata, the so-called Vishnu-sahasranâma. Along with the introductory and final chapters, all those passages generally are distinctly traceable to the activity of the Vishnuitic editor, in which Vishnu (Purusha, Bhagavat, Vâsudeva, &c.) is mentioned, or his dialogue with the goddess of the earth carried on, viz. I ; V, 193; XIX, 24; XX, 16–21; XXII, 93; XXIII, 46 ; XXIV, 35 ; XLVII, 10 ; XLIX ; LXIV, 28, 29; LXV; LXVI; LXVII, 2; XC, 3–5, 17–23; XCVI, 97, 98 ; XCVII, 7–21; XCVIII–C. The short invocation addressed to Vishnu in LXVII, 12 is proved to be ancient by its recurrence in the corresponding chapter of the Kâthaka Grihya-sûtra, and Chapter LXV contains genuine Kâthaka Mantras transferred to a Vishnuitic ceremony. Chapter LXVI, on the other hand, though it does not refer to Vishnu by name, seems to be connected with the same Vishnuitic rite, and becomes further suspected by the recurrence of several of its rules in the genuine Chapter LXXIX. The contents of Chapter XCVII, in which it is attempted to reconcile some of the main tenets of the Sânkhya system, as propounded in the Sânkhya-kârikâ, Sânkhya-pravakanabhâshya, and other works, with the Vaishnava creed and with the Yoga ; the fact that the two Slokas in XCVI (97, 98) and part of the Slokas in XCVII (15–21) have their parallel in similar Slokas of the Bhagavad-gîtâ and of the Bhâgavata-purâna; the terms Mahatpati, Kapila, and Sânkhyâkârya, used as epithets of Vishnu (XCVIII, 26, 85, 86) ; and some other passages in the Vishnuitic chapters seem to favour the supposition that the editor may have been one of those members of the Vishnuitic sect of the Bhâgavatas, who were conspicuous for their leaning towards the Sânkhya and Yoga systems of philosophy. The arrangement of the Vishnu-sûtra in a hundred chapters is no doubt due to the same person, as the Commentary points out that the number of the epithets given to Vish*n*u in XCVIII is precisely equal to the number of chapters into which the laws promulgated by him are divided (II–XCVII); though the number ninety-six is received only by including the introductory and final invocations (XCVIII, 6, 101) among the epithets of Vish*n*u. It seems quite possible, that some chapters were inserted mainly in order to bring up the whole figure to the round number of a hundred chapters, and it is for this reason chiefly that the majority of the following additions, which show no Vish*n*uitic tendencies, may also be attributed to the Vish*n*uitic editor.

1. Most or all of the *S*lokas added at the end of Chapters XX (22–53) and XLIII (32–45) cannot be genuine; the former on account of their great extent and partial recurrence in the Bhagavad-gîtâ[1], Mahâbhârata, and other works of general note, and because they refer to the self-immolation of widows and to Kâla, whom the commentator is probably right in identifying with Vish*n*u; the latter on account of their rather extravagant character and decidedly Purâ*n*ic style, though the Gâru*d*a-purâ*n*a, in its very long description of the hells, offers no strict parallel to the details given here. The verses in which the Brâhma*n*as and cows are celebrated (XIX, 22, 23; XXIII, 57–61) are also rather extravagant; however, some of them are Trish*t*ubhs, and the verses in XIX are closely connected with the preceding Sûtras. The two final *S*lokas in LXXXVI (19, 20) may also be suspected as to their genuineness, because they are wanting in the corresponding chapter of the Kâ*th*aka G*ri*hya-sûtra; and a number of other verses in divers places, because they have no parallel in the Sm*ri*ti literature, or because they have been traced in comparatively modern works, such as the Bhagavad-gîtâ, the Pañ*k*atantra, &c. 2. The week of the later Romans and Greeks, and of modern Europe (LXXVIII, 1–7), the self-immolation of widows (XXV, 14; cf. XX, 39), and the Buddhists and Pâ*s*upatas (LXIII, 36) are not mentioned in any ancient Sanskrit work. Besides, the passages in question may be easily removed, especially the Sûtras referring to the seven days of the week, which

---

[1] Besides the passages quoted in the notes, 50–53 nearly = Bhag.-gîtâ II, 22–25.

form clearly a subsequent addition to the enumeration of
the Nakshatras and Tithis immediately following (LXXVIII,
8–50), and the rule concerning the burning of widows (XXV,
14), which is in direct opposition to the law concerning the
widow's right to inherit (XVII, 4) and to other precepts
regarding widows. That the three terms kâshâyin, pravra-
gita, malina in LXIII, 36 refer to members of religious orders
seems clear, but it may be doubted whether malina denotes
the Pâsupatas, and even whether kâshâyin (cf. pravragitâ
XXXVI, 7) denotes the Buddhists, as dresses dyed with
Kashâya are worn by Brahmanical sects also, and prescribed
for students, and for ascetics likewise, by some of the
Grihya- and Dharma-sûtras. Still the antiquity of the Sûtra
in question can hardly be defended, because the acquaintance of the Vishnuitic editor with the Buddhistic system of
faith is proved by two other Sûtras (XCVIII, 40, 41), and
because the whole subject of good and evil omens is not
treated in any other ancient Smriti. On the other hand,
such terms as vedanindâ and nâstikatâ (XXXVII, 4, 31, &c.)
recur in most Smritis, and can hardly be referred to the
Buddhists in particular. 3. The Tîrthas enumerated in
LXXXV, some of which are sacred to Vishnu and Siva,
belong to all parts of India, and many of them are situated
in the Dekhan, which was certainly not included within the
limits of the 'Âryâvarta' of the ancient Dharma-sûtra
(LXXXIV, 4). As no other Smriti contains a list of this
kind, the whole chapter may be viewed as a later addition.
4. The ceremonies described in XC are not mentioned in
other Smritis, while some of them are decidedly Vishnuitic,
or traceable in modern works; and as all the Sûtras in XC
hang closely together, this entire chapter seems also to be
spurious. 5. The repetitions in the list of articles forbidden
to sell (LIV, 18–22); the addition of the two categories of
atipâtakâni, 'crimes in the highest degree,' and prakîrnakam,
'miscellaneous crimes' (XXXIII, 3, 5; XXXIV; XLII), to
Manu's list of crimes; the frequent references to the Ganges
river; and other such passages, which show a modern
character, without being traceable in the Smritis of Yâgñavalkya and Nârada, may have been added by the Vish-

*n*uitic editor from modern Sm*ri*tis, either for the sake of completeness, or in order to make up the required number of chapters. 6. All the passages hitherto mentioned are such as have no parallel in other ancient Sm*ri*tis. But the Vish*n*uitic editor did evidently not confine himself to the introduction of new matter into the ancient Dharmasûtra. That he did not refrain, occasionally, from altering the original text, has been conjectured above with regard to his readings of some of those *S*lokas, which are found in the code of Manu as well ; and it can be proved quite clearly by comparing his version of the V*ri*shotsarga ceremony (LXXXVI) with the analogous chapter of the Kâ*th*aka G*ri*hya-sûtra. In one case (LI, 64 ; cf. XXIII, 50 = M. V, 131) he has replaced the words, which refer the authorship of the *S*loka in question to Manu, by an unmeaning term. The superior antiquity of Manu's reading (V, 41) is vouched for by the recurrence of the same passage in the G*ri*hya-sûtra of *S*ânkhâyana (II, 16, 1) and in the Vâsish*th*a-sm*ri*ti (IV, 6), and the reference to Manu has no doubt been removed by the Vish*n*uitic editor, because it would have been out of place in a speech of Vish*n*u. References to sayings of Manu and other teachers and direct quotations from Vedic works are more or less common in all Dharmasûtras, and their entire absence in this work is apparently due to their systematical removal by the editor. On the other hand, the lists of Vedic and other works to be studied or recited may have been enlarged in one or two cases by him or by another interpolator, namely, XXX, 37 (cf. V, 191), where the Atharva-veda is mentioned after the other Vedas by the name of 'Âtharva*n*a' (not Atharvâṅgirasas, as in the code of Manu and most other ancient works), and LXXXIII, 7, where Vyâkara*n*a, 'Grammar,' i. e. according to the Commentary the grammars of Pâ*n*ini and others, is mentioned as distinct from the Vedâṅgas. The antiquity of the former passage might indeed be defended by the example of Âpastamba, who, though referring like this work to the 'three Vedas' both separately and collectively, mentions in another place the 'Âtharva*n*a-veda[1].' Besides the above works,

---

[1] See Bühler, Introduction to Âpastamba, p. xxiv.

and those referred to in LVI, the laws of Vish*n*u name no other work except the Purâ*n*as, Itihâsas, and Dharma*s*âstras. 7. As the Vish*n*uitic editor did not scruple to alter the import of a certain number of passages, the modernisation of the language of the whole work, which was probably as rich in archaic forms and curious old terms as the Kâ*th*aka G*ri*hya-sûtra and as the Dharma-sûtra of Âpastamba, may be likewise attributed to him. As it is, the Vish*n*u-sûtra agrees in style and expressions more closely with the Sm*ri*tis of Manu and Yâg*ñ*avalkya than with any other work, and it is at least not inferior to the former work in the preservation of archaic forms. Thus the code of Manu has seven aorist forms[1], while the Vish*n*u-sûtra contains six, not including those occurring in Vedic Mantras which are quoted by their Pratîkas only. Of new words and meanings of words the Vish*n*u-sûtra contains also a certain number; they have lately been communicated by me to Dr. von Böhtlingk for insertion in his new Dictionary.

All the points noticed render it necessary to assign a comparatively recent date to the Vish*n*uitic editor; and if the introduction of the week of the Greeks into the ancient Dharma-sûtra has been justly attributed to him, he cannot be placed earlier than the third or fourth century A. D.[2] The lower limit must be put before the eleventh century, in which the Vish*n*u-sûtra is quoted in the Mitâksharâ of Vig*ñ*âne*s*vara. From that time downwards it is quoted in nearly every law digest, and a particularly large number of quotations occurs in Aparârka's Commentary on Yâg*ñ*avalkya, which was composed in the twelfth century[3]. Nearly all those quotations, as far as they have been examined, are actually found in the Vish*n*u-sûtra; but the whole text is vouched for only by Nandapa*nd*ita's Commentary, called Vaig*a*yantî, which was composed in the

---

[1] Whitney, Indische Grammatik, § 826.

[2] See Jacobi, Journal of the German Oriental Society, XXX, 306. The first author with a known date, who shows an acquaintance with the week of the Greeks, is Varâhamihira (sixth century A. D.)

[3] See Bühler, Ka*s*mîr Report, p. 52. The MSS. used are from the Dekhan College, Pu*n*a.

first quarter of the seventeenth century. The subscriptions
in the London MSS. of the Vaigayantî contain the statement, which is borne out by the Introduction, that it
was composed by Nandapandita, the son of Râmapandita
Dharmâdhikârin, an inhabitant of Benares, at the instiga-
tion of the Mahârâga Kesavanâyaka, also called Tammasâ-
nâyaka, the son of Kodapanâyaka; and a passage added at
the end of the work states, more accurately, that Nandasar-
man (Nandapandita) wrote it at Kâsî (Benares) in the year
1679 of the era of Vikramabhâsvara (=A.D. 1622), by
command of Kesavanâyaka, his own king. These statements regarding the time and place of the composition of
the Vaigayantî are corroborated by the fact that it refers
in several cases to the opinions of Haradatta, who appears
to have lived in the sixteenth century[1], while Nandapandita
is not among the numerous authors quoted in the Vîramitrodaya of Mitramisra, who lived in the beginning of the
seventeenth century[2], and who was consequently a contem-
porary of Nandapandita, if the above statement is correct;
and that he attacks in a number of cases the views of the
'Eastern Commentators' (Prâkyas), and quotes a term from
the dialect of Madhyadesa.

The subjoined translation is based upon the text handed
down by Nandapandita nearly everywhere except in some
of the Mantras, which have been rendered according to the
better readings preserved in the Kâthaka Grihya-sûtra.
The two Calcutta editions of the Vishnu-sûtra, the second of
which is a mere reprint of the first, will be found to agree in
the main with the text here translated. They are doubtless
based upon the Vaigayantî, as they contain several passages
in which portions of Nandapandita's Commentary have
crept into the text of the Sûtras. But the MS. used for
the first Calcutta edition must have been a very faulty one,
as both Calcutta editions, besides differing from the best
MSS. of the Vaigayantî on a very great number of minor
points, entirely omit the greater part of Chapter LXXXI

---

[1] Bühler, Introduction to Âpastamba, p. xliii.
[2] Bühler loc. cit.

(3–22), the genuineness of which is proved by analogous passages in the other Smritis [1]. An excellent copy of the Vaigayantî in possession of Dr. Bühler has, together with three London MSS. of that work and one London MS. containing the text only, enabled me to establish quite positively nearly in every case the readings sanctioned by Nandapandita. I had hoped to publish a new edition of the text prepared from those MSS., and long ready for the press, before publishing my English version. This expectation has not been fulfilled, but it is hoped that in the mean time this attempt at a translation will be welcome to the students of Indian antiquity, and will facilitate the understanding of the text printed in Gîvânanda Vidyâsâgara's cheap edition, which is probably in the hands of most Sanskrit scholars. The precise nature of the relation in which the text of my forthcoming edition stands to the Calcutta editions may be gathered from the large specimens of the text as given in the best MSS., that have been edited by Dr. Bühler in the Bombay Digest, and by myself in two papers published in the Transactions of the Royal Bavarian Academy of Science.

Nandapandita has composed, besides the Vaigayantî, a treatise on the law of adoption, called Dattaka-mî-mâmsâ [2], a commentary on the code of Parâsara, a work called Vidvanmanoharâ-smritisindhu, one called Srâddha-kalpa-latâ, and commentaries on the Mitâksharâ and on Âdityâkârya's Âsaukanirnaya. All these works belong to the province of Hindu law, and both his fertility as a writer in that branch of Indian science, and the reputation enjoyed by some of his works even nowadays, must raise a strong presumption in favour of his knowledge of the subject. The

---

[1] The first edition of the 'Vaishnava Dharmasâstra' was published in Bengali type by Bhavânîkarana; the second, in Devanâgarî type, is contained in Gîvânanda Vidyâsâgara's Dharmashâstrasangraha (1876).

[2] This work has been published repeatedly at Calcutta and Madras, and translated into English by Sutherland (1821), which translation has been reprinted in Stokes' Hindu Law Books. The rest of the above list is made up from an enumeration of Nandapandita's Tîkâs at the end of Dr. Bühler's copy of the Vaigayantî, from an occasional remark in the latter work itself (XV, 9), and from Professor Weber's Catalogue of the Berlin Sanskrit MSS.

general trustworthiness of his Commentary on the Vishnu-sûtra is further confirmed by the frequent references which it contains to the opinions of earlier commentators of that work ; and the wide extent of his reading, though he often makes an unnecessary display of it, has been eminently serviceable to him in tracing the connection of certain chapters and Mantras with the Kâthaka literature[1]. On the other hand, his very learning, combined with a strict adherence to the well-known theory of Hindu commentators regarding the absolute identity between the teaching of all Smritis, has frequently misled him into a too extensive method of interpretation. Even in commenting the Slokas he assigns in many cases an important hidden meaning to such particles as ka, vâ, tathâ, and others, and to unpretending epithets and the like, which have clearly been added for metrical reasons only[2]. This practice, besides being contrary to common sense, is nowhere countenanced by the authority of Kullûka, in his remarks on the numerous identical Slokas found in the code of Manu. With the Sûtras generally speaking the case is different : many of them would be nearly or quite unintelligible without the explanatory remarks added in brackets from Nandapandita's Commentary[3], and in a number of those cases even, where his method jars upon a European mind, the clauses supplied by him are probably correct[4]. The same may be said of his interpretations of the epithets of Vishnu, excepting those which are based on utterly fanciful etymologies[5],

---

[1] See the notes on LXV, 2 seq. ; LXXIII, 5–9 ; LXXXVI, 13. In his Commentary on LXVII also Nandapandita states expressly that the description of the Vaisvadeva is according to the rites of the Katha-sâkhâ.

[2] For instances, see the notes on XX, 45 ; LXIV, 40.

[3] See e. g. Chapter V passim.

[4] Thus nearly all the 'intentionally's' and 'unintentionally's,' &c., as supplied in the section on penances might seem superfluous, or even wrong ; but as in several places involuntary crimes are expressly distinguished from those intentionally committed (see e.g. XXVIII, 48, 51 ; XXXVIII, 7), and as in other cases a clause of this kind must needs be supplied (see XXXIX, 2 ; LII, 3 ; LIII, 5, &c.), Nandapandita is probably right in supplying it from other Smritis in most remaining cases as well. This method has occasionally carried him too far, when his explanations have not been given in the text.

[5] See I, 51, 55 ; XCVIII, 40, 41, 46, &c.

as the style of the introductory and final chapters is as artificial, though in another way, as the Sûtra style. Though,
however, in works composed in the latter style, every *k*a,
vâ, or iti, &c., which is not absolutely required by the sense,
was probably intended by their authors to convey a special
meaning[1], it is a question of evidence in every single case,
whether those meanings which Nandapa*nd*ita assigns to
these and other such particles and expletive words are
the correct ones. In several cases of this or of a similar
kind he is palpably wrong[2], and in many others the interpretations proposed by him are at least improbable, because
the authoritative passages he quotes in support of them are
taken from modern works, which cannot have been known
to the author of the Vish*n*u-sûtra. Interpretations of this
class have, therefore, been given in the notes only; and they
have been omitted altogether in a number of cases where
they appeared quite frivolous, or became too numerous,
or could not be deciphered completely, owing to clerical
mistakes in the MSS. But though it is impossible to agree
with some of his general principles of interpretation, or with
his application of them, Nandapa*nd*ita's interpretations of
difficult terms and Sûtras are invaluable, and I have never
deviated from them in my translation without strong reasons
to the contrary, which have in most cases been stated in the
notes[3]. Besides the extracts given in the notes, a few other
passages from the Commentary and several other additions
will be given in p. 312; and I must apologize to my readers
for having to note along with the Addenda a number of
Corrigenda, which will be found in the same page. In com-
piling the Index of Sanskrit words occurring in this work,
which it has been thought necessary to add to the General
Index, I have not aimed at completeness except as regards

---

[1] For instances of this in the Dharma-sûtras of Âpastamba and Gautama, see
Bühler, Âpast. I, 2, 7, 24; 8, 5; Gaut. V, 5, 14, 17; IX, 44; XIV, 45; XIX,
13-15, 20; XXI, 9, &c.; and see also Dr. Bühler's remarks on G*n*âpaka-sûtras,
Âpast. I, 3, 11, 7; Gaut. I, 31, notes.

[2] See V, 117; VII, 7; XXVII, 10; LI, 26; LXXI, 88; LXXIII, 9;
LXXIV, 1, 2, 7, &c.

[3] See e.g. XVII, 22; XVIII, 44; XXIV, 40; XXVIII, 5, 11; LV, 20; LIX,
27, 29; LXIII, 36; LXIV, 18; LXVII, 6-8; XCII, 4; XCVII, 7.

the names of deities and of penances.   My forthcoming
edition of the Sanskrit text will be accompanied by a full
Index of words.

In conclusion I have to express my thanks in the most
cordial manner to Dr. Bühler, who has constantly assisted
me with his advice in the preparing of this translation, and
has kindly lent me his excellent copy of the Vaigayantî; and
to Dr. von Böhtlingk and Professor Max Müller, who have
favoured me with valuable hints on divers points connected
with this work.   My acknowledgments are due, in the
second place, to K. M. Chatfield, Esq., Director of Public
Instruction, Bombay, to Dr. von Halm, Chief Librarian of
the Royal Library, Munich, to Professor R. Lepsius, Chief
Librarian of the Royal Library of Berlin, and to Dr. R.
Rost, Chief Librarian of the India Office Library, London,
for the valuable aid received from these gentlemen and the
great liberality with which they have placed Sanskrit MSS.
under their care at my disposal.

VISH*N*U.

VISH*N*U

I.

1. THE night of Brahman being over, and the God sprung from the lotus (Brahman) having woke from his slumber, Vish*n*u purposing to create living beings, and perceiving the earth covered with water,

2. Assumed the shape of a boar, delighting to sport in water, as at the beginning of each former Kalpa, and raised up the earth (from the water).

3. His feet were the Vedas; his tusks the sacrificial stakes; in his teeth were the offerings; his mouth was the pyre; his tongue was the fire; his hair was the sacrificial grass; the sacred texts were his head; and he was (endowed with the miraculous power of) a great ascetic.

4. His eyes were day and night; he was of superhuman nature; his ears were the two bundles of Ku*s*a grass (for the Ish*t*is, or smaller sacrifices, and for the animal offerings); his ear-rings were the ends of those bundles of Ku*s*a grass (used for wiping

---

I. 1. Regarding the duration of a night of Brahman, see XX, 14. 'Bhûtâni' means living beings of all the four kinds, born from the womb and the rest. (Nand.) The three other kinds consist of those produced from an egg, from sweat, and from a shoot or germ; see Manu I, 43–46.

2. A Kalpa = a day of Brahman; see XX, 13.

the ladle and other sacrificial implements); his nose
(the vessel containing) the clarified butter; his snout
was the ladle of oblations; his voice was similar in
sound to the chanting of the Sâma-veda; and he
was of huge size.

5. He was full of piety and veracity; beautiful;
his strides and his strength were immense (like
those of Vish*n*u); his large nostrils were penances;
his knees the victim; and his figure colossal.

6. His entrails were the (three) chanters of the
Sâma-veda [1]; his member was the burnt-oblation; his
scrotum was the sacrificial seeds and grains; his
mind was the altar (in the hut for the wives and
domestic uses of the sacrificer); the hindparts (of
Vish*n*u) in his transformation were the Mantras;
his blood was the Soma juice.

7. His shoulders were the (great) altar; his smell
was that of the (sacrificial cake and other) oblations;
his speed was the oblations to the gods and to the
manes and other oblations; his body was the hut for
the wives and domestic uses of the sacrificer; he was
majestic; and instructed with the initiatory ceremonies for manifold sacrifices (lasting one, or two,
three, or twelve years, and others).

8. His heart was the sacrificial fee; he was
possessed of the (sacrificial and other) great Mantras employed in order to effect the union of the
mind with the Supreme; he was of enormous size
(like the long sacrifices lasting more than one day);
his lovely lips were the beginnings of the two

---

6. [1] 'This is because the vital breaths, by which the sound of the
voice is effected, pass through them, it having been said (in 4) that
the sound of his voice was like the chanting of the Sâma-veda.'
(Nand.)

hymns recited at the beginning of the animal sacrifice; his ornaments were the whirlpool of the milk poured into the heated vessel (at the Pravargya ceremony introductory to the Soma-sacrifice).

9. All sorts of sacred texts (the Gâyatrî and others) were his path in marching; the mysterious Upanishads (the Vedânta) were his couch; he was accompanied by his consort *Kh*âyâ (Lakshmî); he was in size like the Ma*nisri*ṅga mountain.

10. The lord, the creator, the great Yogin, plunging into the .one. ocean from love of the world,

11. Raised up, with the edge of his tusks, the earth bounded by the sea together with its mountains, forests, and groves, which was immersed in the water of (the seven oceans now become) one ocean, and created the universe anew.

12. Thus the whole earth, after having sunk into (the lower region called) Rasâtala, was in the first place raised in the boar-incarnation by Vish*n*u, who took compassion upon the living beings.

13, 14. Then, after having raised the earth, the destroyer of Madhu placed and fixed it upon its own (former) seat (upon the oceans) and distributed the waters upon it according to their own (former) station, conducting the floods of the oceans into the oceans, the water of the rivers into the rivers, the water of the tanks into the tanks, and the water of the lakes into the lakes.

15. He created the seven (lower regions called) Pâtâlas [1] and the seven worlds, the seven Dvîpas

---

15. [1] The seven Pâtâlas are, Atala, Vitala, Sutala, Mahâtala, Rasâtala, Talâtala, and Pâtâla; the seven worlds are, Bhûr-loka, Bhuvar-loka, Svar-loka, Mahar-loka, *G*anar-loka, Tapar-loka, and Satya-

and the seven oceans, and fixed their several limits[2].

16. (He created) the rulers of the (seven) Dvîpas and the (eight) guardians of the world (Indra and the rest), the rivers, mountains, and trees, the seven *Ri*shis, who know (and practise) the law, the Vedas together with their Angas, the Suras, and the Asuras.

17. (He created) Pisâ*k*as (ogres), Uragas (serpents), Gandharvas (celestial singers), Yakshas (keepers of Kubera's treasures), Rakshasas (goblins), and men, cattle, birds, deer and other animals, (in short) all the four kinds of living beings[1], and clouds, rainbows, lightnings, and other celestial phenomena or bodies (such as the planets and the asterisms), and all kinds of sacrifices.

18. Bhagavat, after having thus created, in the

---

loka; the seven Dvîpas or divisions of the terrestrial world are, *G*ambu, Plaksha, *S*âlmalî, Ku*s*a, Krau*ñk*a, *S*âka, and Pushkara; each Dvipa is encircled by one of the seven oceans, viz. the seas of Lava*n*a (salt-water), Ikshu (syrup), Sarpi*h* (butter), Dadhi (sour milk), Dugdha (milk), Svâdhu (treacle), and Udaka (water), (Nand.) The enumerations contained in the Vish*n*u-purâ*n*a and other works differ on two or three points only from that given by Nand.—
[2] Besides the interpretation followed in the text, Nand. proposes a second explanation of the term 'sthânâni,' as denoting Bhârata-varsha (India) and the other eight plains situated between the principal mountains.

16. The eight 'guardians of the world' (Lokapâlas) are, Indra, Agni, Yama, Sûrya, Varu*n*a, Pavana, Kubera, and Soma (M.V, 96). The seven *Ri*shis, according to the *S*atapatha-brâhma*n*a, are, Gotama, Bharadvâ*g*a, Vi*s*vâmitra, *G*amadagni, Vasish*th*a, Ka*s*yapa, and Atri. The six Vedângas are, *S*ikshâ (pronunciation), *Kh*andas (metre), Vyâkara*n*a (grammar), Nirukta (etymology), Kalpa (ceremonial), and *G*yotisha (astronomy). See Max Müller, Ancient Sanskrit Literature, p. 108, &c.

17. [1] See 1.

shape of a boar, this world together with all animate and inanimate things in it, went away into a place hidden from the world.

19. *G*anârdana, the chief of the gods, having become invisible, the goddess of the earth began to consider, 'How shall I be able to sustain myself (henceforth)?'

20. 'I will go to Ka*s*yapa to ask : he will tell me the truth. The great Muni has my welfare under constant consideration.'

21. Having thus decided upon her course, the goddess, assuming the shape of a woman, went to see Ka*s*yapa, and Ka*s*yapa saw her.

22. Her eyes were similar to the leaves of the blue lotus (of which the bow of Kâma, the god of love, is made); her face was radiant like the moon in the autumn season; her locks were as dark as a swarm of black bees; she was radiant; her lip was (red) like the Bandhu*g*îva flower; and she was lovely to behold.

23. Her eyebrows were fine; her teeth exceedingly small; her nose handsome; her brows bent; her neck shaped like a shell; her thighs were constantly touching each other; and they were fleshy thighs, which adorned her loins.

24. Her breasts were shining white, firm[1], plump, very close to each other, (decorated with continuous strings of pearls) like the projections on the forehead of Indra's elephant, and radiant like the gold (of the two golden jars used at the consecration of a king).

---

24. [1] Or 'equal in size,' according to the second of the two explanations which Nand. proposes of the term 'samau.'

25. Her arms were as delicate as lotus fibres;
her hands were similar to young shoots; her thighs
were resplendent like golden pillars; and her knees
were hidden (under the flesh), and closely touching
each other.

26. Her legs were smooth and exquisitely
proportioned; her feet exceedingly graceful; her
loins fleshy; and her waist like that of a lion's
cub.

27. Her reddish nails shone (like rubies); her
beauty was the delight of every looker-on; and with
her glances she filled at every step all the quarters
of the sky as it were with lotus-flowers.

28. Radiant with divine lustre, she illuminated all
the quarters of the sky with it; her clothing was
most exquisite and perfectly white; and she was
decorated with the most precious gems.

29. With her steps she covered the earth as it
were with lotuses; she was endowed with beauty
and youthful charms; and made her approach with
modest bearing.

30. Having seen her come near, Kasyapa saluted
her reverentially, and said, 'O handsome lady, O
earth, radiant with divine lustre, I am acquainted
with thy thoughts.

31. 'Go to visit Ganârdana, O large-eyed lady;
he will tell thee accurately, how thou shalt henceforth sustain thyself.

32. 'For thy sake, O (goddess), whose face is
lovely and whose limbs are beautiful, I have found
out, by profound meditation, that his residence is in
the Kshîroda (milk-ocean).'

33. The goddess of the earth answered, 'Yes,
(I shall do as you bid me),' saluted Kasyapa rever-

entially, and proceeded to the Kshîroda sea, in order to see Kesava (Vishnu).

34. She beheld (then) the ocean, from which the Amrita arose. It was lovely, like the rays of the moon, and agitated by hundreds of waves produced by stormy blasts of wind.

35. (With its waves) towering like a hundred Himâlayas it seemed another terrestrial globe, calling near as it were the earth with its hands, the rolling waves.

36. With those hands it was as it were constantly producing the radiancy of the moon; and every stain of guilt was removed from it by Hari's (Vishnu's) residence within its limits.

37. Because (it was entirely free from sin) therefore it was possessed of a pure and shining frame; its colour was white; it was inaccessible to birds; and its seat was in the lower regions.

38. It was rich in blue and tawny gems (sapphires, coral, and others), and looking therefore as if the atmosphere had descended upon the earth, and as if a number of forests adorned with a multitude of fruits had descended upon its surface.

39. Its size was immense, like that of the skin of (Vishnu's) serpent Sesha. After having seen the milk-ocean, the goddess of the earth beheld the dwelling of Kesava (Vishnu) which was in it:

40. (His dwelling), the size of which cannot be expressed in words, and the sublimity of which is also beyond the power of utterance. In it she saw the destroyer of Madhu seated upon Sesha.

41. The lotus of his face was hardly visible on

37. See 15, note.

account of the lustre of the gems decorating the neck of the snake *Sesha*; he was shining like a hundred moons; and his splendour was equal to the rays of a myriad of suns.

42. He was clad in a yellow robe (radiant like gold); imperturbable; decorated with all kinds of gems; and shining with the lustre of a diadem resembling the sun in colour, and with (splendid) ear-rings.

43. Lakshmî was stroking his feet with her soft palms; and his attributes (the shell, the discus, the mace, and the lotus-flower) wearing bodies were attending upon him on all sides.

44. Having espied the lotus-eyed slayer of Madhu, she knelt down upon the ground and addressed him as follows:

45. 'When formerly I was sunk into the region of Rasâtala, I was raised by thee, O God, and restored to my ancient seat, O Vish*n*u, thanks to thy benevolence towards living beings.

46. 'Being there, how am I to maintain myself upon it, O lord of the gods?' Having been thus addressed by the goddess, the god enunciated the following answer:

47. 'Those who practise the duties ordained for each caste and for each order, and who act up strictly to the holy law, will sustain thee, O earth; to them is thy care committed.'

48. Having received this answer, the goddess of the earth said to the chief of the gods, 'Communicate to me the eternal laws of the castes and of the orders.

47. Regarding the four castes and the four orders, see II, 1; III, 3.

49. 'I desire to learn them from thee; for thou art my chief stay. Adoration be to thee, O brilliant[1] chief of the gods, who annihilatest the power of the (Daityas and other) enemies of the gods.

50. 'O Nârâyana (son of Nara), O Gagannâtha (sovereign of the world); thou holdest the shell, the discus, and the mace (in thy hands); thou hast a lotus (Brahman) springing from thy navel; thou art the lord of the senses; thou art most powerful and endowed with conquering strength.

51. 'Thou art beyond the cognisance of the senses; thy end is most difficult to know; thou art brilliant; thou holdest the bow Sârṅga; thou art the boar[1]; thou art terrible; thou art Govinda[2] (the herdsman); thou art of old; thou art Purushottama (the spirit supreme).

52. 'Thy hair is golden; thy eyes are everywhere; thy body is the sacrifice; thou art free from stain; thou art the "field" (the corporeal frame); thou art the principle of life; thou art the ruler

---

49. [1] This is Nand.'s interpretation of the term 'deva,' but it may also be taken in its usual acceptation of 'god.'

51. [1] This is the third of the three interpretations of the term varâha, which Nand. proposes. According to the first, it would mean 'one who kills his worst or most prominent foes;' according to the second, 'one who gratifies his own desires.' But these two interpretations are based upon a fanciful derivation of varâha from vara and â-han. Of many others among the epithets Nand. proposes equally fanciful etymologies, which I shall pass over unnoticed.— [2] This epithet, which literally means 'he who finds or wins cows,' is usually referred to Vishnu's recovering the 'cow,' i.e. the earth, when it was lost in the waters: see Mahâbh. XII, 13228, which verse is quoted both by Nand. and by Sankara in his Commentary on the Vishnu-sahasranâma. It originally refers, no doubt, to Vishnu or Krishna as the pastoral god.

of the world; thou art lying on the bed of the ocean.

53. 'Thou art Mantra (prayer); thou knowest the Mantras; thou surpassest all conception; thy frame is composed of the Vedas and Vedângas; the creation and destruction of this whole world is effected through thee.

54. 'Thou knowest right and wrong; thy body is law; law springs from thee; desires are gratified by thee; thy powers are everywhere; thou art (imperishable like) Am*ri*ta (ambrosia); thou art heaven; thou art the destroyer of Madhu and Kai*l*asa.

55. 'Thou causest the increase of the great; thou art inscrutable; thou art all; thou givest shelter to all; thou art the chief one; thou art free from sin; thou art *G*îmûta; thou art inexhaustible; thou art the creator.

56. 'Thou increasest the welfare (of the world); the waters spring from thee; thou art the seat of intelligence; action is not found in thee; thou presidest over seven chief things[1]; thou art the teacher of religious rites; thou art of old; thou art Purushottama.

57. 'Thou art not to be shaken; thou art unde-

---

55. 'The great (br*i*hat) means time, space, and the like. . . . He is called "all" because he is capable of assuming any shape.' (Nand.)   The sense of the term '*g*îmûta,' as an epithet of divine beings, is uncertain. According to Nand., it would mean 'he who sprinkles living beings;' but this interpretation is based upon a fanciful derivation, from *g*îva and mûtrayati.

56. [1] This refers either to the seven divisions of a Sâman; or to the seven species, of which each of the three kinds of sacrifices, domestic offerings, burnt-offerings, and Soma-sacrifices, consists (cf. Gaut. VIII, 18–20); or to the seven worlds (see 15, note), Bhûr and the rest. (Nand.)

caying; thou art the producer of the atoms; thou art kind to faithful attendants; thou art the purifier (of sinners); thou art the protector of all the gods; thou art the protector of the pious.

58. 'Thou art also the protector of those who know the Veda, O Purushottama. I have come, O *G*agannâtha, to the immovable Vâ*k*aspati (the lord of holy speech), the lord;

59. 'To him, who is very pious; invincible; Vasushe*n*a (who has treasures for his armies); who bestows largesses upon his followers; who is endowed with the power of intense devotion; who is the germ of the ether; from whom the rays (of the sun and moon) proceed;

60. 'To Vâsudeva; the great soul of the universe; whose eyes are like lotuses; who is eternal; the preceptor of the Suras and of the Asuras; brilliant; omnipresent; the great lord of all creatures;

61. 'Who has one body and four faces; who is the producer of (the five grosser elements, ether, air, fire, water, and earth), the producers of the world. Teach me concisely, O Bhagavat, the eternal laws ordained for the aggregate of the four castes,

62. 'Together with the customs to be observed by each order and with the secret ordinances.' The chief of the gods, thus addressed by the goddess of the earth, replied to her as follows:

---

62. According to Nand., the term rahasya, 'secret ordinances or doctrines,' has to be referred either to the laws regarding the occupations lawful for each caste in times of distress (âpaddharma, see II, 15), or to the penances (XLVI seq.) The latter interpretation seems to be the more plausible one, with the limitation, however, that rahasya is only used to denote the penances for secret faults, which are termed rahasya in LV, 1.

63. 'Learn from me, in a concise form, O radiant goddess of the earth, the eternal laws for the aggregate of the four castes, together with the customs to be observed by each order, and with the secret ordinances,

64. 'Which will effect the final liberation of the virtuous persons, who will support thee. Be seated upon this splendid golden seat, O handsome-thighed goddess.

65. 'Seated at ease, listen to me proclaiming the sacred laws.' The goddess of the earth, thereupon, seated at ease, listened to the sacred precepts as they came from the mouth of Vishnu.

II.

1. Brâhmanas, Kshatriyas, Vaisyas, and Sûdras are the four castes.

2. The first three of these are (called) twice-born.

3. For them the whole number of ceremonies, which begin with the impregnation and end with the ceremony of burning the dead body, have to be performed with (the recitation of) Mantras.

4. Their duties are:

5. For a Brâhmana, to teach (the Veda);

6. For a Kshatriya, constant practice in arms;

7. For a Vaisya, the tending of cattle;

8. For a Sûdra, to serve the twice-born;

II. 1. Âpast. I, 1, 1, 3. — 1, 2. M. X, 4; Y. I, 10. — 3. M. II, 26; Y. I, 10. — 4–9. M. I, 88–91; VIII, 410; IX, 326–335; X, 75–79; Y. I, 118–120; Âpast. I, 1, 1, 5, 6; II, 5, 10, 4–7; Gaut. X, 2, 7, 49, 56. — 15. M. X, 81; Y. III, 35; Gaut. VII, 6. — 16, 17. Gaut. VIII, 23; X, 51. 'This chapter treats of the four castes.' (Nand.)

9. For all the twice-born, to sacrifice and to study (the Veda).

10. Again, their modes of livelihood are:

11. For a Brâhma*n*a, to sacrifice for others and to receive alms;

12. For a Kshatriya, to protect the world (and receive due reward, in form of taxes);

13. For a Vai*s*ya, tillage, keeping cows (and other cattle), traffic, lending money upon interest, and growing seeds;

14. For a *S*ûdra, all branches of art (such as painting and the other fine arts);

15. In times of distress, each caste may follow the occupation of that next (below) to it in rank.

16. Forbearance, veracity, restraint, purity, liberality, self-control, not to kill (any living being), obedience towards one's Gurus, visiting places of pilgrimage, sympathy (with the afflicted),

17. Straightforwardness, freedom from covetousness, reverence towards gods and Brâhma*n*as, and freedom from anger are duties common (to all castes).

III.

1. Now the duties of a king are:

2. To protect his people,

---

14. According to Nand., the use of the term sarva, 'all,' implies that *S*ûdras may also follow the occupations of a Vai*s*ya, tillage and the rest, as ordained by Devala.

16. The term Guru, 'superior,' generally denotes the parents and the teacher, or Guru in the narrower sense of the term; see XXXI, 1, 2. It may also include all those who are one's elders or betters; see XXXII, 1–3.

III. 2, 3. M. VII, 35, 144; Gaut. X, 7; XI, 9. — 4, 5. M. VII, 69; Y. I, 320. — 6. M. VII, 70; Y. I, 320; Âpast. II, 10, 25, 2.—

3. And to keep the four castes and the four orders[1] in the practice of their several duties.

4. Let the king fix his abode in a district containing open plains, fit for cattle, and abounding in grain;

5. And inhabited by many Vaisyas and Sûdras.

6. There let him reside in a stronghold (the strength of which consists) either in (its being surrounded·by) a desert, or in (a throng of) armed

---

7–10. M. VII, 115; Âpast. II, 10, 26, 4, 5. — 11–15. M. VII, 116, 117. — 16–21. M. VII, 61, 62; Y. I, 321. — 22–25. M. VII, 130–132; Y. I, 327; Âpast. II, 10, 26, 9; Gaut. X, 24, 25. — 26. M. VII, 133; Âpast. II, 10, 26, 10. — 28. M. VIII, 304; Y. I, 334; Gaut. XI, 11. — 29, 30. M. VII, 128; VIII, 398; Y. II, 161; Gaut. X, 26. — 31. M. VIII, 400; Y. II, 262. — 32. M. VII, 138; Gaut. X, 31–33. — 33. M. IX, 294; Y. I, 352. — 35. M. VII, 122, 184; Y. I, 331, 337. — 36, 37. Y. I, 337. — 38–41. M. VII, 158–161, 182, 183; Y. I, 344–347. — 42. M. VII, 203; Y. I, 342. — 43. M. VII, 215. — 44. M. VII, 88. — 45. M. VII, 89; Y. I, 324; Âpast. II, 10, 26, 2, 3. — 47. M. VII, 202. — 50–52. M. VII, 50, 51. — 55. M. VII, 62; VIII, 39. — 56–58. M. VIII, 37, 38; Y. II, 34; Gaut. X, 43, 44. — 61. Gaut. X, 45. — 62. Y. II, 35. — 63. M. VIII, 35. — 64. M. VIII, 36. — 65. M. VIII, 27, 28; Gaut. X, 48. — 66, 67. M. VIII, 40; Y. II, 36; Âpast. II, 10, 26, 8; Gaut. X, 46, 47. — 68. Gaut. X, 17. — 70. M. VII, 78; Y. I, 312; Gaut. XI, 12. — 71. M. VII, 54, 60; Y. I, 311. — 72. M. VIII, 1; Y. II, 1. — 73. M. VIII, 9; Y. II, 3; Gaut. XIII, 96. — 74. M. VIII, 12–19; Y. II, 2; Âpast. II, 11, 29, 5. — 75. Gaut. XI, 15. — 76, 77. M. VII, 38. — 79, 80 M. VII, 134; Y. I, 338; Âpast. II, 10, 25, 11; Gaut. X, 9, 10. — 81. Âpast. II, 10, 26, 1. — 81, 82. Y. I, 317–319. — 84. M. VII, 82; Y. I, 314. — 85. M. VII, 220. — 87, 88. M. VII, 217, 218. — 89. M. VII, 146. — 91, 92. M. VII, 16; VIII, 126; Y. I, 367; Gaut. X, 8. — 94. M. VIII, 335; Y. I, 357; Âpast. II, 11, 28, 13. — 95. M. VII, 25. — 96. M. VII, 32; Y. I, 333 — 97. M. VII, 33. Chapters III–XVIII contain the section on vyavahâra, 'jurisprudence.' (Nand.)

3.[1] Of student, householder, hermit, and ascetic.

5. 'And there should be many virtuous men in it, as stated by Manu, VII, 69.' (Nand.)

men, or in fortifications (of stone, brick, or others), or in water (enclosing it on all sides), or in trees, or in mountains (sheltering it against a foreign invasion).

7. (While he resides) there, let him appoint chiefs (or governors) in every village;

8. Also, lords of every ten villages;

9. And lords of every hundred villages;

10. And lords of a whole district.

11. If any offence has been committed in a village, let the lord of that village suppress the evil (and give redress to those that have been wronged).

12. If he is unable to do so, let him announce it to the lord of ten villages;

13. If he too is unable, let him announce it to the lord of a hundred villages;

14. If he too is unable, let him announce it to the lord of the whole district.

15. The lord of the whole district must eradicate the evil to the best of his power.

16. Let the king appoint able officials for the working of his mines, for the levying of taxes and of the fares to be paid at ferries, and for his elephants and forests.

17. (Let him appoint) pious persons for performing acts of piety (such as bestowing gifts on the indigent, and the like);

18. Skilled men for financial business (such as examining gold and other precious metals);

---

11. See 67 and Dr. Bühler's note on Âpast. II, 10, 26, 8.

16. The term nâgavana, which has been translated as a Dvandva compound, denoting elephants and forests, may also be taken to mean 'forests in which there are elephants;' or nâga may mean 'situated in the mountains' or 'a mountain fort.' (Nand.)

18. Or, 'he must appoint men skilled in logic as his advisers in knotty points of argument.' (Nand.)

19. Brave men for fighting;

20. Stern men for acts of rigour (such as beating and killing);

21. Eunuchs for his wives (as their guardians).

22. He must take from his subjects as taxes a sixth part every year of the grain;

23. And (a sixth part) of all (other) seeds;

24. Two in the hundred, of cattle, gold, and clothes;

25. A sixth part of flesh, honey, clarified butter, herbs, perfumes, flowers, roots, fruits, liquids and condiments, wood, leaves (of the Palmyra tree and others), skins, earthen pots, stone vessels, and anything made of split bamboo.

26. Let him not levy any tax upon Brâhma*n*as.

27. For they pay taxes to him in the shape of their pious acts.

28. A sixth part both of the virtuous deeds and of the iniquitous acts committed by his subjects goes to the king.

29. Let him take a tenth part of (the price of) marketable commodities (sold) in his own country;

30. And a twentieth part of (the price of) goods (sold) in another country.

31. Any (seller or buyer) who (fraudulently) avoids a toll-house (situated on his road), shall lose all his goods.

---

23. This rule relates to *S*yâmâka grain and other sorts of grain produced in the rainy season. (Nand.)

25. 'Haradatta says that "a sixth part" means "a sixtieth part." But this is wrong, as shown by M. VII, 131.' (Nand.) Haradatta's false interpretation was most likely called forth by Gaut. X, 27.

32. Artizans (such as blacksmiths), manual labourers (such as carpenters), and Sûdras shall do work for the king for a day in each month.

33. The monarch, his council, his fortress, ·his treasure, his army, his realm, and his ally are the seven constituent elements of a state.

34. (The king) must punish those who try to subvert any one among them.

35. He must explore, by means of spies, both the state of his own kingdom and of his foe's.

36. Let him show honour to the righteous;

37. And let him punish the unrighteous.

38. Towards his (neighbour and natural) enemy, his ally (or the power next beyond his enemy), a neutral power (situated beyond the latter), and a power situated between (his natural enemy and an aggressive power)[1] let him adopt (alternately), as the occasion and the time require, (the four modes of obtaining success, viz.) negotiation, division, presents, and force of arms.

39. Let him have resort, as the time demands, to (the six measures of a military monarch, viz.) making alliance and waging war, marching to battle and sitting encamped, seeking the protection (of a more powerful king) and distributing his forces.

---

32. According to Nand., the particle *ka*, 'and,' implies that servile persons, who get their substance from their employers, are also implied. See Manu VII, 138.

35. The particle *ka*, according to Nand., is used in order to include the kingdoms of an ally and of a neutral prince.

38. [1] The term madhyama has been rendered according to Nand.'s and Kullûka's (on M. VII, 155) interpretation of it. Kullûka, however, adds, as a further characteristic, that it denotes a prince, who is equal in strength to one foe, but no match for two when allied.

40. Let him set out on an expedition in the months of *K*aitra or Mârgasîrsha;

41. Or when some calamity has befallen his foe.

42. Having conquered the country of his foe, let him not abolish (or disregard) the laws of that country.

43. And when he has been attacked by his foe, let him protect his own realm to the best of his power.

44. There is no higher duty for men of the military caste, than to risk their life in battle.

45. Those who have been killed in protecting a cow, or a Brâhma*n*a, or a king, or a friend, or their own property, or their own wedded wife, or their own life, go to heaven.

46. Likewise, those (who have been killed) in trying to prevent mixture of castes (caused by adulterous connections).

47. A king having conquered the capital of his foe, should invest there a prince of the royal race of that country with the royal dignity.

48. Let him not extirpate the royal race;

49. Unless the royal race be of ignoble descent.

50. He must not take delight in hunting, dice, women, and drinking;

51. Nor in defamation and battery.

52. And let him not injure his own property (by bootless expenses).

53. He must not demolish (whether in his own town, or in the town of his foe conquered by him,

40. The particle vâ indicates, according to Nand., that he may also set out in the month Phâlguna.

or in a fort) doors which had been built there before his time (by a former king).

54. He must not bestow largesses upon unworthy persons (such as dancers, eulogists, bards, and the like).

55. Of mines let him take the whole produce.

56. Of a treasure-trove he must give one half to the Brâhmanas;

57. He may deposit the other half in his own treasury.

58. A Brâhmana who has found a treasure may keep it entire.

59. A Kshatriya (who has found a treasure) must give one fourth of it to the king, another fourth to the Brâhmanas, and keep half of it to himself.

60. A Vaisya (who has found a treasure) must give a fourth part of it to the king, one half to the Brâhmanas, and keep the (remaining fourth) part to himself.

61. A Sûdra who has found a treasure must divide it into twelve parts, and give five parts to the king, five parts to the Brâhmanas, and keep two parts to himself.

62. Let the king compel him who (having found a treasure) does not announce it (to the king) and is found out afterwards, to give up the whole.

63. Of a treasure anciently hidden by themselves let (members of) all castes, excepting Brâhmanas, give a twelfth part to the king.

64. The man who falsely claims property hidden by another to have been hidden by himself, shall be

---

63. This rule refers to a treasure, which has been found by some one and announced to the king. The original owner is bound to prove his ownership. (Nand.) See M. VIII, 35.

condemned to pay a fine equal in amount to the property falsely claimed by him.

65. The king must protect the property of minors, of (blind, lame or other) helpless persons (who have no guide), and of women (without a guardian).

66. Having recovered goods stolen by thieves, let him restore them entire to their owners, to whatever caste they may belong.

67. If he has been unable to recover them, he must pay (their value) out of his own treasury.

68. Let him appease the onsets of fate by ceremonies averting evil omens and propitiatory ceremonies;

69. And the onsets of his foe (let him repel) by force of arms.

70. Let him appoint as Purohita (domestic priest) a man conversant with the Vedas, Epics, the Institutes of Sacred Law, and (the science of) what is useful in life, of a good family, not deficient in limb, and persistent in the practice of austerities.

71. And (let him appoint) ministers (to help and advise him) in all his affairs, who are pure, free from covetousness, attentive, and able.

72. Let him try causes himself, accompanied by well-instructed Brâhma*n*as.

73. Or let him entrust a Brâhma*n*a with the judicial business.

74. Let the king appoint as judges men of good

---

70. 'The science of what is useful in life' comprises the fine arts, except music, and all technical knowledge.

74. According to Nand., the particle *ka* indicates that the judges should be well acquainted, likewise, with the sacred revelation,

families, for whom the ceremonies (of initiation and so forth) have been performed, and who are eager in keeping religious vows, impartial towards friend and foe, and not likely to be corrupted by litigants either by (ministering to their) lustful desires or by (stimulating them to) wrath or by (exciting their) avarice or by other (such practices).

75. Let the king in all matters listen to (the advice of) his astrologers.

76. Let him constantly show reverence to the gods and to the Brâhma*n*as.

77. Let him honour the aged ;

78. And let him offer sacrifices ;

79. And he must not suffer any Brâhma*n*a in his realm to perish with want ;

80. Nor any other man leading a pious life.

81. Let him bestow landed property upon Brâhma*n*as.

82. To those upon whom he has bestowed (land) he must give a document, destined for the information of a future ruler, which must be written upon a piece of (cotton) cloth, or a copper-plate, and must contain the names of his (three) immediate ancestors, a declaration of the extent of the land, and an imprecation against him who should appropriate the

---

and intent upon performing their daily study of the Veda, as ordained by Yâ*g*ñavalkya, II, 2.

75. According to Nand., the particle *k*a indicates that the king's ministers should also consult the astrologers.

76. 'The particle *k*a is used here in order to imply that the king should bestow presents upon the Brâhma*n*as, as ordained by Manu, VII, 79.' (Nand.) See Introduction.

82. The repeated use of the particle *k*a in this Sûtra signifies that the document in question should also contain the name of the

donation to himself, and should be signed with his own seal.

83. Let him not appropriate to himself landed property bestowed (upon Brâhma*n*as) by other (rulers).

84. Let him present the Brâhma*n*as with gifts of every kind.

85. Let him be on his guard, whatever he may be about.

86. Let him be splendid (in apparel and ornaments).

87. Let him be conversant with incantations dispelling the effects of poison and sickness.

88. Let him not test any aliments, that have not been tried before (by his attendants, by certain experiments).

89. Let him smile before he speaks to any one.

90. Let him not frown even upon (criminals) doomed to capital punishment.

91. Let him inflict punishments, corresponding to the nature of their offences, upon evil-doers.

---

donor, the date of the donation, and the words, written in the donor's own hand, 'What has been written above, by that is my own will declared.' The term dâna*kkh*edopavar*n*anam, 'containing a declaration of the punishment awaiting the robber of a grant,' may also mean, 'indicating the boundaries (such as fields and the like) of the grant.' The seal must contain the figure of a flamingo, boar, or other animal. (Nand.) Numerous grants on copper-plates, exactly corresponding to the above description, have been actually found in divers parts of India. See, particularly, Dr. Burnell's Elements of South Indian Palaeography.

83. According to Nand., the particle *k*a is used in order to include in this prohibition a grant made by himself.

86. Nand. proposes a second interpretation of the term sudar-*s*ana besides the one given above, 'he shall often show himself before those desirous of seeing him.'

92. Let him inflict punishments according to justice (either personally or through his attendants).

93. Let him pardon no one for having offended twice.

94. He who deviates from his duty must certainly not be left unpunished by the king.

95. Where punishment with a black hue and a red eye advances with irresistible might, the king deciding causes justly, there the people will prosper.

96. Let a king in his own domain inflict punishments according to justice, chastise foreign foes with rigour, behave without duplicity to his affectionate friends, and with lenity to Brâhma*n*as.

97. Of a king thus disposed, even though he subsist by gleaning, the fame is far spread in the world, like a drop of oil in the water.

98. That king who is pleased when his subjects are joyful, and grieved when they are in grief, will obtain fame in this world, and will be raised to a high station in heaven after his death.

IV.

1. The (very small mote of) dust which may be discerned in a sun-beam passing through a lattice is called trasare*n*u (trembling dust).

2. Eight of these (trasare*n*us) are equal to a nit.

3. Three of the latter are equal to a black mustard-seed.

4. Three of these last are equal to a white mustard-seed.

5. Six of these are equal to a barley-corn.

6. Three of these equal a K*r*ish*n*ala.

IV. 1–14. M. VIII, 132–138; Y. I, 361–365.

6. K*r*ish*n*ala (literally, 'seed of the Guñgâ creeper') is another

7. Five of these equal a Mâsha.

8. Twelve of these are equal to half an Aksha.

9. The weight of half an Aksha, with four Mâshas added to it, is called a Suvarna.

10. Four Suvarnas make a Nishka.

11. Two Krishnalas of equal weight are equal to one Mâshaka of silver.

12. Sixteen of these are equal to a Dharana (of silver).

13. A Karsha (or eighty Raktikâs) of copper is called Kârshâpana.

14. Two hundred and fifty (copper) Panas are declared to be the first (or lowest) amercement, five hundred are considered as the middlemost, and a thousand as the highest.

V.

1. Great criminals should all be put to death.

---

name for Raktikâ or Ratî, the lowest denomination in general use. According to Prinsep (Useful Tables, p. 97) it equals 1.875 grains = 0.122 grammes of the metrical system. According to Thomas (see Colebrooke's Essays, ed. by Cowell, I, p. 529, note) it equals 1.75 grains.

7–10. These names refer to weights of gold.

V. 2, 3. M. VIII, 124; IX, 239, 241; Gaut. XII, 46, 47. — 3–7. M. IX, 237. — 8. M. IX, 241; VIII, 380. — 9, 11. M. IX, 232. — 12, 13. M. VIII, 320, 321. — 18. M. VIII, 371. — 19. M. VIII, 279; Y. II, 215; Âpast. II, 10, 27, 14; Gaut. XII, 1. — 20–22. M. VIII, 281, 282; Âpast. II, 10, 27, 15; Gaut. XII, 7. — 23. M. VIII, 270; Âpast. II, 10, 27, 14. — 24. M. VIII, 272. — 25. M. VIII, 271. — 26–28. M. VIII, 273–275. — 27. Y. II, 204. — 29, 30. Y. II, 210. — 31–33. Y. II, 211. — 35. M. VIII, 269. — 36. M. VIII, 268; Gaut. XII, 12. — 40, 41. M. VIII, 382–385. — 40, 44. Y. II, 286, 289. — 45. M. VIII, 224. — 47. M. VIII, 225. — 49. Y. II, 297. — 50, 52. M. VIII, 296–298; Y. II, 225, 226. — 55–58. M. VIII, 285; Y. II, 227–229. — 60, 61. M. VIII, 280. — 60–73. Y. II, 216–221. — 66–68. M. VIII, 283, 284. — 74. M. IX, 274. —

2. In the case of a Brâhma*n*a no corporal punishment must be inflicted.

3. A Brâhma*n*a must be banished from his own country, his body having been branded.

---

75. M.VIII, 287 ; Y. II, 222. — 77. M.VIII, 325. — 79. M.VIII, 320. — 81, 82. M.VIII, 322. — 83, 84. M.VIII, 326–329. — 85, 86. M.VIII, 330 ; Gaut. XII, 18. — 89, 90. Y. II, 270. — 94. M. VIII, 392 ; Y. II, 263. — 96, 97. M.VIII, 393. — 98–103. Y. II, 296. — 104. Y. II, 234. — 106, 107. M. IX, 282. — 108. Y. II, 223. — 110. Y. II, 224. — 111. Y. II, 236. — 113. M.VIII, 389; Y. II, 237. — 115–123. Y. II, 232, 235, 236, 239–241. — 124–126. Y. II, 246, 250. — 127. Y. II, 254. — 127, 128. Colebrooke, Dig. III, 3, XXII. — 129. Y. II, 255. — 130. M.VIII, 399 ; Y. II, 261. — 131. Y. II, 263. — 132. M.VIII, 407. — 134, 135. Y. II, 202. — 136. M. IX, 277 ; Y. II, 274. — 137, 138. M.VIII, 235 ; Y. II, 164. — 137–139. Colebrooke, Dig. III, 4, XIV. — 140. Y. II, 159. — 141. Gaut. XII, 19. — 142–145. Y. II, 159, 160. — 142–144. Gaut. XII, 22–25. — 140–146. Colebrooke, Dig. III, 4, XLV, 4. — 146. M.VIII, 241 ; Y. II, 161 ; Gaut. XII, 19. — 147, 148. M.VIII, 238, 240 ; Y. II, 162 ; Gaut. XII, 21. — 147–149. Colebrooke, Dig. III, 4, XXI. — 150. M.VIII, 242 ; Y. II, 163. — 151. M.VIII, 412 ; Y. II, 183 ; Colebrooke, Dig. III, 1, LVIII. — 152. Y. II, 183. — 153, 154. M.VIII, 215 ; Y. II, 193 ; Âpast. II, 11, 28, 2, 3. — 153–159. Colebrooke, Dig. III, 1, LXXX. — 155, 156. Y. II, 197. — 160. M. IX, 71 ; Y. I, 65. — 162. M. IX, 72 ; Y. I, 66. — 163. M.VIII, 389. — 162, 163. Colebrooke, Dig. IV, 1, LX. — 164, 165. M.VIII, 202 ; Y. II, 170. — 166. Y. II, 168. — 167, 168. Y. II, 187. — 169–171. M.VIII, 191. — 172. M. IX, 291 ; Y. II, 155. — 174. M. IX, 285 ; Y. II, 297. — 175–177. M. IX, 284 ; Y. II, 242. — 178. Y. II, 232. — 179. M. VIII, 123 ; Y. II, 81 ; Âpast. II, 11, 29, 8 ; Gaut. XIII, 23. — 180. Y. I, 338. — 183. Colebrooke, Dig. I, 3, CXXX. — 189. M. VIII, 350. — 190. M.VIII, 351. — 194. M.VIII, 126 ; Y. I, 367. — 195. M.VIII, 128 ; Y. II, 243, 305.

1. The crimes by the commission of which a man becomes a Mahâpatakin, 'mortal sinner,' will be enumerated below, XXXV.

2. The use of the particle *k*a implies, according to Nand. and a passage of Yama quoted by him, that, besides branding him, the criminal should be shorn, his deed publicly proclaimed, and himself mounted upon an ass and led about the town.

4. For murdering another Brâhma*n*a, let (the figure of) a headless corpse be impressed on his forehead;

5. For drinking spirits, the flag of a seller of spirituous liquor;

6. For stealing (gold), a dog's foot;

7. For incest, (the mark of) a female part.

8. If he has committed any other capital crime, he shall be banished, taking with him all his property, and unhurt.

9. Let the king put to death those who forge royal edicts;

10. And those who forge (private) documents;

11. Likewise poisoners, incendiaries, robbers, and killers of women, children, or men;

12. And such as steal more than ten Kumbhas of grain,

13. Or more than a hundred Mâshas of such things as are usually sold by weight (such as gold and silver);

14. Such also as aspire to sovereignty, though being of low birth;

15. Breakers of dikes;

---

10. The use of the particle *k*a indicates that this rule includes those who corrupt the king's ministers, as stated by Manu, IX, 232. (Nand.)

11. Nand. infers from the use of the particle *k*a, and from a passage of Kâtyâyana, that false witnesses are also intended here.

12. Nand. here refers *k*a to women who have committed a capital offence, as mentioned by Yâg*ñ*avalkya (II, 278). A Kumbha is a measure of grain equal to twenty Dro*n*as, or a little more than three bushels and three gallons. Nand. mentions, as the opinion of some, that 1 Kumbha = 2 Dro*n*as. For other computations of the amount of a Kumbha, see Colebrooke's Essays, I, 533 seq.

13. Regarding the value of a Mâsha, see IV, 7, 11.

15. Nand. infers from the use of the particle *k*a and from a

16. And such as give shelter and food to robbers,

17. Unless the king be unable (to protect his subjects against robbers);

18. And a woman who violates the duty which she owes to her lord, the latter being unable to restrain her.

19. With whatever limb an inferior insults or hurts his superior in caste, of that limb the king shall cause him to be deprived.

20. If he places himself on the same seat with his superior, he shall be banished with a mark on his buttocks.

21. If he spits on him, he shall lose both lips;

22. If he breaks wind against him, his hindparts;

23. If he uses abusive language, his tongue.

24. If a (low-born) man through pride give instruction (to a member of the highest caste) concerning his duty, let the king order hot oil to be dropped into his mouth.

25. If a (low-born man) mentions the name or caste of a superior revilingly, an iron pin, ten inches long, shall be thrust into his mouth (red hot).

26. He who falsely denies the sacred knowledge, the country, or the caste (of such), or who says

---

passage of Manu (IX, 280), that robbers who forcibly enter the king's treasury, or the arsenal, or a temple, are likewise intended here.

17. In the case to which this Sûtra refers, the villagers may satisfy the demands of the robbers with impunity, as they are obliged to do so out of regard for their own safety. (Nand.)

20. The particle *ka* indicates here that if he urines against a superior his organ shall be cut off. (Nand.) See M. VIII, 282.

26. This Sûtra has been rendered in accordance with Kullûka's gloss on M. VIII, 273, Nand.'s interpretation of it being palpably wrong.

that his religious duties have not been fulfilled by
(or that the initiatory and other sacramental rites
have not been performed for) him, shall be fined
two hundred Pa*n*as.

27. If a man is blind with one eye, or lame, or
defective in any similar way, and another calls him
so, he shall be fined two Kârshâpa*n*as, though he
speaks the truth.

28. He shall be fined a hundred Kârshâpa*n*as for
defaming a Guru.

29. He shall pay the highest amercement for
imputing to another (a great crime) entailing loss
of caste;

30. The second amercement for (imputing to
another) a minor offence (such as the slaughter of
a cow);

31. The same for reviling a Brâhma*n*a versed in
the three Vedas, or an old man, or a (whole) caste
or corporation (of judges or others ;

32. For reviling a village or district, the lowest
amercement;

33. For using insulting language (such as 'I shall
visit your sister,' or 'I shall visit your daughter'), a
hundred Kârshâpa*n*as;

34. For insulting a man by using bad language
regarding his mother (such as 'I shall visit your
mother' or the like speeches), the highest amercement.

35. For abusing a man of his own caste, he shall
be fined twelve Pa*n*as.

36. For abusing a man of a lower caste, he shall
be fined six (Pa*n*as).

---

32. Nand. infers from the use of the particle *k*a that 'a family'
is also intended here.

37. For insulting a member of the highest caste or of his own caste (he having been insulted by him) at the same time, the same fine is ordained ;

38. Or (if he only returns his insult, a fine amounting to) three Kârshâpa*n*as.

39. The same (punishment is ordained) if he calls him bad names.

40. An adulterer shall be made to pay the highest amercement if he has had connection with a woman of his own caste ;

41. For adultery with women of a lower caste, the second amercement ;

42. The same (fine is ordained) for a bestial crime committed with a cow.

43. He who has had connection with a woman of one of the lowest castes, shall be put to death.

44. For a bestial crime committed with cattle (other than cows) he shall be fined a hundred Kârshâpa*n*as.

45. (The same fine is ordained) for giving a (blemished) damsel in marriage, without indicating her blemish (whether the bride be sick, or no longer a maid, or otherwise faulty) ;

46. And he shall have to support her.

47. He who says of an unblemished damsel, that she has a blemish (shall pay) the highest amerce-ment.

48. For killing an elephant, or a horse, or a camel, or a cow, (the criminal) shall have one hand, or one foot, lopped off.

---

43. The lowest castes (antyâ*h*), according to Aṅgiras, are the following seven, *K*and*â*las, *S*vapa*k*as, Kshattr*i*s, Sûtas, Vaidehakas, Mâgadhas, and Âyogavas.

49. A seller of forbidden meat (such as pork, shall be punished in the same way).

50. He who kills domestic animals, shall pay a hundred Kârshâpanas.

51. He shall make good their value to the owner of those animals.

52. He who kills wild animals, shall pay five hundred Kârshâpanas.

53. A killer of birds, or of fish, (shall pay) ten Kârshâpanas.

54. A killer of insects shall pay one Kârshâpana.

55. A feller of trees yielding fruit (shall pay) the highest amercement.

56. A feller of trees yielding blossoms only (shall pay) the second amercement.

57. He who cuts creepers, shrubs, or climbing plants (shall pay) a hundred Kârshâpanas.

58. He who cuts grass (shall pay) one Kârshâpana.

59. And all such offenders (shall make good) to the owners (of the trees or plants cut down by them) the revenue which they yield.

60. If any man raises his hand (against his equal in caste, with intent to strike him, he shall pay) ten Kârshâpanas;

61. If he raises his foot, twenty;

62. If he raises a piece of wood, the first amerce-ment;

63. If he raises a stone, the second amercement;

64. If he raises a weapon, the highest amerce-ment.

65. If he seizes him by his feet, by his hair, by

---

53. Nand. infers from a passage of Kâtyâyana that the particle *ka* is used here in order to include serpents.

his garment, or by his hand, he shall pay ten Pa*n*as as a fine.

66. If he causes pain to him, without fetching blood from him, (he shall pay) thirty-two Pa*n*as;

67. For fetching blood from him, sixty-four.

68. For mutilating or injuring a hand, or a foot, or a tooth, and for slitting an ear, or the nose, the second amercement (is ordained).

69. For rendering a man unable to move about, or to eat, or to speak, or for striking him (violently, the same punishment is ordained).

70. For wounding or breaking an eye, or the neck, or an arm, or a bone, or a shoulder, the highest amercement (is ordained).

71. For striking out both eyes of a man, the king shall (confine him and) not dismiss him from jail as long as he lives;

72. Or he shall order him to be mutilated in the same way (i. e. deprived of his eyes).

73. Where one is attacked by many, the punishment for each shall be the double of that which has been ordained for (attacks by) a single person.

74. (The double punishment is) likewise (ordained) for those who do not give assistance to one calling for help, though they happen to be on the spot, or (who run away) after having approached it.

75. All those who have hurt a man, shall pay the expense of his cure.

76. Those who have hurt a domestic animal (shall also pay the expense of his cure).

77. He who has stolen a cow, or a horse, or a camel, or an elephant, shall have one hand, or one foot, cut off;

78. He who has stolen a goat, or a sheep, (shall have) one hand (cut off).

79. He who steals grain (of those sorts which grow in the rainy season), shall pay eleven times its value as a fine;

80. Likewise, he who steals grain (of those sorts, which grow in winter and spring, such as rice and barley).

81. A stealer of gold, silver, or clothes, at a value of more than fifty Mâshas, shall lose both hands.

82. He who steals a less amount than that, shall pay eleven times its value as a fine.

83. A stealer of thread, cotton, cow-dung, sugar, sour milk, milk, butter-milk, grass, salt, clay, ashes, birds, fish, clarified butter, oil, meat, honey, basket-work, canes of bamboo, earthenware, or iron pots, shall pay three times their value as a fine.

84. (The same fine is ordained for stealing) dressed food.

85. For stealing flowers, green (grain), shrubs, creepers, climbing plants or leaves, (he shall pay) five Krishnalas.

86. For stealing pot-herbs, roots, or fruits (the same punishment is ordained).

87. He who steals gems, (shall pay) the highest amercement.

88. He who steals anything not mentioned above, (shall make good) its value (to the owner).

89. Thieves shall be compelled to restore all stolen goods to the owners.

90. After that, they shall suffer the punishment that has been ordained for them.

91. He who does not make way for one for

whom way ought to be made, shall be fined twenty-five Kârshâpa*n*as.

92. (The same fine is ordained) for omitting to offer a seat to (a guest or others) to whom it ought to be offered.

93. For neglecting to worship such as have a claim to be worshipped, (the same fine is ordained);

94. Likewise, for neglecting to invite (at a *S*râddha) a Brâhma*n*a, one's neighbour;

95. And for offering him no food, after having invited him.

96. He who does not eat, though he has received and accepted an invitation, shall give a gold Mâshaka as a fine;

97. And the double amount of food to his host.

98. He who insults a Brâhma*n*a by offering him uneatable food (such as excrements and the like, or forbidden food, such as garlic, must pay) sixteen Suvar*n*as (as a fine).

99. (If he insults him by offering him) such food as would cause him to be degraded (were he to taste it, he must pay) a hundred Suvar*n*as.

100. (If he offers him) spirituous liquor, he shall be put to death.

101. If he insults a Kshatriya (in the same way), he shall have to pay half of the above amercement;

102. If he insults a Vai*s*ya, half of that again;

103. If he insults a *S*ûdra, the first amercement.

104. If one who (being a member of the *K*a*nd*âla or some other low caste) must not be touched, inten-

---

93. Those persons 'have a claim to be worshipped' who are worthy to receive the Madhuparka or honey-mixture. (Nand.) See M. III, 119, 120; Y. I, 110; Âpast. II, 4, 8, 5–9; Gaut. V, 27; Weber, Ind. Stud. X, 125.

tionally defiles by his touch one who (as a member of a twice-born caste) may be touched (by other twice-born persons only), he shall be put to death.

105. If a woman in her courses (touches such a person), she shall be lashed with a whip.

106. If one defiles the highway, or a garden, or the water (by voiding excrements) near them (or in any other way), he shall be fined a hundred Pa*n*as;

107. And he must remove the filth.

108. If he demolishes a house, or a piece of ground (a court-yard or the like), or a wall or the like, he shall have to pay the second amercement;

109. And he shall have it repaired (at his own cost).

110. If he throws into another man's house (thorns, spells, or other) such things as might hurt some one, he shall pay a hundred Pa*n*as.

111. (The same punishment is ordained) for falsely denying the possession of common property;

112. And for not delivering what has been sent (for a god or for a Brâhma*n*a).

113. (The same punishment is) also (ordained) for father and son, teacher (and pupil), sacrificer and officiating priest, if one should forsake the other, provided that he has not been expelled from caste.

114. And he must return to them (to the parents and the rest).

115. (The same punishment is) also (ordained) for hospitably entertaining a *S*ûdra or religious ascetic at an oblation to the gods or to the manes;

116. And for following an unlawful occupation

---

115. According to Nand., the particle *ka* indicates here, that the same punishment is ordained for him who visits a widow by his own accord, as mentioned by Yâg*ñ*avalkya (II, 234).

(such as studying the Vedas without having been initiated);

117. And for breaking open a house on which (the king's) seal is laid;

118. And for making an oath without having been asked to do so (by the king or a judge);

119. And for depriving cattle of their virility.

120. The fine for the witnesses in a dispute between father and son shall be ten Panas.

121. For him who acts as surety for either of the two parties in such a contest, the highest amercement (is ordained).

122. (The same punishment is ordained) for forging a balance, or a measure;

123. Also, for pronouncing them incorrect, although they are correct.

124. (The same punishment is) also (ordained) for selling adulterated commodities;

125. And for a company of merchants who prevent the sale of a commodity (which happens to be abroad) by selling it under its price.

126. (The same punishment is ordained) for those (members of such a company) who sell (an article belonging to the whole company for more than it is worth) on their own account.

127. He who does not deliver to the purchaser a commodity (sold), after its price has been paid to him, shall be compelled to deliver it to him with interest;

---

117. Nand. considers the particle *ka* to imply that the exchange of sealed goods for others shall be punished in the same way. But this assertion rests upon a false reading (samudraparivarta for samudgaparivarta) of Y. II, 247, which passage Nand. quotes in support of his view.

128. And he shall be fined a hundred Pa*n*as by the king.

129. If there should be a loss upon a commodity purchased, which the purchaser refuses to accept (though it has been tendered to him), the loss shall fall upon the purchaser.

130. He who sells a commodity on which the king has laid an embargo, shall have it confiscated.

131. A ferry-man who takes a toll payable (for commodities conveyed) by land shall be fined ten Pa*n*as.

132. Likewise, a ferry-man, or an official at a toll-office, who takes a fare or toll from a student, or Vânaprastha (hermit), or a Bhikshu (ascetic or religious mendicant), or a pregnant woman, or one about to visit a place of pilgrimage;

133. And he shall restore it to them.

134. Those who use false dice in gaming shall lose one hand.

135. Those who resort to (other) fraudulent practices in gaming shall lose two fingers (the thumb and the index).

136. Cutpurses shall lose one hand.

137. Cattle being attacked, during day-time, by wolves or other ferocious animals, and the keeper not going (to repel the attack), the blame shall fall upon him;

138. And he shall make good to the owner the value of the cattle that has perished.

139. If he milks a cow without permission, (he shall pay) twenty-five Kârshâpa*n*as (as a fine).

---

131. The toll mentioned here is the duty on marketable commodities mentioned above, III, 29, 30. (Nand.)

140. If a female buffalo damages grain, her keeper shall be fined eight Mâshas.

141. If she has been without a keeper, her owner (shall pay that fine).

142. (For mischief done by) a horse, or a camel, or an ass (the fine shall be the same).

143. (For damage done by) a cow, it shall be half.

144. (For damage done by) a goat, or a sheep, (it shall be) half of that again.

145. For cattle abiding (in the field), after having eaten (grain), the fine shall be double.

146. And in every case the owner (of the field) shall receive the value of the grain that has been destroyed.

147. There is no offence if the damage has been done near a highway, near a village, or (in a field adjacent to) the common pasture-ground for cattle;

148. Or (if it has been done) in an uninclosed field;

149. Or if the cattle did not abide long;

150. Or if the damage has been done by bulls that have been set at liberty, or by a cow shortly after her calving.

151. He who commits members of the highest (or Brâhma*n*a) caste to slavery, shall pay the highest amercement.

152. An apostate from religious mendicity shall become the king's slave.

153. A hired workman who abandons his work before the term has expired shall pay the whole amount (of the stipulated wages) to his employer;

154. And he shall pay a hundred Pa*n*as to the king.

155. What has been destroyed through his want of care, (he must make good) to the owner;

156. Unless the damage have been caused by an accident.

157. If an employer dismisses a workman (whom he has hired) before the expiration of the term, he shall pay him his entire wages;

158. And (he shall pay) a hundred Pa*n*as to the king;

159. Unless the workman have been at fault.

160. He who, having promised his daughter to one suitor, gives her in marriage to another, shall be punished as a thief;

161. Unless the (first) suitor have a blemish.

162. The same (punishment is ordained for a suitor) who abandons a faultless girl;

163. (And for a husband who forsakes) a (blameless) wife.

164. He who buys unawares in open market the property of another man (from one not authorised to sell it) is not to blame;

165. (But) the owner shall recover his property.

166. If he has bought it in secret and under its price, the purchaser and the vendor shall be punished as thieves.

167. He who embezzles goods belonging to a corporation (of Brâhma*n*as, and which have been sent to them by the king or by private persons), shall be banished.

168. He who violates their established rule (shall) also (be banished).

169. He who retains a deposit shall restore the commodity deposited to the owner, with interest.

170. The king shall punish him as a thief.

171. (The same punishment is ordained for him) who claims as a deposit what he never deposited.

172. A destroyer of landmarks shall be compelled to pay the highest amercement and to mark the boundary anew with landmarks.

173. He who (knowingly) eats forbidden food effecting loss of caste shall be banished.

174. He who sells forbidden food (such as spirituous liquor and the like), or food which must not be sold, and he who breaks an image of a deity, shall pay the highest amercement;

175. Also, a physician who adopts a wrong method of cure in the case of a patient of high rank (such as a relative of the king's);

176. The second amercement in the case of another patient;

177. The lowest amercement in the case of an animal.

178. He who does not give what he has promised, shall be compelled to give it and to pay the first amercement.

179. To a false witness his entire property shall be confiscated.

180. (The same punishment is ordained) for a judge who lives by bribes.

181. He who has mortgaged more than a bull's hide of land to one creditor, and without having redeemed it mortgages it to another, shall be corporally punished (by whipping or imprisonment).

---

171. According to Nand., the particle *ka* indicates that those who state the nature or amount of a deposit wrongly are also intended here.

173. Thus according to Nand., who says expressly that the causative form cannot here mean causing to eat, because the punishment for the latter offence has been mentioned in Sûtra 98.

182. If the quantity be less, he shall pay a fine of sixteen Suvar*n*as.

183. That land, whether little or much, on the produce of which one man can subsist for a year, is called the quantity of a bull's hide.

184. If a dispute should arise between two (creditors) concerning (a field or other immovable property) which has been mortgaged to both at the same time, that mortgagee shall enjoy its produce who holds it in his possession, without having obtained it by force.

185. What has been possessed in order and with a legitimate title (such as purchase, donation, and the like), the possessor may keep; it can never be taken from him.

186. Where (land or other) property has been held in legitimate possession by the father (or grandfather), the son's right to it, after his death, cannot be contested; for it has become his own by force of possession.

187. If possession has been held of an estate by three (successive) generations in due course, the fourth in descent shall keep it as his property, even without a written title.

188. He who kills (in his own defence a tiger or other) animal with sharp nails and claws, or a (goat or other) horned animal (excepting cows), or a (boar or other) animal with sharp teeth, or an assassin, or an elephant, or a horse, or any other (ferocious animal by whom he has been attacked), commits no crime.

189. Any one may unhesitatingly slay a man who attacks him with intent to murder him, whether his spiritual teacher, young or old, or a Brâhma*n*a,

or even (a Brâhma*n*a) versed in many branches of sacred knowledge.

190. By killing an assassin who attempts to kill, whether in public or in private, no crime is committed by the slayer: fury recoils upon fury.

191. Assassins should be known to be of seven kinds: such as try to kill with the sword, or with poison, or with fire, such as raise their hand in order to pronounce a curse, such as recite a deadly incantation from the Atharva-veda, such as raise a false accusation which reaches the ears of the king,

192. And such as have illicit intercourse with another man's wife. The same designation is given to other (evil-doers) who deprive others of their worldly fame or of their wealth, or who destroy religious merit (by ruining pools, or other such acts), or property (such as houses or fields).

193. Thus I have declared to thee fully, O Earth, the criminal laws, enumerating at full length the punishments ordained for all sorts of offences.

194. Let the king dictate due punishments for other offences also, after having ascertained the class and the age (of the criminal) and the amount (of the damage done or sum claimed), and after having consulted the Brâhma*n*as (his advisers).

195. That detestable judge who dismisses without punishment such as deserve it, and punishes such as deserve it not, shall incur twice as heavy a penalty as the criminal himself.

196. A king in whose dominion there exists neither thief, nor adulterer, nor calumniator, nor robber, nor murderer, attains the world of Indra.

VI.

1. A creditor shall receive his principal back from his debtor exactly as he had lent it to him.

2. (As regards the interest to be paid), he shall take in the direct order of the castes two, three, four, or five in the hundred by the month (if no pledge has been given).

3. Or let debtors of any caste pay as much interest as has been promised by themselves.

4. After the lapse of one year let them pay interest according to the above rule, even though it have not been agreed on.

5. By the use of a pledge (to be kept only) interest is forfeited.

VI. 2. M. VIII, 142; Y. II, 37. — 1, 2. Colebrooke, Dig. I, 2, XXXI. — 3. M. VIII, 157; Y. II, 38. — 4. Colebrooke, Dig. I, 2, LII. — 5. M. VIII, 143; Y. II, 59; Gaut. XII, 32; Colebrooke, Dig. I, 2, LXXVIII. — 6. Y. II, 59; Colebrooke, Dig. I, 3, LXXXII. — 7. M. VIII, 151; Gaut. XII, 31; Colebrooke, Dig. I, 3, CX. — 8. Colebrooke loc. cit. — 9. Colebrooke, Dig. I, 3, CVII. — 10. Y. II, 44; Colebrooke, Dig. I, 2, LXXVII. — 11–15. M. VIII, 151; Y. II, 39; Gaut. XII, 36; Colebrooke, Dig. I, 2, LXIV. — 16, 17. Colebrooke, Dig. I, 2, LXX. — 18, 19. M. VIII, 50, 176; Y. II, 40; Colebrooke, Dig. I, 6, CCLII. — 20, 21. M. VIII, 139; Y. II, 42; Colebrooke, Dig. I, 6, CCLXXVII. — 22. Y. II, 20. — 24, 25. Y. II, 94; Colebrooke, Dig. I, 6, CCLXXXIII. — 26. Y. II, 93; Colebrooke, Dig. I, 6, CCLXXXVI. — 27. Y. II, 50; Colebrooke, Dig. I, 5, CLXVIII. — 28. Colebrooke, Dig. I, 5, CLXVIII. — 29. Gaut. XII, 40. — 29, 30. Y. II, 51; Colebrooke, Dig. I, 5, CCXX. — 31–33. Y. II, 46; Colebrooke, Dig. I, 5, CCVIII. — 34–36. M. VIII, 166; Y. II, 45. — 38, 39. M. VIII, 166, 167; Y. II, 45; Colebrooke, Dig. I, 5, CXCII. — 41. M. VIII, 158, 160; Y. II, 53; Colebrooke, Dig. I, 4, CXLIV. — 42, 43. Y. II, 55, 56; Colebrooke, Dig. I, 4, CLVI, CLXI.

1, 2. Colebrooke loc. cit. seems to have translated a different reading.

6. The creditor must make good the loss of a pledge, unless it was caused by fate or by the king.

7. (The pledge must) also (be restored to the debtor) when the interest has reached its maximum amount (on becoming equal to the principal, and has all been paid).

8. But he must not restore an immovable pledge without special agreement (till the principal itself has been paid).

9. That immovable property which has been delivered, restorable when the sum borrowed is made good, (the creditor) must restore when the sum borrowed has been made good.

10. Property lent bears no further interest after it has been tendered, but refused by the creditor.

11. On gold the interest shall rise no higher than to make the debt double;

12. On grain, (no higher than to make it) three-fold;

13. On cloth, (no higher than to make it) four-fold;

14. On liquids, (no higher than to make it) eight-fold;

15. Of female slaves and cattle, the offspring (shall be taken as interest).

16. On substances from which spirituous liquor

---

7. Colebrooke loc. cit. connects this Sûtra with the next. My rendering rests on Nand.'s interpretation.

8. Nand. cites as an instance of an agreement of this kind one made in the following form, ' You shall have the enjoyment of this or that mango grove as long as interest on the principal lent to me has not ceased to accrue.'

is extracted, on cotton, thread, leather, weapons, bricks, and charcoal, the interest is unlimited.

17. On such objects as have not been mentioned it may be double.

18. A creditor recovering the sum lent by any (lawful) means shall not be reproved by the king.

19. If the debtor, so forced to discharge the debt, complains to the king, he shall be fined in an equal sum.

20. If a creditor sues before the king and fully proves his demand, the debtor shall pay as a fine to the king a tenth part of the sum proved;

21. And the creditor, having received the sum due, shall pay a twentieth part of it.

22. If the whole demand has been contested by the debtor, and even a part of it only has been proved against him, he must pay the whole.

23. There are three means of proof in case of a demand having been contested, viz. a writing, witnesses, and proof by ordeal.

24. A debt contracted before witnesses should be discharged in the presence of witnesses.

25. A written contract having been fulfilled, the writing should be torn.

26. Part only being paid, and the writing not being at hand, let the creditor give an acquittance.

27. If he who contracted the debt should die, or

17. Nand. infers from a passage of Kâtyâyana that this rule refers to gems, pearls, coral, gold, silver, cotton, silk, and wool.

18. The 'lawful means' are mediation of friends and the four other modes of compelling payment of an unliquidated demand. (Nand.) See M. VIII, 49.

22. 'The particle api indicates that he must pay a fine to the king besides, as ordained by Yâgñavalkya II, 11.' (Nand.)

become a religious ascetic, or remain abroad for twenty years, that debt shall be discharged by his sons or grandsons;

28. But not by remoter descendants against their will.

29. He who takes the assets of a man, leaving or not leaving male issue, must pay the sum due (by him);

30. And (so must) he who has the care of the widow left by one who had no assets.

31. A woman (shall) not (be compelled to pay) the debt of her husband or son;

32. Nor the husband or son (to pay) the debt of a woman (who is his wife or mother);

33. Nor a father to pay the debt of his son.

34. A debt contracted by parceners shall be paid by any one of them who is present.

35. And so shall the debt of the father (be paid) by (any one of) the brothers (or of their sons) before partition.

36. But after partition they shall severally pay according to their shares of the inheritance.

37. A debt contracted by the wife of a herdsman, distiller of spirits, public dancer, washer, or hunter shall be discharged by the husband (because he is supported by his wife).

38. (A debt of which payment has been previously) promised must be paid by the householder;

39. And (so must he pay that debt) which was

38, 39. Regarding these two Sûtras see Jolly, Indisches Schuldrecht, in the Transactions of the Royal Bavarian Academy of Sciences, 1877, p. 309, note.

contracted by any person for the behoof of the family.

40. He who on receiving the whole amount of a loan, promises to repay the principal on the following day (or some other date near at hand), but from covetousness does not repay it, shall give interest for it.

41. Suretiship is ordained for appearance, for honesty, and for payment; the first two (sureties, and not their sons), must pay the debt on failure of their engagements, but even the sons of the last (may be compelled to pay it).

42. When there are several sureties (jointly bound), they shall pay their proportionate shares of the debt; but when they are bound severally, the payment shall be made (by any of them), as the creditor pleases.

43. If the surety, being harassed by the creditor, discharges the debt, the debtor shall pay twice as much to the surety.

VII.

1. Documents are of three kinds:

2. Attested by the king, or by (other) witnesses, or unattested.

3. A document is (said to be) attested by the king when it has been executed (in a court of judicature), on the king ordering it, by a scribe, his

---

42. In the first case the agreement is made in the following form, 'I shall pay so and so much to you, in the way agreed on.' In the second case the sum is not divided between the sureties, and each of them liable for the whole debt therefore. (Nand.)

VII. 4. Y. II, 84–88. — 5–7. Y. II, 89. — 6. M. VIII, 168. — 12. Y. II, 92.

servant, and has been signed by his chief judge, with his own hand.

4. It is (said to be) attested by witnesses when, having been written anywhere, and by any one, it is signed by witnesses in their own hands.

5. It is (said to be) unattested when it has been written (by the party himself) with his own hand.

6. Such a document, if it has been caused to be written by force, makes no evidence.

7. Neither does any fraudulent document (make evidence);

8. Nor a document (which), though attested, (is vitiated) by the signature of a witness bribed (by one party) or of bad character;

9. Nor one written by a scribe of the same description;

10. Nor one executed by a woman, or a child, or a dependant person, or one intoxicated or insane, or one in danger or in bodily fear.

11. (That instrument is termed) proof which is not adverse to peculiar local usages, which defines clearly the nature of the pledge given[1], and is free from confusion in the arrangement of the subject matter and (in the succession of) the syllables.

12. If the authenticity of a document is contested, it should be ascertained by (comparing with it other)

---

7. According to Nand., the particle *ka* is used here in order to include documents that have been executed by a person intoxicated, by one under duress, by a female, by a child, by force, and by intimidation (see Nârada IV, 61). Most of these categories are, however, mentioned in Sûtra 10.

11. [1] I have translated the reading vyaktâdhividhilakshaṇam, which, though not occurring in the text of any MS., is mentioned by Nand., and is found in an identical passage of the Institutes of Nârada (see Nârada IV, 60, and Appendix, p. 123).

letters or signs (such as the flourish denoting the word *Sri* and the like) or documents executed by the same man, by (enquiring into) the probabilities of the case, and by (finding out such writings as show) a mode of writing similar (to that contained in the disputed document).

13. Should the debtor, or creditor, or witness, or scribe be dead, the authenticity of the document has to be ascertained by (comparing with it other) specimens of their handwriting.

VIII.

1. Now follow (the laws regarding) witnesses.

2. The king cannot be (made a witness); nor a learned Brâhma*n*a; nor an ascetic; nor a gamester; nor a thief; nor a person not his own master; nor a woman; nor a child; nor a perpetrator of the acts called sâhasa[1] (violence); nor one over-aged (or more than eighty years old); nor one intoxicated or insane; nor a man of bad fame; nor an outcast;

VIII. 2, 3, 5. M.VIII, 64–67; Y. II, 70, 71. — 4, 5. Gaut. XIII, 5. — 6. M.VIII, 72; Y. II, 72; Gaut. XIII, 9. — 8. M. VIII, 62, 63; Y. II, 68, 69; Âpast. II, 11, 29, 7; Gaut. XIII, 2. — 9. M. VIII, 77; Y. II, 72. — 10, 11. Y. II, 17. — 14. M. VIII, 81; Âpast. II, 11, 29, 10; Gaut. XIII, 7. — 15, 16. M.VIII, 104–106; Y. II, 83. — 15. Gaut. XIII, 24. — 18. M. VIII, 25, 26; Y. II, 13–15. — 19. M.VIII, 87; Y. II, 73; Âpast. II, 11, 29, 7; Gaut. XIII, 12. — 20–23. M.VIII, 88. — 24–26. M.VIII, 89, 90; Y. II, 73–75. — 37. M.VIII, 107; Y. II, 77; Gaut. XIII, 6. — 38. Y. II, 79. — 39. M.VIII, 73; Y. II, 78. — 40. M.VIII, 117.

2. [1] There are three kinds of sâhasa. (Nand.) They are, in the enumeration of Nârada, 1. spoiling fruits or the like; 2. injuring more valuable articles; 3. offences directed against the life of a human being, and approaching another man's wife. See Nârada XIV, 4–6.

nor one tormented by hunger or thirst; nor one oppressed by a (sudden) calamity (such as the death of his father or the like), or wholly absorbed in evil passions;

3. Nor an enemy or a friend; nor one interested in the subject matter; nor one who does forbidden acts; nor one formerly perjured; nor an attendant;

4. Nor one who, without having been appointed, comes and offers his evidence;

5. Nor can one man alone be made a witness.

6. In cases of theft, of violence, of abuse and assault, and of adultery the competence of witnesses must not be examined too strictly.

7. Now (those who are fit to be) witnesses (shall be enumerated):

8. Descendants of a noble race, who are virtuous and wealthy, sacrificers, zealous in the practice of religious austerities, having male issue, well versed in the holy law, studious, veracious, acquainted with the three Vedas, and aged (shall be witnesses).

9. If he is endowed with the qualities just mentioned, one man alone can also be made a witness.

10. In a dispute between two litigants, the witnesses of that party have to be examined from which the plaint has proceeded.

11. Where the claim has been refuted as not agreeing with the facts (as e. g. the sum claimed

---

5. According to Nand., who argues from a passage of Nârada (5, 37), the use of the particle *ka* implies here, that two witnesses are also not sufficient. But the MSS. of Nârada exhibit a different reading of the passage in question, which reading is supported by the Vîramitrodaya.

8. The particle *ka* is used here, according to Nand., who argues from a passage of Yâgñavalkya (II, 68), in order to include liberality among the qualities required in a witness.

having been repaid by the debtor), there the witnesses of the defendant have to be examined as well.

12. An appointed witness having died or gone abroad, those who have heard his deposition may give evidence.

13. (The evidence of) witnesses is (of two kinds): either of what was seen, or of what was heard.

14. Witnesses are free from blame if they give true evidence.

15. Whenever the death of a member of any of the four castes (would be occasioned by true evidence, they are free from blame) if they give false evidence.

16. In order to expiate the sin thus committed, (such a witness), if he belongs to a twice-born caste, must pour an oblation in the fire, consecrating it with the texts called Kûshmâ*ndî*.

17. If he is a *S*ûdra, he must feed ten cows for one day.

18. A false witness may be known by his altered looks, by his countenance changing colour, and by his talk wandering from the subject.

19. Let the judge summon the witnesses, at the time of sunrise, and examine them after having bound them by an oath.

20. A Brâhma*n*a he must address thus, 'Declare.'

21. A Kshatriya he must address thus, 'Declare the truth.'

---

16. Vâ*g*asan. Sa*m*h. XX, 14–16, or Taitt. Âra*n*y. X, 3–5. Nand. considers the term Kûshmâ*ndî* to be used in a general sense here, so as to include all the other texts mentioned in an analogous passage of Manu (VIII, 106).

22. A Vaisya he must address thus, ' Thy kine, grain, and gold (shall yield thee no fruit, if thou wert to give false evidence).'

23. A Sûdra he must address thus, ' Thou shalt have to atone for all (possible) heavy crimes (if thou wert to give false evidence).'

24. Let him exhort the witnesses (with the following speeches) :

25. ' Whatever places (of torture) await (the killer of a Brâhma*n*a and other) great criminals and (the killer of a cow and other) minor offenders, those places of abode are ordained for a witness who gives false evidence;

26. ' And the fruit of every virtuous act he has done, from the day of his birth to his dying day, shall be lost to him.

27. ' Truth makes the sun spread his rays.

28. ' Truth makes the moon shine.

29. ' Truth makes the wind blow.

30. ' Truth makes the earth bear (all that is upon it).

31. ' Truth makes waters flow.

32. ' Truth makes the fire burn.

33. ' The atmosphere exists through truth.

34. ' So do the gods.

35. ' And so do the offerings.

36. ' If veracity and a thousand horse-sacrifices

22, 23. Nand.'s interpretation of these two Sûtras, which has been followed above, does not agree with Kullûka's, of M. VIII, 88. But in another passage of Manu (VIII, 113), where the same terms recur, he interprets them like Nand.

36. This *S*loka is also found in the Mahâbhârata I, 3095 &c., in the Mârka*nd*eya-purâ*n*a VIII, 42, in the Hitopade*s*a IV, 129, and, in a somewhat modified form, in the Râmâya*n*a II, 61, 10. See Böhtlingk, Ind. Sprüche, 731 &c.

are weighed against each other, (it is found that) truth ranks even higher than a thousand horse-sacrifices.

37. 'Those who, though acquainted with the facts, and appointed to give evidence, stand mute, are equally criminal with, and deserve the same punishment as, false witnesses.' (After having addressed them) thus, let the king examine the witnesses in the order of their castes.

38. That plaintiff whose statement the witnesses declare to be true, shall win his suit; but he whose statement they declare to be wrong, shall certainly lose it.

39. If there is contradictory evidence, let the king decide by the plurality of witnesses; if equality in number, by superiority in virtue; if parity in virtue, by the evidence of the best among the twice-born.

40. Whenever a perjured witness has given false evidence in a suit, (the king) must reverse the judgment; and whatever has been done, must be considered as undone.

IX.

1. Now follows (the rule regarding) the performance of ordeals.

---

39. Nand. takes the term dvigottama, 'the best among the twice-born,' as an equivalent for 'Brâhmanas.' Kullûka (on M. VIII, 73) refers it to 'twice-born men, who are particularly active in the discharge of their religious duties.'

IX. 2. Y. II, 96, 99. — 11. M. VIII, 114, 115; Y. II, 95. — 20–22. Y. II, 95, 96, 99. — 23. Y. II, 98. — 33. Y. II, 97. The whole section on ordeals (IX–XIV) agrees very closely with the corresponding section of the Institutes of Nârada (5, 107–9, 8).

2. In cases of a criminal action directed against the king, or of violence[1] (they may be administered) indiscriminately.

3. In cases of (denial of) a deposit or of (alleged) theft or robbery they must be administered each according to the value (of the property claimed).

4. In all such cases the value (of the object claimed) must be estimated in gold.

5. Now if its value amounts to less than one Krishnala, a Sûdra must be made to swear by a blade of Dûrvâ grass, (which he must hold in his hand);

6. If it amounts to less than two Krishnalas, by a blade of Tila;

7. If it amounts to less than three Krishnalas, by a blade of silver;

8. If it amounts to less than four Krishnalas, by a blade of gold;

9. If it amounts to less than five Krishnalas, by a lump of earth taken from a furrow;

10. If it amounts to less than half a Suvarna, a Sûdra must be made to undergo the ordeal by sacred libation;

11. If it exceeds that amount, (the judge must administer to him) any one of the (other) ordeals, viz. the ordeal by the balance, by fire, by water, or by poison, considering duly (the season, &c.)

12. If the amount (of the matter in contest) is twice as high (as in each of the last-mentioned cases), a Vaisya must (in each case) undergo that ordeal which has (just) been ordained (for a Sûdra);

13. A Kshatriya (must undergo the same ordeals), if the amount is thrice as high;

---

2. [1] See VIII, 2, note.

14. A Brâhma*n*a, if it is four times as high. He is, however, not subject to the ordeal by sacred libation.

15. No judge must administer the (ordeal by) sacred libation to a Brâhma*n*a;

16. Except if it be done as a preliminary proof of his dealing fairly in some future transaction.

17. Instead of (administering the ordeal by) sacred libation to a Brâhma*n*a (in suits regarding an object, the value of which amounts to less than two Suvar*n*as), let the judge cause him to swear by a lump of earth taken from a furrow.

18. To one formerly convicted of a crime (or of perjury) he must administer one of the ordeals, even though the matter in contest be ever so trifling.

19. But to one who is known (and esteemed) among honest men and virtuous, he must not (administer any ordeal), even though the matter in contest be ever so important.

20. The claimant must declare his willingness to pay the fine (which is due in case of his being defeated);

21. And the defendant must go through the ordeal.

22. In cases of a criminal action directed against the king, or of violence (an ordeal may be administered) even without (the claimant) promising to pay the fine (due in case of defeat in ordinary suits).

23. To women, Brâhma*n*as, persons deficient in an organ of sense, infirm (old) men, and sick persons, the (ordeal by the) balance must be administered.

24. But it must not be administered to them while a wind is blowing.

25. The (ordeal by) fire must not be administered to lepers, to infirm persons, or to blacksmiths;

26. Nor must it ever be administered in autumn or summer.

27. The (ordeal by) poison must not be administered to lepers, bilious persons, or Brâhma*n*as;

28. Nor during the rainy season.

29. The (ordeal by) water must not be administered to persons afflicted with phlegm or (another) illness, to the timid, to the asthmatic, nor to those who gain their subsistence from water (such as fishermen and the like);

30. Nor during (the two cold seasons) Hemanta and *Si*sira (or from middle of November to middle of March);

31. The (ordeal by) sacred libation must not be administered to atheists;

32. Nor when the country is afflicted with disease or pestilence.

33. Let the judge summon the defendant at the time of sunrise, after having fasted on the previous day and bathed in his clothes, and make him go through all the ordeals in the presence of (images of) the gods and of the (assessors and other) Brâhma*n*as.

X.

1. Now follows the (rule regarding the ordeal by) balance.

---

29. Nand. infers from a text of Nârada (not found in his Institutes), that the plural is made use of in this Sûtra in order to include women, children, sickly, old, and feeble persons.

32. According to Nand., the particle *ka* is used here in order to include fire, wind, grasshoppers, and other plagues.

X. 5, 6. Y. II, 100.

2. The transverse beam, by which the balance is to be suspended, should be fastened upon two posts, four Hastas above the ground (each), and should be made two Hastas long.

3. The beam of the balance should be made of strong wood (such as that of the Khadira or Tinduka trees), five Hastas long, and the two scales must be suspended on both sides of it, (and the whole suspended upon the transverse beam by means of an iron hook).

4. A man out of the guild of goldsmiths, or of braziers, should make it equal on both sides.

5. Into the one scale the person (who is to be tried by this ordeal) should be placed, and a stone (or earth or bricks) or some other (equivalent) of the same weight into the other.

6. The equivalent and the man having been made equal in weight and (the position of the scales) well marked, the man should be caused to descend from the balance.

---

2. One Hasta, 'cubit,' the modern 'hath,' equals two Vitasti, 'spans,' and 24 Aṅgulas, 'digits,' the modern Aṅgul. See Prinsep, Useful Tables, p. 122.

3. See the plate of balance, according to the statements of Indian legislators, in Professor Stenzler's Essay, 'Über die ind. Gottesurtheile,' Journal of the German Oriental Society, IX.

4. Nand. infers from the use of the plural number and from a passage of Pitâmaha and Nârada (see the Institutes of the latter, 5, 122), that merchants may also be appointed for this purpose.

6. Nand. refers the term su*k*ihnitau kr*i*tvâ to the man and to the equivalent, both having to be marked 'with the king's seal or in some other way, in order that no one may suspect the weight of the equivalent or of the man to have been increased or lessened by the addition or removal of other objects, or of clothes, ornaments, and the like.' 'Others' explain the term in the way in which it has been rendered above.

7. Next (the judge) should adjure by (the following) imprecations the balance

8. And the person appointed to look after the weighing :

9. 'Those places of torture which have been prepared for the murderer of a Brâhma*n*a, or for a false witness, the same places are ordained for a person appointed to look after the weighing, who acts fraudulently in his office.

10. 'Thou, O balance (dha*t*a), art called by the same name as holy law (dharma); thou, O balance, knowest what mortals do not comprehend.

11. 'This man, being arraigned in a cause, is weighed upon thee. Therefore mayest thou deliver him lawfully from this perplexity.'

12. Thereupon the judge should have him placed into the one scale again. If he rises in it, he is freed from the charge according to law.

13. In case of the strings bursting, or of the splitting of the transverse beam, the man should be placed in the scale once more. Thus the facts will be ascertained positively, and a just sentence be the result.

XI.

1. Now follows the (rule regarding the ordeal by) fire.

2. He must make seven circles, sixteen Aṅgulas [1] in breadth each, the intervals being of the same breadth.

3. Thereupon he must place seven leaves of the

XI. 2–9. Y. II, 103, 105–107. — 11. Y. II, 104.

2. [1] See X, 2, note.

3. Nand. takes the term tata*h*, 'thereupon,' to imply that he

holy fig-tree into the hands of the person (about to perform the ordeal), who must turn his face towards the east and stretch out both arms.

4. Those (leaves) and his hands he must bind together with a thread.

5. Then he must place into his hands a ball made of iron, red-hot, fifty Palas in weight, and smooth.

6. Having received this, the person must proceed through the (seven) circles, without either walking at a very hurried pace, or lingering on his way.

7. Finally, after having passed the seventh circle, he must put down the ball upon the ground.

8. That man whose hands are burnt ever so little, shall be deemed guilty; but if he remains wholly unburnt, he is freed from the charge.

9. If he lets the ball drop from fear, or if there exists a doubt as to whether he is burnt or not, let him take the ball once more, because the proof has not been decided.

10. At the beginning (of the whole ceremony) the judge shall cause the person to rub some rice in his hands, and shall mark (with red sap, or the like, the already existing scars, eruptions of the skin, &c., which will thus have become visible). Then the judge, after having addressed the iron ball (with the following prayer), shall place it in his hands:

---

must previously examine the hands of the person about to perform the ordeal and mark existing scars or eruptions of the skin, as prescribed in Sûtra 10.

4. The particle *ka* implies, according to Nand., that he must further place seven Samî leaves, unbroken grains, Dûrvâ leaves, and grain smeared with sour milk upon his hands, as ordained in a passage of Pitâmaha.

11. 'Thou, O fire, dwellest ·in the ·interior of all creatures, like a witness. O fire, thou knowest what mortals do not comprehend.

12. 'This man being arraigned in a cause, desires to be cleared from guilt. Therefore mayest thou deliver him lawfully from this perplexity.'

XII.

1. Now follows the (rule regarding the ordeal by) water.

2. (The defendant must enter) water which is free from mud, aquatic plants, (crabs and other) vicious animals, (porpoises or other) large rapacious animals living in water, fish, leeches, and other (animals or plants).

3. The water ·having been addressed with the Mantras (mentioned hereafter), he must enter it, seizing the knees of another man, who must be free from friendship or hatred, and must dive into the water up to his navel.

4. At the same time another man must discharge an arrow from a bow, which must neither be too strong nor too weak.

5. That arrow must be fetched quickly by another man.

6. He who is not seen above the water in the mean time is proclaimed innocent. But in the contrary case he is (declared) guilty, even though one limb of his only has become visible.

7. 'Thou, O water, dwellest in the interior of all creatures, like a witness. O water, thou knowest what mortals do not comprehend.

XII. 3–6. Y. II, 1 o8, 1o9.

8. 'This man being arraigned in a cause, desires to be cleared from guilt. Therefore mayest thou deliver him lawfully from this perplexity.'

XIII.

1. Now follows the (rule regarding the ordeal by) poison.

2. All (other) sorts of poison must be avoided (in administering this ordeal),

3. Except poison from the *Sringa* tree, which grows on the Himâlayas.

4. (Of that) the judge must give seven grains, mixed with clarified butter, to the defendant (while reciting the prayer hereafter mentioned).

5. If the poison is digested easily, without violent symptoms, he shall recognise him as innocent, and dismiss him at the end of the day.

6. 'On account of thy venomous and dangerous nature thou art destruction to all living creatures; thou, O poison, knowest what mortals do not comprehend.

7. 'This man being arraigned in a cause, desires to be cleared from guilt. Therefore mayest thou deliver him lawfully from this perplexity.'

XIV.

1. Now follows the (rule regarding the ordeal by) sacred libation.

2. Having invoked terrible deities (such as Durgâ, the Âdityas or others, the defendant) must drink three handfuls of water in which (images of) those deities have been bathed,

---

XIII. 3, 5-7. Y. II, 110, 111.
XIV. 2, 4, 5. Y. II, 112, 113.

3. Uttering at the same time the words, 'I have not done this,' with his face turned towards the deity (in question).

4. He to whom (any calamity) happens within a fortnight or three weeks (such as an illness, or fire, or the death of a relative, or a heavy visitation by the king),

5. Should be known to be guilty; otherwise (if nothing adverse happens to him), he is freed from the charge. A just king should honour (with presents of clothes, ornaments, &c.) one who has cleared himself from guilt by an ordeal.

XV[1].

1. Now there are twelve kinds of sons.

2. The first is the son of the body, viz. he who is begotten (by the husband) himself on his own lawfully wedded wife.

3. The second is the son begotten on a wife, viz. one begotten by a kinsman allied by funeral oblations, or [1] by a member of the highest caste, on an appointed (wife or widow).

XV. 1–29. M. IX, 127, 136, 158–181; Y. II, 127–132; Gaut. XXVIII, 18, 19, 32, 33; Colebrooke, Dig. V, 4, CLXXXV; V, 4, CCXXV. — 28–30. Colebrooke, Dig. V, 4, CCXCIX. — 30. M. IX, 163. — 31. Colebrooke, Dig. V, 3, CXXI. — 32–34. M. IX, 201–203; Y. II, 140, 141; Gaut. XXVIII, 43, 44. — 32. Âpast. II, 6, 14, 1. — 34–38. Colebrooke, Dig. V, 5, CCCXXVII. — 40. M. IX, 180; Y. II, 132. — 41, 42. M. IX, 182, 183. — 44. M. IX, 138; Colebrooke, Dig. V, 4, CCCII. — 45–47. M. IX, 106, 137, 139. Of Chapters XV and XVII an excellent translation has been published by Dr. Bühler in the Bombay Digest (I, [1] 338–343). I have followed him literally almost throughout.

3. [1] I have translated the reading votpâdita*h*, which was no doubt

4. The third is the son of an appointed daughter.

5. She is called an appointed daughter, who is given away by her father with the words, 'The son whom she bears be mine.'

6. A damsel who has no brother is also (in every case considered) an appointed daughter, though she has not been given away according to the rule of an appointed daughter.

7. The son of a twice-married woman is the fourth.

8. She who, being still a virgin, is married for the second time is called twice married (punarbhû).

9. She also is called twice married (punarbhû) who, though not legally married more than once, has lived with another man before her lawful marriage.

---

the reading of Nandapan*d*ita, as he paraphrases the whole clause as follows, 'begotten by an elder or younger brother of the husband ; on failure of such, by a kinsman allied by funeral oblations ; on failure of him, by one belonging to the same gotra (race) as the husband ; on failure of him, by one descended from the same *R*ishi ancestors as he ; on failure of him, by a member of the highest caste, i. e. a Brâhma*n*a.' The above reading is also found in the London MS. of the text and in the two Calcutta editions. Dr. Bühler's MS., in which Nand.'s Commentary on this chapter is wanting, has *k*otpâdita*h*, and he translates accordingly, 'begotten by a kinsman . . ., who belongs to the highest caste.' The same reading is found in a quotation contained in *G*agannâtha and Colebrooke's Dig. loc. cit. (I quote from a very good though fragmentary Bengali MS. in my possession), where, however, this clause runs as follows, niyuktâyâ*m* savar*n*ena *k*otpâdita*h*, 'begotten by a man of equal class on a widow duly appointed,' Colebrooke. The other Smr*i*tis do not speak of the appointment of others than kinsmen to beget a son on a widow, or wife of a eunuch, &c., unless Yâ*g*ñavalkya's words (II, 128) sagotre*n*etare*n*a vâ, 'by a Sagotra or by another,' may be rendered, contrary to Vi*g*ñânesvara's interpretation, by 'a kinsman or one who is no kinsman.'

10. The son of an unmarried damsel is the fifth.

11. (He is called so who is) born by an unmarried daughter in the house of her father.

12. And he belongs to the man who (afterwards) marries the mother.

13. The son who is secretly born in the house is the sixth.

14. He belongs to him in whose bed he is born.

15. The son received with a bride is the seventh.

16. He (is called so who) is the son of a woman married while she was pregnant.

17. And he belongs to the husband (of the pregnant bride).

18. The adopted son (dattaka) is the eighth.

19. And he belongs to him to whom he is given by his mother or father.

20. The son bought is the ninth.

21. And he belongs to him by whom he is bought.

22. The son self-given is the tenth.

23. And he belongs to him to whom he gave himself.

24. The son cast away is the eleventh.

25. (He is called so) who was forsaken by his father or mother (or by both).

26. And he belongs to him by whom he is received.

27. The son born by any woman whomsoever [1] is the twelfth.

---

27. [1] Yatra kva*k*anotpâdita, 'born wherever,' means, according to Nand., ' begotten anyhow, but otherwise than the above-mentioned sons, upon a woman, whether one's own wife, or another man's wife, whether equal in caste or not, whether legally married to the

28. Amongst these (sons) each preceding one is preferable (to the one next in order).

29. And he takes the inheritance (before the next in order).

30. And let him maintain the rest.

31. He should marry unmarried (sisters) in a manner correspondent with the amount of his property.

32. Outcasts, eunuchs, persons incurably diseased, or deficient (in organs of sense or actions, such as blind, deaf, dumb, or insane persons, or lepers) do not receive a share.

33. They should be maintained by those who take the inheritance.

34. And their legitimate sons receive a share.

35. But not the children of an outcast;

36. Provided they were born after (the commission of) the act on account of which the parents were outcasted.

37. Neither do children begotten (by husbands of

---

begetter or not, whether still a virgin or not,' &c. But he adds a very lengthy discussion, the upshot of which is, that the term yatra kva*k*anotpâdita is applicable to adopted sons only, who, although they are considered as the sons of the adopter, or of the legitimate husband of the woman, upon whom they were begotten by another, may also become heirs to the begetter, in case he has no other son. 'Or this term refers to the son of a *S*ûdra concubine, whom Manu calls Pâra*s*ava' (M. IX, 178). The latter interpretation agrees with the one proposed by Dr. Bühler, who identifies the yatra kva*k*anotpâdita with the 'Nishâda and Pâra*s*ava of other lawyers,' especially of Baudhâyana (II, 2, 22), and with the view taken by *G*agannâtha, who thinks that the *S*audra (son of a *S*ûdra woman) is meant.

32. 'The particle tu, "but," indicates that those who have entered the order of ascetics must also be understood here.' (Nand.)

34. 'The particle *k*a indicates that sons begotten on their wives (Kshetra*g*as) shall also receive a share.' (Nand.)

an inferior caste) on women of a higher caste receive a share.

38. Their sons do not even receive a share of the wealth of their paternal grandfathers.

39. They should be supported by the heirs.

40. And he who inherits the wealth, presents the funeral oblation (to the deceased).

41. Amongst wives of one husband also the son of one is the son of all (and must present funeral oblations to them after their death).

42. Likewise, amongst brothers begotten by one (father, the son of one is the son of all, and must present funeral oblations to them all).

43. Let a son present the funeral oblations to his father, even though he inherit no property.

44. Because he saves (trâyate) his father from the hell called Put, therefore (a male child) is called put-tra (protector from Put, son) by Svayambhû himself.

45. He (the father) throws his debt on him (the son); and the father obtains immortality, if he sees the face of a living son.

46. Through a son he conquers the worlds, through a grandson he obtains immortality, and through the son's grandson he gains the world of the sun.

47. No difference is made in this world between the son of a son and the son of a daughter; for even a daughter's son works the salvation of a childless man, just like a son's son.

---

44. 'Svayambhû means the Veda.' (Nand.)

XVI.

1. On women equal in caste (to their husbands) sons are begotten, who are equal in caste (to their fathers).

2. On women of lower caste than their husbands sons are begotten, who follow the caste of their mothers.

3. On women of higher caste than their husbands sons are begotten, who are despised by the twice-born.

4. Among these, the son of a *Sûdra* with a Vaisya woman is called Âyogava.

5. The Pukkasa and Mâgadha are sons of a Vaisya and *Sûdra* respectively with a Kshatriya woman.

6. The *Kand*âla, Vaidehaka, and Sûta are the sons of a *Sûdra*, Vaisya, and Kshatriya respectively with a Brâhma*n*a woman.

7. Besides these, there are innumerable other mixed castes produced by further intermixture between those that have been mentioned.

8. Âyogavas must live by artistic performances (such as public wrestling, dancing, and the like).

9. Pukkasas must live by hunting.

10. Mâgadhas must live by calling out in public the good qualities (of saleable commodities).

11. *Kand*âlas must live by executing criminals sentenced to death.

XVI. 1. M. X, 5; Y. I, 90; Âpast. II, 6, 13, 1. — 4–6. M. X, 11, 12; Y. I, 93, 94; Gaut. IV, 17. — 7. M. X, 31. — 8–15. M. X, 47–53. — 17. M. X, 57. — 18. M. X, 62.

10. According to Manu (X, 47) the Mâgadhas are to live by traffic.

12. Vaidehakas must live by keeping (dancing girls and other public) women and profiting by what they earn.

13. Sûtas must live by managing horses.

14. *Kand*âlas must live out of the town, and their clothes must be the mantles of the deceased. In this their condition is different (from, and lower than, that of the other mixed castes).

15. All (members of mixed castes) should have intercourse (of marriage, and other community) only between themselves.

16. (In the lower castes also) the son inherits the property of his father.

17. All members of those mixed castes, whether their descent has been kept secret or is generally known, may be found out by their acts.

18. Desertion of life, regardless of reward, in order to save a Brâhma*n*a, or a cow, or for the sake of a woman or child, may confer heavenly bliss even upon (members of those) base castes.

XVII.

1. If a father makes a partition with his sons, he may dispose of his self-acquired property as he thinks best.

XVII. 1. Y. II, 114. — 2. Y. II, 121. — 3. M. IX, 216; Y. II, 122; Gaut. XXVIII, 29; Colebrooke, Dig. V, 2, CII. — 4–16. M. IX, 185–189; Y. II, 135–137; Âpast. II, 6, 14, 2–5; Gaut. XXVIII, 21. — 4–13, 15. Colebrooke, Dig. V, 8, CCCCXVII; V, 8, CCCCLIX. — 17. M. IX, 211, 212; Y. II, 138; Gaut. XXVIII, 28. — 18. M. IX, 194, 195; Y. II, 143, 144; Colebrooke, Dig. V, 9, CCCCLVII. — 19. M. IX, 196; Y. II, 145. — 20. M. IX, 197; Y. II, 145. — 21. M. IX, 192; Y. II, 145; Gaut. XXVIII, 24; Colebrooke, Dig. V, 9, CCCCXCIV. — 22. M. IX, 200; Colebrooke, Dig. V, 9, CCCCLXXIII. — 23. Y. II, 120.

2. But in regard to wealth inherited of the paternal grandfather, the ownership of father and son is equal.

3. (Sons), who have separated from their father, should give a share to (a brother) who is born after partition.

4. The wealth of a man who dies without male issue goes to his wife;

5. On failure of her, to his daughter;

6. On failure of her, to his father;

7. On failure of him, to his mother;

8. On failure of her, to his brother;

9. On failure of him, to his brother's son;

10. On failure of him, to the relations called Bandhu;

11. On failure of them, to the relations called Sakulya;

12. On failure of them, to a fellow-student;

13. On failure of him, it goes to the king, with the exception of a Brâhma*n*a's property.

14. The property of a Brâhma*n*a goes to (other) Brâhma*n*as.

---

8. 'On failure of brothers the sister inherits.' (Nand.)

9. 'On failure of a brother's son the sister's son inherits.' (Nand.)

10. Bandhu means Sapi*nd*a (allied by funeral oblations). The inheritance goes first to the Sapi*nd*as on the father's side in the following order: (the brother's son), the brother's grandson, the grandfather, his son, grandson, and great-grandson, the great-grandfather, his son, grandson, and great-grandson. Then follow the mother's Sapi*nd*as in the same order. (Nand.)

11. Sakulya means distant kinsmen, beginning with the fifth in descent and ascent. On failure of such, the inheritance goes to the spiritual teacher; on failure of him, to a pupil of the deceased, as ordained by Âpastamba (II, 6, 14, 3); and on failure of him, to a fellow-student, as stated in Sûtra 12. (Nand.)

15. The wealth of a (deceased) hermit shall be taken by his spiritual teacher;

16. Or his pupil (may take it).

17. But let a reunited coparcener take the share of his reunited coparcener who has died (without issue), and a uterine brother that of his uterine brother, and let them give (the shares of their deceased coparceners and uterine brothers) to the sons of the latter.

18. What has been given to a woman by her father, mother, sons, or brothers, what she has received before the sacrificial fire (at the marriage ceremony), what she receives on supersession, what has been given to her by her relatives, her fee (Sulka), and a gift subsequent, are called 'woman's property' (Strîdhana).

19. If a woman married according to (one of the first) four rites, beginning with the Brâhma rite, dies without issue, that (Strîdhana) belongs to her husband.

20. (If she has been married) according to (one of) the other (four reprehensible rites), her father shall take it.

---

18. 'Sulka, "fee," denotes the price or value of a house or other valuable object presented to the bride by her father; or it means the fee paid for her by the bridegroom.' (Nand.) The latter interpretation is evidently the correct one. The bride's 'fee' (see Gaut. XXVIII, 25), from being originally the price due to the parents or guardian of the bride for surrendering her to the bridegroom, became in after times a wedding present, which the bride received from the bridegroom either directly or through her parents. This is the only way to account for the Sulka being enumerated among the constituent parts of Strîdhana in this place. See also I. D. Mayne, Hindu Law and Usage, §§ 77, 566; Mayr, Indisches Erbrecht, 170 seq.; Jolly, Stellung der Frauen, 23, note.

19, 20. See XXIV, 17–27.

21. If she dies leaving children, her wealth goes in every case to her daughter.

22. Ornaments worn by women when their husbands were alive, the heirs shall not divide among themselves; if they divide them, they become outcasts.

23. (Coparceners) descended from different fathers must adjust their shares according to the fathers. Let each take the wealth due to his father, no other (has a right to it).

XVIII.

1. If there are four sons of a Brâhma*n*a (springing from four different wives) of the four castes, they shall divide the whole estate of their father into ten parts.

2. Of these, let the son of the Brâhma*n*a wife take four parts;

3. The son of the Kshatriya wife, three parts;

4. The son of the Vai*s*ya wife, two parts;

5. The son of the *S*ûdra wife, a single part.

---

22. My rendering of this *S*loka is based upon Kullûka's interpretation of the identical passage of Manu (IX, 200), which is supported by Vig*ñ*âne*s*vara (Mitâksharâ I, 4, 19 in Colebrooke's version), Mâdhava (Burnell, Dâya-Vibhâga 51), Varadarâ*g*a (Burnell, Varadarâ*g*a's Vyavahâranir*n*aya 49), and others. Nand. proposes a different interpretation, on which rests Dr. Bühler's rendering, 'Those ornaments, which the wives usually wear, should not be divided by the heirs whilst the husbands are alive.'

XVIII. 1–5. M. IX, 149, 151–153; Y. II, 125. — 11, 25–27. Y. II, 125. — 1–31, 38–40. Colebrooke, Dig. V, 3, CLIII. — 32–37. Colebrooke, Dig. V, 3, CLXXII; V, 2, LXXXVI; V, 1, LIV. — 36. Y. II, 114; Âpast. II, 6, 14, 1. — 41. M. IX, 210. — 42, 43. M. IX, 208, 209; Y. II, 118, 119. — 44. M. IX, 219; Gaut. XXVIII, 46, 47. — 43, 44. Colebrooke, Dig. V, 2, XCI; V, 5, CCCLXIII.

6. Again, if there are three sons of a Brâhma*n*a (by wives of different castes), but no son by a *S*ûdra (wife) among them, they shall divide the estate into nine parts.

7. (Of these) let them take, each in the order of his caste, shares amounting to four, three, and two parts of the whole respectively.

8. (If there are three sons by wives of different castes, but) no Vai*s*ya among them, they shall divide the estate into eight parts, and take four parts, three parts, and one part respectively.

9. (If there are three sons, but) no Kshatriya among them, they shall divide it into seven parts, and take four parts, two parts, and a single part respectively.

10. If there is no Brâhma*n*a among them, they shall divide it into six parts, and take three parts, two parts, and a single part respectively.

11. If there are sons of a Kshatriya by a Kshatriya, a Vai*s*ya, and a *S*ûdra wife, the mode of division shall be the same (i. e. the estate shall be divided into six parts, &c.)

12. Again, if there are two sons of a Brâhma*n*a, the one belonging to the Brâhma*n*a and the other to the Kshatriya caste, they shall divide the estate into seven parts; and of these the Brâhma*n*a son shall take four parts;

13. The Kshatriya son, three parts.

14. Again, if there are two sons of a Brâhma*n*a, and the one belongs to the Brâhma*n*a and the other to the Vai*s*ya caste, the estate shall be divided into six parts; and of these, the Brâhma*n*a shall take four parts;

15. The Vai*s*ya, two parts.

16. Again, if there are two sons of a Brâhmana, and the one belongs to the Brâhmana and the other to the Sûdra caste, they shall divide the estate into five parts;

17. And of these, the Brâhmana shall take four parts;

18. The Sûdra, a single part.

19. Again, if there are two sons of a Brâhmana or a Kshatriya, and the one belongs to the Kshatriya and the other to the Sûdra caste, they shall divide the estate into five parts;

20. And of these, the Kshatriya shall take three parts;

21. The Sûdra, one part.

22. Again, if there are two sons of a Brâhmana or a Kshatriya, and the one belongs to the Kshatriya, the other to the Sûdra caste, they shall divide the estate into four parts;

23. And of these, the Kshatriya shall take three parts;

24. The Sûdra, a single part.

25. Again, if there are two sons of a Brâhmana or a Vaisya or a Sûdra, and the one belongs to the Vaisya, the other to the Sûdra caste, they shall divide the estate into three parts;

26. And of these, the Vaisya shall take two parts;

27. The Sûdra, a single part.

28. If a Brâhmana has an only son, he shall take the whole estate, provided he be a Brâhmana, Kshatriya, or Vaisya.

29. If a Kshatriya has (an only son who is) either a Kshatriya or a Vaisya, (the rule shall be the same.)

30. If a Vaisya has (an only son who is) a Vaisya, (the rule shall also be the same);

31. (And so shall the only) son of a Sûdra (be sole heir) to his Sûdra (father).

32. A Sûdra, who is the only son of a father belonging to a twice-born caste, shall inherit one half of his property;

33. The other half shall devolve in the same way as the property of one who died without leaving issue.

34. Mothers shall receive shares proportionate to their sons' shares;

35. And so shall unmarried daughters.

36. Sons, who are equal in caste (to their father), shall receive equal shares.

37. A best part (the twentieth part of the inheritance, &c.) shall be given to the eldest, as his additional share.

38. If there are two sons by a Brâhmana wife, and one son by a Sûdra wife, the estate shall be divided into nine parts; and of these, the two sons of the Brâhmana wife shall take two parts, the one son of the Sûdra wife, a single part.

39. If there are two sons by a Sûdra, and one son by a Brâhmana wife, the estate shall be divided into six parts; and of these, the son of the Brâhmana wife shall take four parts, and the two sons of the Sûdra wife together shall take two parts.

40. Upon the same principles the shares have to be adjusted in other cases also.

---

33. See XVII, 4 seq.

34. 'That is to say, a Brâhmana wife shall take four parts, a Kshatriya wife, three parts,' &c. (Nand.)

37. See Gaut. XXVIII, 5.

41. If (brothers), who after a previous division of the estate live again together as parceners, should make a second partition, the shares must be equal in that case, and the eldest has no right to an additional share.

42. What a brother has acquired by his own efforts, without using the patrimony, he must not give up (to his brothers or other co-heirs), unless by his own free will; for it was gained by his own exertion.

43. And if a man recovers (a debt or other property), which could not before be recovered by his father, he shall not, unless by his own free will, divide it with his sons; for it is an acquisition made by himself.

44. Apparel, vehicles[1] (carriages or riding-horses), and ornaments (such as are usually worn according to the custom of the caste), prepared food, water (in a well or pool), females (slaves or mistresses of the deceased), property destined for pious uses or sacrifices, a common pasture-ground[2], and a book, are indivisible.

---

42. The term svayamîhitalabdham has been translated according to Kullûka (on M. IX, 208). Nand. interprets this *S*loka thus, 'What a brother has acquired by his own efforts, and what has been given to him, at his desire (by friends or others), he must not give up,' &c.

43. Here again I have followed Kullûka (on M. IX, 209), and deviated from Nand.'s interpretation, who renders this *S*loka as follows, 'If a man recovers property, &c., or if he gains property by himself (by his learning or valour, &c.) . . .'

44. [1] The term pattra has been rendered above in accordance with the first interpretation proposed by Nand., and with Kullûka's interpretation (on M. IX, 219). Vig*ñ*âne*s*vara (in his comment upon the same passage of Manu) refers it to written documents, such especially as relate to a debt to be paid to the deceased; and

XIX.

1. He must not cause a member of a twice-born caste to be carried out by a *Sûdra* (even though he be a kinsman of the deceased);

2. Nor a *Sûdra* by a member of a twice-born caste.

3. A father and a mother shall be carried out by their sons (who are equal in caste to their parents).

4. But *Sûdras* must never carry out a member of a twice-born caste, even though he be their father.

5. Those Brâhma*n*as who carry out (or follow the corpse of) a (deceased) Brâhma*n*a who has no relatives shall attain a mansion in heaven.

6. Those who have carried out a dead relative and burnt his corpse, shall walk round the pile from left to right, and then plunge into water, dressed in their clothes.

7. After having offered a libation of water to the deceased, they must place one ball of rice on blades of Ku*s*a grass, (and this ceremony has to be repeated on each subsequent day, while the period of impurity lasts.)

8. Then, having changed their dress, they must

---

this interpretation is mentioned by Nand. also. But there is no reason why an unliquidated demand should not be divided ; and written documents are only twice referred to in the code of Manu (VIII, 168, and IX, 232). — [2] In translating the term pra*k*âra I have again followed Kullûka loc. cit. ; see also Petersburg Dictionary s. v. Nand. interprets this term as denoting ' a path leading to or from the house.'

XIX. 1. M.V, 104. — 2. Y. III, 26. — 6. M.V, 103 ; Y. III, 26. — 7, 8. Y. III, 7, 12, 13. — 14–17. M. V, 73 ; Y. III, 16. ' Chapters XIX–XXXII contain the section on Â*k*âra, " Holy Usage." ' (Nand.)

bite Nimba leaves between their teeth, and having stepped upon the stone threshold, they must enter the house.

9. Then they must throw unbroken grains into the fire.

10. On the fourth day they must collect the bones that have been left.

11. And they must throw them into water from the Ganges.

12. As many bones of a man are contained in the water of the Ganges, so many thousands of years will he reside in heaven.

13. While the term of impurity lasts, they must continually offer a libation of water and a ball of rice to the deceased.

14. And they must eat food which has been bought, or which they have received unsolicited.

15. And they must eat no meat.

16. And they must sleep on the ground.

17. And they must sleep apart.

18. When the impurity is over, they must walk forth from the village, have their beards shaved, and having cleansed themselves with a paste of sesamum, or with a paste of mustard-seed, they must change their dress and re-enter the house.

19. There, after reciting a propitiatory prayer, they must honour the Brâhma*n*as.

---

13. The duration of the impurity varies according to the caste &c. of the deceased.   See XXII.

14. The particle *k*a, according to Nand., indicates that factitious salt must also not be used by them, as stated in a Sm*ri*ti.

15. Nand. refers the particle *k*a to an implied prohibition to eat fish, which he quotes from a text of Gautama (not found in his Institutes).

20. The gods are invisible deities, the Brâhma*n*as are visible deities.

21. The Brâhma*n*as sustain the world.

22. It is by the favour of the Brâhma*n*as that the gods reside in heaven; a speech uttered by Brâhma*n*as (whether a curse or a benediction) never fails to come true.

23. What the Brâhma*n*as pronounce, when highly pleased (as, if they promise sons, cattle, wealth, or some other boon to a man), the gods will ratify; when the visible gods are pleased, the invisible gods are surely pleased as well.

24. The mourners, who lament the loss of a relative, shall be addressed by men gifted with a tranquil frame of mind with such consolatory speeches as I shall now recite to thee, O Earth, who art cherished to my mind.

XX.

1. The northern progress of the sun is a day with the gods.

2. The southern progress of the sun is (with them) a night.

3. A year is (with them) a day and a night;

4. Thirty such are a month;

5. Twelve such months are a year.

6. Twelve hundred years of the gods are a Kaliyuga.

XX. 1–3. M. I, 67. — 6–9. M. I, 69, 70. — 10. M. I, 71. — 11. M. I, 79. — 12–14. M. I, 72. — 30. Y. III, 11.

6. The Kaliyuga itself consists of a thousand years only; but it is both preceded and followed by a twilight lasting a hundred years. It is similar with the three other Yugas. (Nand.)

7. Twice as many (or two thousand four hundred) are a Dvâpara (Yuga).

8. Thrice as many (or three thousand six hundred) are a Tretâ (Yuga).

9. Four times as many (or four thousand eight hundred) are a K*ri*ta Yuga.

10. (Thus) twelve thousand years make a *K*atur-yuga (or period of four Yugas).

11. Seventy-one *K*aturyugas make a Manvantara (or period of a Manu).

12. A thousand *K*aturyugas make a Kalpa.

13. And that is a day of the forefather (Brahman).

14. His night also has an equal duration.

15. If so many such nights and days are put together that, reckoned by the month and by the year, they make up a period of a hundred years (of Brahman) it is called the age of one Brahman.

16. A day of Purusha (Vish*n*u) is equal in duration to the age of one Brahman.

17. When it ends, a Mahâkalpa is over.

18. The night following upon it is as long.

19. The days and nights of Purusha that have gone by are innumerable;

20. And so are those that will follow.

21. For Kâla (time) is without either beginning or end.

22. Thus it is, that in this Kâla (time), in whom there is nothing to rest upon, and who is everlasting, I can espy nothing created in which there is the least stability.

23. The sands in the Ganges and (the waters pouring down from the sky) when Indra sends rain

21. 'Kâla means Vish*n*u in this place.' (Nand.)

can be counted, but not the number of 'Forefathers' (Brahmans) who have passed away.

24. In each Kalpa, fourteen chiefs of the gods (Indras) go to destruction, as many rulers of the world (kings), and fourteen Manus.

25. And so have many thousands of Indras and hundred thousands of princes of the Daityas (such as Hira*n*yaka*s*ipu, Hira*n*yâksha, and others) been destroyed by Kâla (time). What should one say of human beings then?

26. Many royal *Ri*shis too (such as Sagara), all of them renowned for their virtues, gods and Brahmanical *Ri*shis (such as Ka*s*yapas) have perished by the action of Kâla.

27. Those even who have the power of creating and annihilating in this world (the sun, moon, and other heavenly bodies) continually perish by the act of Kâla; for Kâla (time) is hard to overcome.

28. Every creature is seized upon by Kâla and carried into the other world. It is the slave of its actions (in a former existence). Wherefore then should you wail (on its death)?

29. Those who are born are sure to die, and those who have died are sure to be born again. This is inevitable, and no associate can follow a man (in his passage through mundane existence).

30. As mourners will not help the dead in this world, therefore (the relatives) should not weep, but perform the obsequies to the best of their power.

31. 'As both his good and bad actions will follow

27. Here also Kâla, the god of time, is another name for Vish*n*u. (Nand.)

29. The same proverb occurs in the Râmâya*n*a II, 84, 21, and in the Bhagavadgîtâ II, **27**. See Böhtlingk, Ind. Sprüche, 2383.

him (after death) like associates, what does it matter to a man whether his relatives mourn over him or no?

32. But as long as his relatives remain impure, the departed spirit finds no rest, and returns to visit (his relatives), whose duty it is to offer up to him the funeral ball of rice and the water libation.

33. Till the Sapindikarana[1] has been performed, the dead man remains a disembodied spirit (and is afflicted with hunger and thirst). Give rice and a jar with water to the man who has passed into the abode of disembodied spirits.

34. Having passed into the abode of the manes (after the performance of the Sapindikarana) he enjoys in the shape of celestial food his portion of the Srâddha (funeral oblation) ; offer the Srâddha, therefore, to him who has passed into the abode of the manes.

35. Whether he has become a god, or stays in hell, or has entered the body of an animal, or of a human being, he will receive the Srâddha offered to him by his relatives.

36. The dead person and the performer of the Srâddha are sure to be benefitted by its performance. Perform the Srâddha always, therefore, abandoning bootless grief.

37. This is the duty which should be constantly discharged towards a dead person by his kinsmen ; by mourning a man will neither benefit the dead nor himself.

38. Having seen that no help is to be had from this world, and that his relations are dying (one after

---

33. [1] See XXI, 12.

the other), you must choose virtue for your only associate, O ye men.

39. Even were he to die with him, a kinsman is unable to follow his dead relative : all excepting his wife are forbidden to follow him on the path of Yama.

40. Virtue alone will follow him, wherever he may go; therefore do your duty unflinchingly in this wretched world.

41. To-morrow's business should be done to-day, and the afternoon's business in the forenoon; for death will not wait, whether a person has done it or not.

42. While his mind is fixed upon his field, or traffic, or his house, or while his thoughts are engrossed by some other (beloved) object, death suddenly carries him away as his prey, as a she-wolf catches a lamb.

43. Kâla (time) is no one's friend and no one's enemy : when the effect of his acts in a former existence, by which his present existence is caused, has expired, he snatches a man away forcibly.

44. He will not die before his time has come, even though he has been pierced by a thousand shafts; he will not live after his time is out, even though he has only been touched by the point of a blade of Kusa grass.

45. Neither drugs, nor magical formulas, nor

---

39. This is an allusion to the custom of Sattee. (Nand.) See XXV, 14.

41. This proverb is found in the Mahâbhârata also (XII, 6536, &c.) See Böhtlingk, Ind. Sprüche, 6595.

43. This proverb is also found in the Mahâbhârata XI, 68, and Râmâyana IV, 18, 28, and other works. See Böhtlingk, 3194.

45. 'Neither will presents of gold (to Brâhmanas) or other such

burnt-offerings, nor prayers will save a man who is in the bonds of death or old age.

46. An impending evil cannot be averted even by a hundred precautions; what reason then for you to complain?

47. Even as a calf finds his mother among a thousand cows, an act formerly done is sure to find the perpetrator.

48. Of existing beings the beginning is unknown, the middle (of their career) is known, and the end again unknown; what reason then for you to complain?

49. As the body of mortals undergoes (successively the vicissitudes of) infancy, youth, and old age, even so will it be transformed into another body (hereafter); a sensible man is not mistaken about that.

50. As a man puts on new clothes in this world, throwing aside those which he formerly wore, even so the self of man puts on new bodies, which are in accordance with his acts (in a former life).

51. No weapons will hurt the self of man, no fire burn it, no waters moisten it, and no wind dry it up.

52. It is not to be hurt, not to be burnt, not to be moistened, and not to be dried up; it is imperishable, perpetual, unchanging, immovable, without beginning.

---

acts of liberality save him, as the use of the particle *ka* implies.' (Nand.)

47. This proverb is also found in the Mahâbhârata XII, 6760, Pañ*k*atantra II, 134, and other works. See Böhtlingk, Ind. Sprüche, 5114.

48. This proverb is also found in the Bhagavadgîtâ II, 28. See Böhtlingk, Ind. Sprüche, 704.

50. Regarding transmigration, see below, XLIV, XLV.

53. It is (further) said to be immaterial, passing all thought, and immutable. Knowing the self of man to be such, you must not grieve (for the destruction of his body).

XXI.

1. Now then [1], (on the day) after the impurity is over, let him bathe duly (during the recitation of Mantras), wash his hands and feet duly, and sip water duly, (and having invited some Brâhma*n*as), as many as possible, who must cleanse themselves in the same way and turn their faces towards the north, let him bestow presents of perfumes, garlands, clothes and other things (a lamp, frankincense, and the like) upon them, and hospitably entertain them.

2. At the Ekoddish*t*a (or *S*râddha for one recently deceased) let him alter the Mantras [1] so as to refer to (the) one person (deceased) [2].

XXI. 1–11. Âsv. IV, 7; Pâr. III, 10, 48–53; Sânkh. IV, 2; M. III, 247; Y. III, 250, 251, 255. — 12–23. Sânkh. IV, 3; V, 9; Y. I, 252–254. Regarding the parallel passages of the Kâ*th*aka Gr*i*hya-sûtra, see the Introduction.

1. [1] 'Having said, in the previous Chapter (XX, 30), that "the obsequies should be performed," he now goes on to describe that part of the obsequies which has not yet been expounded, viz. the "first *S*râddha."' (Nand.)

2. [1] The Mantras here referred to are those contained in the description of the Pârva*n*a and other ordinary *S*râddhas in Chapter LXXIII. Thus, the Mantra, 'This is your (share), ye manes' (LXXIII, 12, 13), has to be altered into, 'This is thy (share), father;' and so on. Devapâla, in his Commentary on the Kâ*th*aka Gr*i*hya-sûtra, gives an accurate statement of all the modifications which the ordinary Mantras have to undergo at the Ekoddish*t*a.—[2] Nand. states that not only the Mantras, but the whole ritual should be modified. The nature of the latter modifications is stated by Yâg*ñ*avalkya loc. cit. and by *S*ânkhâyana loc. cit.

3. Close to the food left (by the Brâhma*n*as) let him offer a ball of rice, at the same time calling out his name and (that of) his race.

4. The Brâhma*n*as having taken food and having been honoured with a gift, let him offer, as imperishable food, water to the Brâhma*n*as, after having called out the name and Gotra of the deceased; and let him dig three trenches, each four Angulas in breadth, their distance from one another and their depth also measuring (four Angulas), and their length amounting to one Vitasti (or twelve Angulas).

5. Close by the trenches let him light three fires, and having added fuel to them, let him make three oblations (of boiled rice) in each (fire, saying),

6. 'Svadhâ and reverence to Soma, accompanied by the manes.

7. 'Svadhâ and reverence to Agni, who conveys the oblations addressed to the manes.

8. 'Svadhâ and reverence to Yama Angiras.'

9. Then let him offer balls of rice as (ordained) before (in Sûtra 3) on the three mounds of earth (adjacent to the three trenches).

10. After having filled the three trenches with

---

3. This must be done with the Mantra, 'This is for you.' (Nand.)   Regarding this Mantra, see note on Sûtra 10.

4. The 'imperishable water,' akshayyodakam, derives its name from the Mantra, with which it is delivered, expressing the wish that the meal 'may give imperishable satisfaction' (akshayyam astu).   This is the explanation which Nand. gives of the term akshayyodakam in his gloss on LXXIII, 27.   In his comment on the present Sûtra he says that the 'imperishable water' must be presented with the (further?) Mantras, 'Let arrive' and 'Be satisfied.'   See Y. I, 251; *S*ânkh. IV, 2, 5, 6.

10. The whole Mantra runs as follows, 'This is for you, father,

rice, sour milk, clarified butter, honey, and meat, let him mutter (the Mantra), 'This is for you.'

11. This ceremony he must repeat monthly, on the day of his death.

12. At the close of the year let him give food to the Brâhma*n*as, after having fed the gods first, in honour of the deceased and of his father, grandfather, and great-grandfather.

13. At (the Ekoddish*t*a belonging to) this ceremony let him perform the burnt-offering, the invitation, and (the offering of) water for washing the feet.

14. Then he must pour the water for washing the feet and the Arghya (water libation) destined for the deceased person into the three vessels containing the water for washing the feet, and the three other vessels containing the Arghya of his three ancestors. At the same time he must mutter

---

and for those after you.' But in the present case (at a 'first *S*râddha') the name of the deceased has to be substituted for the word 'father.' (Nand.) Although Nand. quotes this Mantra from Â*s*valâyana's *S*rauta-sûtra, it seems probable that the author of the Vish*n*u-sûtra took it from the Kâ*th*aka (IX, 6 of the Berlin MS.)

11. The Sûtras following next refer to the Sapi*nd*îkara*n*a or 'ceremony of investing a dead person with the rights of a Sapi*nd*a.'

12. 'He must invite six Brâhma*n*as altogether, four as representatives of the deceased person and of his three ancestors, two for the offering to be addressed to the Vi*s*vedevâs. The Brâhma*n*a, who represents the deceased person, must be fed according to the rule of the Ekoddish*t*a, and the three Brâhma*n*as, who represent the three ancestors, must be fed according to the rule of the Pârva*n*a *S*râddha, as laid down in Chapter LXXIII.' (Nand.)

13. The import of this Sûtra is, that those three ceremonies must not be omitted in the present case, as is otherwise the case at an Ekoddish*t*a. (Nand.)

14. [1] The following is a translation of the whole of this Mantra,

(the two Mantras), 'May earth unite thee[1],' and ' United your minds[2].'

15. Near the leavings he must make (and put) four balls of rice.

16. Let him show out the Brâhma*n*as, after they have sipped water duly and have been presented by him with their sacrificial fee.

17. Then let him knead together the ball of the deceased person with the three balls (of the three ancestors), as (he has mixed up) his water for washing the feet and his Arghya (with theirs).

18. Let him do the same (with the balls placed) near the three trenches.

19. Or (see Sûtra 12) the Sapi*nd*îkara*n*a must be performed on the thirteenth, after the monthly *S*râddha has been performed on the twelfth[1] day.

20. For *S*ûdras it should be performed on the twelfth day, without Mantras.

21. If there be an intercalary month in that year, he must add one day to the (regular days of the) monthly *S*râddha.

22. The ceremony of investing women with the relationship of Sapi*nd*a has to be performed in the same manner. Later, he must perform a *S*râddha every year, while he lives, (on the anniversary of the deceased relative's death)[1].

which is quoted at full in the Kâ*th*aka Gri*h*ya-sûtra, 'May P*ri*thivî (the earth), Vâyu (air), Agni (fire), and Pra*g*âpati (the lord of creatures) unite thee with thy ancestors, and may you ancestors unite with him.' Regarding the particular ancestors implied here, see below, LXXV. — [2] Rig-veda X, 191, 4.

19. [1] I. e. on that day on which the period of impurity expires. (Nand.)

22. [1] The meaning is, that he must give him food and water, as prescribed in 23. (Nand.)

23. He, for whom the ceremony of investing him with the relationship of Sapi*nd*a is performed after the lapse of a year, shall be honoured by the gift, (on each day) of that year, of food and a jar with water to a Brâhma*n*a.

XXII.

1. The impurity of a Brâhma*n*a caused by the birth or death of Sapi*nd*as lasts ten days.

2. In the case of a Kshatriya (it lasts) twelve days.

3. In the case of a Vai*s*ya (it lasts) fifteen days.

4. In the case of a *S*ûdra (it lasts) a month.

5. The relationship of Sapi*nd*a ceases with the seventh man (in descent or ascent).

6. During the period of impurity oblations (to the Vi*s*vedevâs), gifts and receiving of alms, and study have to be interrupted.

XXII. 1–4. M. V, 83; Y. III, 18, 22; Âpast. I, 5, 16, 18; Gaut. XIV, 1–4. — 5. M. V, 60; Âpast. II, 6, 15, 2; Gaut. XIV, 13. — 25. M. V, 66; Y. III, 20; Gaut. XIV, 17. — 27. Y. III, 23; Gaut. XIV, 44. — 28. M. V, 69; Y. III, 1. — 29, 30. M. V, 67; Y. III, 23. — 35. M. V, 79; Y. III, 20; Gaut. XIV, 6. — 36, 37. Gaut. XIV, 7, 8. — 38. M. V, 79; Y. III, 20. — 39–41. M. V, 75, 76; Y. III, 21; Gaut. XIV, 19. — 42. M. V, 80; Y. III, 24. — 43. Y. III, 25. — 44. M. V, 80, 81; Y. III, 24; Gaut. XIV, 20. — 45. M. V, 82; Y. III, 25. — 46. M. V, 81; Gaut. XIV, 20. — 47. M. V, 89; Y. III, 21, 27; Gaut. XIV, 10–12. — 48–55. M. V, 93–95; Y. III, 27–29. — 48, 49. Gaut. XIV, 45, 46. — 56. M. V, 89; Y. III, 21; Gaut. XIV, 12. — 63–65. M. V, 103; Y. III, 26; Gaut. XIV, 31. — 67. M. V, 144. — 69. M. V, 85; Y. III, 30; Âpast. II, 1, 2, 8, 9; Gaut. XIV, 30. — 70. M. V, 87. — 75. M. V, 145; Y. I, 196; Âpast. I, 5, 16, 14; Gaut. I, 37. — 81. M. V, 135. — 82. M. XI, 95. — 84. M. XI, 96. — 85. M. V, 65. — 86. M. V, 91. — 87. M. V, 88. — 88–93. M. V, 105–110; Y. III, 31–34.

7. No one must eat the food of one impure (unless he be a Sapi*nd*a of his).

8. He who eats but once the food of Brâhma*n*as or others, while they are impure, will remain impure as long as they.

9. When the (period of) impurity is over, he must perform a penance (as follows):

10. If a twice-born man has eaten (the food) of a member of his own caste, while the latter was impure, he must approach a river and plunge into it, mutter the (hymn of) Aghamarsha*n*a [1] three times, and, after having emerged from the water, must mutter the Gâyatrî [2] one thousand and eight times.

11. If a Brâhma*n*a has eaten the food of a Kshatriya, while the latter was impure, he is purified by performing the same penance and by fasting (on the previous day).

12. (The same penance is ordained for) a Kshatriya who has eaten the food of a Vai*s*ya, while the latter was impure.

13. (The same penance is ordained for) a Brâhma*n*a (who has eaten the food) of an impure Vai*s*ya; but he must fast besides during the three (previous) days.

14. If a Kshatriya or a Vai*s*ya (have eaten the food) of a Brâhma*n*a or a Kshatriya respectively, who were impure, they must approach a river and mutter the Gâyatrî five hundred times.

15. A Vai*s*ya, who has eaten the food of a Brâhma*n*a, while the latter was impure, must (go to a river and) mutter the Gâyatrî one hundred and eight times.

---

10. [1] Rig-veda X, 190. — [2] Rig-veda III, 62, 10.

16. A twice-born man (who has eaten the food) of a Sûdra, while the latter was impure, must (go to a river and) perform the Prâgâpatya (penance).

17. A Sûdra (who has eaten the food) of an impure man of a twice-born caste must bathe (in a river).

18. A Sûdra (who has eaten the food) of another Sûdra, while the latter was impure, must bathe (in a river) and drink Pañkagavya.

19. Wives and slaves in the direct order of the castes (i. e. who do not belong to a higher·caste than their lord) remain impure as long as their lord.

20. If their lord is dead (or if they live apart from him, they remain impure) as long as (members of) their own caste.

21. If Sapindas of a higher caste (are born or have died) the period of impurity has for their lower caste relations the same duration as for members of the higher caste.

22. A Brâhmana (to whom) Sapindas of the Kshatriya, Vaisya, or Sûdra castes (have been born or have died) becomes pure within six nights, or three nights, or one night, respectively.

23. A Kshatriya (to whom Sapindas of the) Vaisya or Sûdra castes (have been born or have died) is purified within six and three nights, respectively.

24. A Vaisya (to whom Sapindas of the) Sûdra caste (have been born or have died) becomes pure within six nights.

---

16. Regarding the Prâgâpatya penance, see below, XLVI, 10.

18. The Pañkagavya, or five productions of a cow, consist of milk, sour milk, butter, urine, and cow-dung.

25. In a number of nights equal to the number of months after conception, a woman is purified from an abortion.

26. The relatives of children that have died immediately after birth (before the cutting of the navel-string), and of still-born children, are purified at once.

27. (The relatives) of a child that has died before having teethed (are also purified) at once.

28. For him no ceremony with fire is performed, nor offering of water.

29. For a child that has teethed but has not yet been shorn, purity is obtained in one day and night;

30. For a child that has been shorn but not initiated, in three nights;

31. From that time forward (i. e. for initiated persons) in the time that has been mentioned above (in Sûtra 1 seq.)

32. In regard to women, the marriage ceremony is (considered as their) initiation.

33. For married women there is no impurity for the relatives on the father's side.

34. If they happen to stay at their father's house during childbirth or if they die there, (their distant relatives are purified) in one night, and their parents (in three nights).

35. If, while the impurity caused by a birth lasts,

---

26. 'The meaning is, that the relatives of such children do not become impure.' (Nand.)

28. 'The meaning is, that he must not be burnt.' (Nand.)

32. The import of this Sûtra is this, that the full period of impurity is ordained on the death of women also, in case they were married, as the marriage ceremony takes with them the place of the initiation of males.

another impurity caused by childbirth intervenes, it ends when the former impurity terminates.

36. If it intervenes when one night (only of the period of impurity remains, the fresh impurity terminates) two days later.

37. If it intervenes when one watch (only of the last night remains, the impurity ends) three days later.

38. The same rule is observed if a relative dies during a period of impurity caused by the death (of another relative).

39. If a man, while staying in another country, hears of the birth or death (of a relative), he becomes purified after the lapse of the period still wanting (to the ten days).

40. If the period of impurity, but not a whole year, has elapsed, (he is purified in one night.)

41. After that time (he is purified) by a bath.

42. If his teacher or maternal grandfather has died, (he is purified) in three nights.

43. Likewise, if sons other than a son of the body have been born or have died, and if wives who had another husband before have been delivered of a child or have died.

---

40. 'Although the general term impurity is used in this Sûtra, it refers to impurity caused by a death only.' (Nand.)

42. 'The use of the particle *ka* implies, that this rule extends to the death of a maternal grandmother, as ordained in the Shadasîtismr*i*ti.' (Nand.)

43. The twelve kinds of sons have been enumerated above, XV, 2–27. Of these, the three species of adopted sons, the son bought, and the son cast off cannot cause impurity, because their sonship dates from a period subsequent to their birth; but their offspring may cause impurity. (Nand.) Parapûrvâs, or 'wives who had another husband before,' are either of the punarbhû or of the svairi*nî* kind. (Nand.) See XV, 8, 9, and Nârada XII, 46–54.

44. (He becomes pure) in one day, if the wife or son of his teacher, or his Upâdhyâya (sub-teacher [1]), or his maternal uncle, or his father-in-law, or a brother-in-law, or a fellow-student, or a pupil has died.

45. The impurity has the same duration (as in the cases last mentioned), if the king of that country in which he lives has died.

46. Likewise, if a man not his Sapi*nd*a has died at his house.

47. The relatives of those who have been killed by (falling from) a precipice, or by fire, or (have killed themselves by) fasting, or (have been killed by) water, in battle, by lightning, or by the king (on account of a crime committed by them), do not become impure;

48. Nor do kings (become impure) while engaged in the discharge of their duties (such as the protection of their subjects, the trial of lawsuits, &c.)

49. Devotees fulfilling a vow (also do not become impure);

50. Nor do sacrificers engaged in a sacrificial ceremony;

51. Nor workmen (such as carpenters or others) while engaged in their work;

52. Nor those who perform the king's orders, if the king wishes them to be pure.

53. Nor (can impurity arise) during the installation of the monument of a deity, nor during

---

44. [1] See XXIX, 2.

49. The term vratin, 'a devotee fulfilling a vow,' may be referred to students as well, who, however, become impure by the death of their parents. (Nand.)

53. A marriage ceremony is said to have actually begun when the Nândîmukha, or *S*râddha preliminary to marriage, has taken place. (Nand.)

a marriage ceremony, if those ceremonies have actually begun;

54. Nor when the whole country is afflicted with a calamity;

55. Nor in times of great public distress (such as an epidemic or a famine).

56. Suicides and outcasts do not cause impurity or receive offerings of water.

57. On the death-day of an outcast a female slave of his must upset a pot with water with her feet, (saying, 'Drink thou this.')

58. He who cuts the rope by which (a suicide) has hung himself, becomes pure by performing the Taptak*rikkh*ra ('hot penance').

59. So does he who has been (in any way) concerned with the funeral of a suicide;

60. And he who sheds tears for such.

61. He who sheds tears for any deceased person together with the relations of the latter (becomes pure) by a bath.

62. If he has done so, before the bones (of the deceased) had been collected, (he becomes pure) by bathing with his apparel.

63. If a member of a twice-born caste has followed the corpse of a dead *S*ûdra, he must go to a river, and having plunged into it, mutter the Aghamarsha*n*a three times, and then, after having emerged from it, mutter the Gâyatrî one thousand and eight times.

64. (If he has followed) the corpse of a dead member of a twice-born caste, (the same expiation

---

is ordained, but he must mutter the Gâyatrî) one hundred and eight times only.

65. If a *S*ûdra has followed the corpse of a member of a twice-born caste, he must bathe.

66. Members of any caste, who have come near to the smoke of a funeral pile, must bathe.

67. (Bathing is also ordained) after sexual intercourse, bad dreams (of having been mounted upon an ass, or the like), when blood has issued from the throat, and after having vomited or been purged;

68. Also, after tonsure of the head;

69. And after having touched one who has touched a corpse (a carrier of a corpse), or a woman in her courses, or a *K*ân*d*âla (or other low-caste persons, such as *S*vapa*k*as), or a sacrificial post;

70. And (after having touched) the corpse of a five-toed animal, except of those kinds that may be eaten [1], or their bones still moist with fat.

71. In all such ablutions he must not wear his (defiled) apparel without having washed it before.

72. A woman in her courses becomes pure after four days by bathing.

73. A woman in her courses having touched another woman in her courses, who belongs to a lower caste than she does, must not eat again till she is purified.

74. If she has (unawares) touched a woman of her own caste, or of a higher caste than her own, she becomes pure at once, after having taken a bath.

75. Having sneezed, having slept, having eaten,

---

70. [1] See LI, 6.

75. Nand. argues from a passage of Yâg*ñ*avalkya (I, 196) and from texts of Âpastamba (not found in his Dharma-sûtra) and of Pra*k*etas, that the particle *k*a refers to repeated sipping of water.

going to eat or to study, having drunk (water),
having bathed, having spat, having put on his garment, having walked on the high road, having
discharged urine or voided excrements, and having
touched the bones no longer moist with fat of a
five-toed animal, he must sip water;

76. Likewise, if he has talked to a *Kând*âla or to
a Mle*kkh*a (barbarian).

77. If the lower part of his body, below the
navel, or one of his fore-arms, has been defiled by
one of the impure excretions of the body, or by one
of the spirituous liquors or of the intoxicating drinks
(hereafter mentioned), he is purified by cleansing
the limb in question with earth and water.

78. If another part of his body (above the navel)
has been defiled, (he becomes pure by cleansing it)
with earth and water, and by bathing.

79. If his mouth has been defiled (he becomes
pure) by fasting, bathing, and drinking Pañ*k*agavya;

80. Likewise, if his lip has been defiled.

81. Adeps, semen, blood, dandruff, urine, fæces, ear-
wax, nail-parings, phlegm, tears, rheum, and sweat
are the twelve impure excretions of the body.

82. Distilled from sugar, or from the blossoms of
the Madhûka (Mâdhvî wine [1]), or from flour: these
three kinds of spirituous liquor have to be discerned; as one, so are all: none of them must be
tasted by the twice-born.

83. Again, distilled from the blossoms of the

---

76. Regarding the meaning of Mle*kkh*a, see LXXXIV, 4.

82, 83. [1] How the Mâdhvî, Mâdhûka, and Mâdhvîka wines differ
from one another, does not become clear. Nand. explains the
term Mâdhûka as denoting an extract from Madhûka blossoms
(bassia latifolia), and Mâdhvî and Mâdhvîka as two different preparations from Madhu. Now Madhu might be rendered by 'honey;'

Madhûka tree (Mâdhûka wine), from molasses, from
the fruits of the *T*aṅka (or Kapittha tree), of the
jujube tree, of the Khar*g*ûra tree, or of the bread-
fruit tree, from wine-grapes, from Madhûka blossoms
(Mâdhvîka wine), Maireya, and the sap of the cocoa-
nut tree :

84. These ten intoxicating drinks are unclean for
a Brâhma*n*a ; but a Kshatriya and a Vai*s*ya commit
no wrong in touching (or drinking) them.

85. A pupil having performed (on failure of
other mourners) the funeral of his dead Guru, becomes pure after ten nights, like those (kinsmen)
who carry out the dead.

86. A student does not infringe the rules of his
order by carrying out, when dead, his teacher, or his
sub-teacher, or his father, or his mother, or his Guru.

87. A student must not offer a libation of water
to a deceased relative (excepting his parents) till
the term of his studentship has expired; but if,
after its expiration, he offers a libation of water, he
becomes pure after three nights.

88. Sacred knowledge (see 92), religious austerities (see 90), fire (see XXIII, 33), holy food (Pañ-
*k*agavya), earth (see 91), the mind, water (see
91), smearing (with cow-dung and the like, see
XXIII, 56), air (see XXIII, 41), (the morning and
evening prayers and other) religious acts, the sun

---

but Kullûka, in his comment on the term Mâdhvî (M. XI, 95),
states expressly that it means 'Madhûka blossom,' and Hârîta (as
quoted by Nand.) says that Mâdhûka, Mâdhvî and Mâdhvîka are
all preparations from Madhu, i. e. Madhûka blossoms. Maireya,
according to the lexicographer Vâ*k*aspati, as quoted by Nand., is an
intoxicating drink prepared from the flowers of the grislea tormen-
tosa, mixed with sugar, grain, and water, or, according to the reading
of the *S*abdakalpadruma (see the Petersburg Dictionary), with sorrel.

(see XXIII, 40), and time (by the lapse of the ten days of impurity and the like) are purifiers of animate objects.

89. Of all pure things, pure food is pronounced the most excellent; for he who eats pure food only, is truly pure, not he who is only purified with earth and water.

90. By forgiveness of injuries the learned are purified; by liberality, those who have done forbidden acts; by muttering of prayers, those who have sinned in secret; by religious austerities, those who best know the Veda.

91. By water and earth is purified what should be purified (because it has been defiled); a river is purified by its current (carrying away all slime and mud); a woman, whose thoughts have been impure, by her menses; and the chief among the twice-born (the Brâhmanas), by renouncing the world.

92. Bodies (when defiled) are purified by water; the mind is purified (from evil thoughts) by truth; the soul (is purified or freed from worldly vanity) by sacred learning and austerities; the understanding (when unable to resolve some doubt), by knowledge.

93. Thus the directions for purifying animate bodies have been declared to thee; hear now the rules for cleaning all sorts of inanimate objects.

XXIII.

1. What has been defiled by the impure excretions of the body, by spirits, or by intoxicating drinks, is impure in the highest degree.

XXIII. 2. Âpast. I, 5, 17, 10; Gaut. I, 29. — 4. Y. I, 185; Gaut. I, 29, 31. — 5. M. V, 123; Gaut. I, 34. — 7-11. M. V, 111, 112, 116, 117; Y. I, 182, 183. — 7, 8. Gaut. I, 29, 30. — 13–

2. All vessels made of iron (or of other metals or of composition metals such as bell-metal and the like), which are impure in the highest degree, become pure by exposure to the fire.

3. Things made of gems or stones or water-shells, (such as conch-shells or mother-of-pearl, become pure) by digging them into the earth for seven days.

4. Things made of horns (of rhinoceroses or other animals), or of teeth (of elephants or other animals), or of bone (of tortoises or other animals, become pure) by planing them.

5. Vessels made of wood or earthenware must be thrown away.

6. Of a garment, which has been defiled in the highest degree, let him cut off that part which, having been washed, is changed in colour.

7. Objects made of gold, silver, water-shells, or gems, when (they are only defiled by leavings of food and the like, and) not smeared (with greasy substances), are cleansed with water.

8. So are stone cups and vessels used at Soma-sacrifices (when not smeared).

---

15. M.V, 118, 119; Y. I, 184, 182. — 16. M.V, 122. — 17. M. V, 126; Y. I, 191. — 18. M.V, 118. — 19–22. M.V, 120; Y. I, 186, 187. — 25, 26. M. V, 114; Y. I, 190. — 27. M.V, 115; Y. I, 185; Âpast. I, 5, 17, 12; Gaut. I, 29. — 28. Y. I, 185. — 30. M.V, 115; Y. I, 190. — 33. M. V, 122; Y. I, 187. — 38, 39. M.V, 125, 126. — 38. Y. I, 189. — 40. Y. I, 194. — 41. Y. I, 197. — 47–52. M. V, 127–133. — 53–55. M.V, 141–143. — 53. Y. I, 195; Âpast. I, 5, 16, 12; Gaut. I, 38, 41. — 55. Gaut. I, 28. — 56, 57. M.V, 122, 124; Y. I, 188.

7. The defilement in the highest degree having been treated of in the six preceding Sûtras, he now goes on to discuss the various cases of lesser defilement. (Nand.)

8–11. Regarding the shape of the sacrificial implements men-

9. Sacrificial pots, ordinary wooden ladles, and wooden ladles with two collateral excavations (used for pouring clarified butter on a sacrificial fire) are cleansed with hot water (when not smeared).

10. Vessels used for oblations (of butter, fruits, and the like are cleansed) by rubbing them with the hand (with blades of Kusa grass) at the time of the sacrifice.

11. Sword-shaped pieces of wood for stirring the boiled rice, winnowing baskets, implements used for preparing grain, pestles and mortars (are cleansed) by sprinkling water over them.

12. So are beds, vehicles, and seats (when defiled even by the touch of a Sûdra)[1].

13. Likewise, a large quantity (of anything).

14. Grain, skins (of antelopes, &c.), ropes, woven cloth, (fans and the like) made of bamboo, thread, cotton, and clothes (which have only just come from the manufactory, or which are dyed with saffron and will not admit of washing for that reason, are cleansed in the same way, when there is a large quantity of them);

15. Also, pot-herbs, roots, fruits, and flowers;

16. Likewise, grass, firewood, dry cow-dung (used as fuel), and leaves (of the Madhûka, Palâsa, or other trees).

---

tioned in these Sûtras, see the plates in Professor Max Müller's paper, 'Die Todtenbestattung bei den Brahmanen,' in the Journal of the German Oriental Society, IX, LXXVIII–LXXX.

12. [1] This Sûtra and the following ones relate to defilement caused by touch. (Nand.)

13. 'I. e. more than one man can carry, as Baudhâyana says.' (Nand.)

14. The use of the particle *ka* implies that resin and other objects mentioned by Devala must be included in this enumeration. (Nand.)

17. The same (when smeared with excrements and the like, are cleansed) by washing.

18. And so (have the objects mentioned in Sûtra 14, if defiled without being smeared, to be cleansed by washing), when there is only a small quantity of them;

19. Silk and wool, with saline earths;

20. (Blankets or plaids) made of the hair of the mountain-goat, with the fruits of the soap plant;

21. Clothes made of the bark of trees[1], with Bèl fruit;

22. Linen cloth, with white sesamum;

23. Likewise, things made of . horns, bone, or teeth;

24. (Rugs or covers) made of deer's hair, with lotus-seeds;

25. Vessels of copper, bell-metal, tin, and lead, with acidulated water;

26. Vessels of white copper and iron, with ashes;

27. Wooden articles, by planing;

28. Vessels made of fruits (such as cocoa-nuts, bottle-gourds, and Bèl fruits), by (rubbing them with) cows' hair.

29. Many things in a heap, by sprinkling water over them;

30. Liquids (such as clarified butter, milk, &c.), by straining them;

---

17. 'All the objects mentioned in Sûtras 12–16 must be washed, but so as to avoid injuring them, in case they have been defiled by excrements or other such impure substances.' (Nand.)

21. The term *amsupatta* has been rendered in accordance with Nand.'s interpretation, which agrees with Vignânesvara's (on Y. V, 186). Kullûka (on M. V, 120; see the Petersburg Dictionary) appears to refer it to two different sorts of clothes.

30–37. These Sûtras relate to defilement caused by insects, &c. (Nand.)

31. Lumps of sugar and other preparations from the sugar-cane [1], stored up in large quantities (exceeding a Drona) and kept in one's own house [2], by water and fire [3];

32. All sorts of salt, in the same manner;

33. Earthern vessels (if smeared with excrements and the like), by a second burning;

34. Images of gods (if smeared), by cleansing them in the same way as the material (of which they are made is generally cleansed), and then installing them anew (in their former place).

35. Of undressed grain let him remove so much only as has been defiled, and the remainder let him pound in a mortar and wash.

36. A quantity of prepared grain not exceeding a Drona is not spoiled by being defiled (by dogs, crows, and other unclean animals).

37. He must throw away thus much of it only as has been defiled, and must sprinkle over the remainder water, into which a piece of gold has been dropped, and over which the Gâyatrî has been pronounced, and must hold it up before a goat (or before a horse) and before the fire.

---

31. [1] Such as raw sugar, candied sugar, &c. — [2] If there is no large quantity of them, they require to be sprinkled with water only; and if they are kept elsewhere than in the house, as if they are exposed for sale in a fair, they require no purification at all. — [3] They must be encircled with fire, and sprinkled with water afterwards. (Nand.)

32. Nand. mentions as the main species of salt, rock-salt, sea-salt, sochal-salt, and Sâmbhala-salt. The last term refers perhaps to salt coming from the famous salt-lake of Sâkambharî or Shambar in Râgputana.

37. 'A quantity less than a Drona having been defiled must be thrown away, as stated by Parâsara.' (Nand.) One Drona = 4 Âdhakas = 1024 Mushtis or handfuls. The meaning of Âdhaka,

38. That (food) which has been nibbled by a bird (except a crow or other such birds that must not be eaten or touched), smelt at by a cow, sneezed on, or defiled by (human) hair, or by insects or worms, is purified by earth scattered over it.

39. As long as the scent or moisture, caused by any unclean substance, remains on the defiled object, so long must earth and water be constantly applied in all purifications of inanimate objects.

40. A goat and a horse are pure, as regards their mouths, but not a cow, nor the impure excretions of a man's body; roads are purified by the rays of the moon and of the sun, and by the winds.

41. Mire and water upon the high road, that has been touched by low-caste people, by dogs, or by crows, as well as buildings constructed with burnt bricks, are purified by the wind.

42. For everybody let him (the Â*k*ârya or spiritual guide) carefully direct the performance of purificatory ceremonies, with earth and water, when he has been defiled in the highest degree.

43. Stagnant water, even if a single cow only has quenched her thirst with it, is pure, unless it is quite filled with (hair or other) unclean objects; it is the same with water upon a rock (or upon the top of a mountain).

44. From a well, in which a five-toed animal (whether man or beast, but not one of the five-toed

---

however, according to Nand.'s observation, varies in different countries. See Colebrooke's Essays, I, 533 seq.

38. In explanation of the term amedhya, 'unclean substance,' Nand. quotes the following passage of Devala, 'Human bones, a corpse, excrements, semen, urine, the menstrual discharge, adeps, sweat, the rheum of the eyes, phlegm, and spirituous liquors are called unclean substances.'

animals whose flesh may be eaten)[1] has died, or which has been defiled in the highest degree, he must take out all the waters and dry up the remainder with a cloth.

45. If it is a well constructed with burnt bricks (or stones,) he must light a fire and afterwards throw Pañ*k*agavya into it, when fresh water is coming forth.

46. For small reservoirs of water and for ponds the same mode of purification has been prescribed as for wells, O Earth; but large tanks (excepting Tîrthas) are not defiled (by dead animals, &c.)

47. The gods have declared, as peculiar to Brâh-ma*n*as, three causes effecting purity: if an (existing) impurity has not been perceived by them; if they sprinkle the object (supposed to be impure) with water; and if they commend it, in doubtful cases, with their speech, (saying, ' This or that shall be pure.')

48. The hand of a (cook or other) artizan, things exposed for sale in a shop (though they may have passed through the hands of many customers), food given to a Brâhma*n*a (by other Brâhma*n*as, or by Kshatriyas, &c., but not by *S*ûdras), and all manufactories or mines (of sugar, salt, and the like, but not distilleries of spirituous liquor), are always pure.

49. The mouth of a woman is always pure (for the purpose of a kiss); a bird is pure on the fall of fruit (which he has pecked); a sucking calf (or child), on the flowing of the milk; a dog, on his catching the deer.

50. Flesh of an animal which has been killed by dogs is pronounced pure; and so is that of an

---

44. [1] See LI, 6.

animal slain by other carnivorous creatures (such as tigers) or by huntsmen such as *Kand*âlas (*S*vapa*k*as, Kshatt*ri*s, or other low-caste men).

51. The cavities above the navel must be considered as pure; those below it are impure; and so are all excretions that fall from the body.

52. Flies, saliva dropping from the mouth, a shadow, a cow, an elephant, a horse, sun-beams, dust, the earth, air, fire, and a cat are always pure.

53. Such drops as fall from the mouth of a man upon any part of his body do not render it impure, nor do hairs of the beard that enter his mouth, nor remnants of his food adhering to his teeth.

54. Drops which trickle on the feet of a man holding water for others to sip it, are considered as equal to waters springing from the earth: by them he is not soiled.

55. He who is anyhow touched by anything impure, while holding things in his hands, is purified by sipping water, without laying the things on the ground.

---

51. There are, according to Indian views, nine cavities or apertures of the body: the mouth, the two ears, the two nostrils, the two eyes, and the organs of excretion and generation. The two last are impure, the rest are pure.

55. Nand. and Kullûka (on M. V, 143) explain that hasta, 'hand,' here means 'arm,' as it would be impossible to sip water without using the hand. The former adds that, if the things are being carried with the hand, they must be placed in the cavity formed by the fore-arm. He refutes the opinion of the 'Eastern Commentators,' who, arguing from another Sm*ri*ti, contend that the things have to be placed on the ground and to be sprinkled with water; and he further tries to account for the seemingly contradictory rules propounded by Vâsish*th*a (Benares ed., III, 43) and Gautama (I, 28) by explaining that a large quantity of things should be laid on the ground, and a small quantity placed upon

56. A house is purified by scouring it with a broom and plastering the ground with cow-dung, and a manuscript or book by sprinkling water over it. Land is cleansed by scouring, by plastering it with cow-dung,

57. By sprinkling [1], by scraping, by burning, or by letting cows (or goats) pass (a day and a night) on it. Cows are auspicious purifiers, upon cows depend the worlds,

58. Cows alone make sacrificial oblations possible (by producing sacrificial butter), cows take away every sin. The urine of cows, their dung, clarified butter, milk, sour milk, and Gorokanâ :

59. Those six excellent (productions) of a cow are always propitious. Drops of water falling from the horns of a cow are productive of religious merit, and have the power to expiate all sins (of those who bathe in, or rub themselves with, them).

60. Scratching the back of a cow destroys all guilt, and giving her to eat procures exaltation in heaven.

---

some other limb, and further, that food should always be placed on the ground, but that a garment, a stick, and the like should be kept in the hand. Compare Dr. Bühler's note on Gaut. loc. cit. It may be remarked, incidentally, that Nand. quotes the reading ukkhishto 'nidhâya in the passage of Gautama referred to.

56. ' The term pustaka refers to MSS. or books, whether made of palm leaves, or of prepared hemp, or of prepared reeds (sara).' (Nand.) It may be that Nand. means by the last term a sort of paper, though paper is usually called by its Arabian name (kâgad) in Indian works. See regarding the materials used for writing in ancient India, Burnell's Palæography, p. 84 seq. (2nd ed.)

57. [1] The term seka, ' sprinkling,' either refers to the earth being sprinkled by rain, or to Pañkagavya being poured over it. (Nand.)

58. Gorokanâ is a bright yellow pigment which is said to be prepared from the urine or bile of a cow.

61. In the urine of cows dwells the Ganges, prosperity (dwells) in the dust (rising from their couch), good fortune in cow-dung, and virtue in saluting them. Therefore should they be constantly saluted.

XXIV.

1. Now a Brâhma*n*a may take four wives in the direct order of the (four) castes;

2. A Kshatriya, three;

3. A Vai*s*ya, two;

4. A *S*ûdra, one only.

5. Among these (wives), if a man marries one of his own caste, their hands shall be joined.

6. In marriages with women of a different class, a Kshatriya bride must hold an arrow in her hand;

7. A Vai*s*ya bride, a whip;

8. A *S*ûdra bride, the skirt of a mantle.

9. No one should marry a woman belonging to the same Gotra, or descended from the same *R*ishi ancestors, or from the same Pravaras.

XXIV. 1–4. Weber, Ind. Stud. X, 21, 74; M. III, 12–14; Y. I, 56, 57. — 5. M. III, 43; Y. I, 62. — 6–8. M. III, 44; Y. I, 62. — 9, 10. Weber loc. cit. 75; M. III, 5; Y. I, 53; Âpast. II, 5, 11, 15, 16; Gaut. IV, 2–5. — 12–16. M. III, 8. — 12. Y. I, 53. — 17–26. M. III, 20, 21, 27–34; Y. I, 58–61; Âpast. II, 5, 11, 17– II, 5, 12, 2; Gaut. IV, 6–13. — 27, 28. M. III, 23–26, 39; Âpast. II, 5, 12, 3; Gaut. IV, 14, 15. — 29–32. M. III, 37, 38; Y. I, 58–60; Gaut. IV, 30–33. — 38. M. V, 151; Y. I, 63. — 39. Y. I, 62. — 40. M. IX, 90; Y. I, 64. — 41. M. IX, 93.

1. This chapter opens the section on Sa*m*skâras or sacraments, i. e. the ceremonies on conception and so forth. (Nand.) This section forms the second part of the division treating of Â*k*âra. See above, XIX.

9. According to Nand., the term Gotra refers to descent from one of the seven *R*ishis, or from Agastya as the eighth; the term Ârsha (*R*ishi ancestors), to descent from the Ârsh*r*ishe*n*as or Mudgalas,

10. Nor (should he marry) one descended from his maternal ancestors within the fifth, or from his paternal ancestors within the seventh degree;

11. Nor one of a low family (such as an agriculturer's, or an attendant of the king's family);

12. Nor one diseased;

13. Nor one with a limb too much (as e. g. having six fingers);

14. Nor one with a limb too little;

15. Nor one whose hair is decidedly red;

16. Nor one talking idly.

17. There are eight forms of marriage:

18. The Brâhma, Daiva, Ârsha, Prâgâpatya, Gândharva, Âsura, Râkshasa, and Paisâ*k*a forms.

19. The gift of a damsel to a fit bridegroom, who has been invited, is called a Brâhma marriage.

20. If she is given to a *R*itvi*g* (priest), while he is officiating at a sacrifice, it is called a Daiva marriage.

21. If (the giver of the bride) receives a pair of kine in return, it is called an Ârsha marriage.

22. (If she is given to a suitor) by his demand, it is called a Prâgâpatya marriage.

---

or from some other subdivision of the Bh*r*igus or Âṅgirasas, excepting the *G*âmadagnas, Gautamas, and Bhâradvâ*g*as; and the term Pravara, to the Mantrak*ri*ts of one's own race, i. e. the ancestors invoked by a Brâhma*n*a at the commencement of a sacrifice. Nand.'s interpretation of the last term is no doubt correct; but it seems preferable to take Gotra in the sense of 'family name' (laukika gotra), and to refer the term samânârsha to descent from the same *R*ishi (vaidika gotra). See Dr. Bühler's notes on Âpast. II, 5, 11, 15, and Gaut. XVIII, 6; Max Müller, History of Ancient Sanskrit Literature, pp. 379–388; Weber, Ind. Stud. X, 69–81. If ârsha were connected with pravara, the whole compound samânârshapravarâ would denote 'a woman descended from the same *R*ishi' = samanârshâ, Y. I, 53, and samânapravarâ, Gaut. XVIII, 6.

23. A union between two lovers, without the consent of mother and father, is called a Gândharva marriage.

24. If the damsel is sold (to the bridegroom), it is called an Âsura marriage.

25. If he seizes her forcibly, it is called a Râkshasa marriage.

26. If he embraces her in her sleep, or while she is unconscious, it is called a Paisâ*k*a marriage.

27. Among those (eight forms of marriage), the four first forms are legitimate (for a Brâhma*n*a);

28. And so is the Gândharva form for a Kshatriya.

29. A son procreated in a Brâhma marriage redeems (or sends into the heavenly abodes hereafter mentioned) twenty-one men (viz. ten ancestors, ten descendants, and him who gave the damsel in marriage).

30. A son procreated in a Daiva marriage, fourteen;

31. A son procreated in an Ârsha marriage, seven;

32. A son procreated in a Prâ*g*âpatya marriage, four.

33. He who gives a damsel in marriage according to the Brâhma rite, brings her into the world of Brahman (after her death, and enters that world himself).

34. (He who gives her in marriage) according to the Daiva rite, (brings her) into Svarga (or heaven, and enters Svarga himself).

35. (He who gives her in marriage) according to the Ârsha rite, (brings her) into the world of Vish*n*u (and enters that world himself).

36. (He who gives her in marriage) according to the Prâ*g*âpatya rite, (brings her) into the world of the gods (and enters that world himself).

37. (He who gives her in marriage) according to the Gândharva rite, will go to the world of Gandharvas.

38. A father, a paternal grandfather, a brother, a kinsman, a maternal grandfather, and the mother (are the persons) by whom a girl may be given in marriage.

39. On failure of the preceding one (it devolves upon) the next in order (to give her in marriage), in case he is able.

40. When she has allowed three monthly periods to pass (without being married), let her choose a husband for herself; three monthly periods having passed, she has in every case full power to dispose of herself (as she thinks best).

41. A damsel whose menses begin to appear (while she is living) at her father's house, before she has been betrothed to a man, has to be considered as a degraded woman : by taking her (without the consent of her kinsmen) a man commits no wrong.

---

39. Regarding the causes effecting legal disability, such as love, anger, &c., see Nârada 3, 43.

40. Nand., arguing from a passage of Baudhâyana (see also M. IX, 90), takes *ri*tu, 'monthly period,' as synonymous with varsha, 'year.' But *ri*tu, which occurs in two other analogous passages also (Gaut. XVIII, 20, and Nârada XII, 24), never has that meaning.

41. Nand. observes, that the rules laid down in this and the preceding *S*loka refer to young women of the lower castes only. Nowadays the custom of outcasting young women, who have not been married in the proper time, appears to be in vogue in Brahmanical families particularly. Sm*ri*ti passages regarding the illegality of marriages concluded with such women have been collected by me, Über die rechtl. Stellung der Frauen, p. 9, note 17. The

XXV.

1. Now the duties of a woman (are as follows):

2. To live in harmony with her husband;

3. To show reverence (by embracing their feet and such-like attentions) to her mother-in-law, father-in-law, to Gurus (such as elders), to divinities, and to guests;

4. To keep household articles (such as the winnowing basket and the rest) in good array;

5. To maintain saving habits;

6. To be careful with her (pestle and mortar and other) domestic utensils;

7. Not to practise incantations with roots (or other kinds of witchcraft);

8. To observe auspicious customs;

9. Not to decorate herself with ornaments (or to partake of amusements) while her husband is absent from home;

10. Not to resort to the houses of strangers (during the absence of her husband);

---

custom of Svayamvara or 'self-choice,' judging from the epics, was confined to females of the kingly caste, and in reality was no doubt of very rare occurrence.

XXV. 1–13. Colebrooke, Dig. IV, 2, XCII. — 2. M.V, 154; Y. I, 77. — 3. Y. I, 83. — 4–6. M.V, 150; Y. I, 83. — 9, 10. M. IX, 75; Y. I, 84. — 12, 13. M.V, 148; IX, 3; Y. I, 85; Gaut. XVIII, 1. — 14. M.V, 158; Colebrooke, Dig. IV, 3, CXXXIII. — 15. M.V, 155. — 17. M.V, 160. 15 is also found in the Mârkandeya-purâna XVI, 61, and, in a modified form, in other works. See Böhtlingk, Ind. Sprüche, 3686, 3679. 16 is also found, in a modified form, in Vriddhakânakhya's Proverbs XVII, 9; and 17 in Sârṅgadhara's Paddhati, Sadâkâra, 10. See Böhtlingk, Ind. Sprüche, 3900, 4948.

10. 'Strangers' means any other persons than her parents-in-law, her brother, maternal uncle, and other near relatives. (Nand.)

11. Not to stand near the doorway or by the windows (of her house);

12. Not to act by herself in any matter;

13. To remain subject, in her infancy, to her father; in her youth, to her husband; and in her old age, to her sons.

14. After the death of her husband, to preserve her chastity, or to ascend the pile after him.

15. No sacrifice, no penance, and no fasting is allowed to women apart from their husbands; to pay obedience to her lord is the only means for a woman to obtain bliss in heaven.

16. A woman who keeps a fast or performs a penance in the lifetime of her lord, deprives her husband of his life, and will go to hell.

17. A good wife, who perseveres in a chaste life after the death of her lord, will go to heaven like (perpetual) students, even though she has no son.

XXVI.

1. If a man has several wives of his own caste,

---

14. Nand. states that the self-immolation of widows (Sattee) is a specially meritorious act, and not obligatory. Besides, he quotes several passages from other Smritis and from the Brihannâradîya-purâna, to the effect that in case the husband should have died abroad, a widow of his, who belongs to the Brâhmana caste, may not commit herself to the flames, unless she can reach the place, where his corpse lies, in a day; and that one who is in her courses, or pregnant, or whose pregnancy is suspected, or who has an infant child, is also forbidden to burn herself with her dead husband. English renderings of all the texts quoted by Nand. may be found in Colebrooke's Essay on the Duties of a Faithful Hindu Widow. See also above, XX, 39. Nand., arguing from a passage of Baudhâyana, takes the particle vâ, 'or,' to imply that the widow is at liberty to become a female ascetic instead of burning herself.

XXVI. 2. M. IX, 86. — 4. M. IX, 87. — 1–4. Colebrooke, Dig.

he shall perform his religious duties together with the eldest (or first-married) wife.

2. (If he has several) wives of divers castes (he shall perform them) even with the youngest wife if she is of the same caste as himself.

3. On failure of a wife of his own caste (he shall perform them) with one belonging to the caste next below his own; so also in cases of distress (i. e. when the wife who is equal in caste to him happens to be absent, or when she has met with a calamity);

4. But no twice-born man ever with a *Sûdra* wife.

5. A union of a twice-born man with a *Sûdra* wife can never produce religious merit; it is from carnal desire only that he marries her, being blinded by lust.

6. Men of the three first castes, who through folly marry a woman of the lowest caste, quickly degrade their families and progeny to the state of *Sûdras*.

7. If his oblations to the gods and manes and (his hospitable attentions) to guests are offered principally through her hands, the gods and manes (and the guests) will not eat such offerings, and he will not go to heaven.

XXVII.

1. The Nishekakarman (ceremony of impregna-

IV, 1, XLIX. — 5–7. M. III, 12, 14, 15, 18; Y. I, 56; Weber, Ind. Stud. X, 74. — 7. Colebrooke, Dig. IV, 1, LII.

XXVII. 1–14. Âsv. I, 4–18; Gobh. II, 1–9; Pâr. I, 4–II, 1; *S*ânkh. I, 12–28; M. II, 29–35, 66, 67; Y. I, 11–13; Gaut. VIII, 14. — 15–24, 26, 27. Weber, Ind. Stud. X, 21; M. II, 38–47; Y. I,

tion) must be performed when the season fit for procreating children [1] distinctly appears (for the first time).

2. The Pumsavana (ceremony to cause the birth of a male) must be performed before the embryo begins to move.

3. The Sîmantonnayana (ceremony of parting the hair) should take place in the sixth or eighth month (of pregnancy).

4. The Gâtakarman (birth-ceremony) should take place on the birth of the child.

5. The Nâmadheya (naming-rite) must be performed as soon as the term of impurity (caused by the birth of the child) is over.

6. (The name to be chosen should be) auspicious in the case of a Brâhmana;

7. Indicating power in the case of a Kshatriya;

8. Indicating wealth in the case of a Vaisya;

9. Indicating contempt in the case of a Sûdra.

14, 37, 38; Âpast. I, 1, 1, 18–21; I, 1, 2, 33–3, 6; Gaut. I, 5, 11–26. — 25. Weber, Ind. Stud. X, 22; M. II, 49; Y. I, 30; Âpast. I, 1, 3, 28–30; Gaut. II, 36. — 28, 29. M. II, 174, 64.

1. [1] 'Garbha' here means 'ritu,' i.e. the time favourable for procreation, following immediately upon the menstrual evacuation, and the above ceremony should be performed once only, in order to consecrate the mother once for all. (Nand.)

2, 3. The embryo begins to move in the fourth month of pregnancy, and the Pumsavana must be performed in the second or third month of every pregnancy. Thus Nand., who combats expressly the opinion that this ceremony has the consecration of the mother, and not the consecration of the fœtus, for its object. Regarding the Sîmantonnayana he seems to consider both views as admissible. According to the former view it would have to be performed only once, like the Nishekakarman.

6–9. Nand. quotes as instances of such names: 1. Lakshmîdhara; 2. Yudhishthira; 3. Arthapati; 4. Lokadâsa; or (observing,

10. The Âdityadarsana (ceremony of taking the child out to see the sun) should take place in the fourth month (after birth).

11. The Annaprâsana (ceremony of first feeding) should take place in the sixth month.

12. The Kûdâkarana (tonsure rite) should take place in the third year [1].

13. For female children the same ceremonies, (beginning with the birth ceremony, should be performed, but) without Mantras.

14. The marriage ceremony only has to be performed with Mantras for them.

15. The initiation of Brâhmanas (should take place) in the eighth year after conception [1];

16. Of Kshatriyas, in the eleventh year after conception [1];

17. Of Vaisyas, in the twelfth year after conception [1];

18. Their girdles should be made of Muñga grass, a bow-string, and Balbaga (coarse grass) respectively.

19. Their sacrificial strings and their garments should be made of cotton, hemp, and wool respectively.

---

at the same time, another rule regarding the second part of a compound name), 1. Vishnusarman; 2. Bhîmavarman; 3. Devagupta; 4. Dharmadâsa.

10. According to Nand., who quotes a passage of Yama in support of his opinion, this Sûtra has to be divided into two, which would, however, require several words to complete their sense, the import of the first being, that the child should be taken out to see the sun in the third month, and to see the moon in the fourth month. See the Introduction.

12. [1] 'The third year,' i. e. either after conception, or after birth. (Nand.)

15–17: [1] Nand., 'or after birth.' See Pâr. and Âsv. loc. cit.

20. The skins (which they wear) should be those of a black antelope, of a tiger, and of a he-goat respectively.

21. Their staves should be made of Palâsa, Khadira, and Udumbara wood respectively.

22. Their staves should be of such a length as to reach the hair, the forehead, and the nose respectively.

23. Or all (kinds of staves may be used for all castes indiscriminately).

24. And they should not be crooked, nor should the bark be stripped off.

25. In begging alms, they should put in the word ' Lady ' at the beginning, in the middle, and at the end of their request (according to their caste).

26. The ceremony of initiation must not be delayed beyond the sixteenth year in the case of a Brâhma*n*a; beyond the twenty-second, in the case of a Kshatriya; and beyond the twenty-fourth, in the case of a Vai*s*ya.

27. After that, the youths belonging to any of those three castes, who have not been initiated at the proper time, are excluded from initiation, and contemned by the twice-born, and are called Vrâtyas.

28. That skin, that cord, that girdle, that staff, and that garment which has been given to any one (on his initiation), that he must for ever wear when performing any religious observance.

29. His girdle, his skin, his staff, his string, and his ewer he must throw into the water when broken (or spoiled by use), and receive others consecrated with Mantras.

XXVIII.

1. Now[1] students shall dwell at their Guru's (spiritual teacher's) house.

2. They shall recite their morning and evening prayers.

3. (A student) shall mutter the morning prayer standing, and the evening prayer sitting.

4. He shall perform twice a day (in the mornings and evenings) the religious acts of sprinkling the ground (round the altar) and of putting fuel on the fire.

5. He must plunge into the waters like a stick.

XXVIII. passim. Âsv. Grihya-s. I, 22; III, 7–9; Gobh. Grihya-s. II, 10, 42–III, 4; Pâr. Grihya-s. II, 4–6; Sânkh. Grihya-s. II, 6, 9–12; III, 1. — 1. Âpast. I, 1, 2, 11. — 3. M. II, 101; Y. I, 24, 25; Gaut. II, 11. — 4. M. II, 108; Y. I, 25; Âpast. I, 1, 4, 16. — 5. Âpast. I, 1, 2, 30. — 6, 7. M. II, 73, 182; Y. I, 27; Âpast. I, 2, 5, 27; I, 1, 4, 23; Gaut. I, 54; II, 29, 30. — 8. M. II, 41–47; Y. I, 29; Âpast. I, 1, 2, 33–I, 1, 3, 10; Gaut. I, 15, 16, 22. — 9, 10. M. II, 183, 184, 51; Y. I, 29, 31; Âpast. I, 1, 3, 25, 32; Gaut. II, 35, 37–39. — 11, 12. M. II, 177–179, &c.; Y. I, 33, &c.; Âpast. I, 1, 2, 23–28, &c.; Gaut. II, 13, &c. — 13–23. M. II, 194, 71, 72, 122–124, 195–198; Âpast. I, 2, 4, 28; I, 2, 5, 12, 23; I, 2, 6, 5–9, 14; Gaut. II, 21, 25–28; I, 52; II, 14. — 17. Y. I, 26. — 24–26. M. II, 199, 200. — 27, 28. M. II, 204; Âpast. I, 2, 8, 11, 13. — 29, 30. M. II, 205; Âpast. I, 2, 8, 19–21. — 31–33. M. II, 208, 209; Âpast. I, 2, 7, 28, 30; Gaut. II, 31, 32. — 34–36. M. III, 2; II, 168. — 37–40. M. II, 169–172; Y. II, 39; Âpast. I, 1, 1, 15–17; Gaut. I, 8. — 41. M. II, 219; Âpast. I, 1, 2, 31, 32; Gaut. I, 27. — 42. M. II, 245; Y. I, 51; Âpast. I, 11, 30, 1; Gaut. IX, 1. — 43–46. M. II, 243, 247, 248; Y. I, 49; Âpast. I, 2, 4, 29; Gaut. II, 5–8. — 47. M. II, 249; Gaut. III, 9. — 48–53. M. XI, 121, 123, 124; II, 181, 187, 220. — 51, 52. Y. III, 278, 281; Gaut. XXIII, 20.

1. [1]'I. e. after the performance of the initiation ceremony.' (Nand.)

5. The sense of this injunction, according to Nand., is, that he must not pronounce any bathing Mantras. But more probably it

6. Let him study when called (by his teacher).

7. He shall act so as to please his Guru (spiritual teacher) and to be serviceable to him.

8. He shall wear his girdle, his staff, his skin, and his sacrificial string.

9. He shall go begging at the houses of virtuous persons, excepting those of his Guru's (and of his own) relatives.

10. He may eat (every morning and evening) some of the food collected by begging, after having received permission to do so from his Guru.

11. He must avoid Srâddhas, factitious salt, food turned sour [1], stale food, dancing, singing, women, honey, meat, ointments, remnants of the food (of other persons than his teacher), the killing of living beings, and rude speeches.

12. He must occupy a low couch.

13. He must rise before his Guru and go to rest after him.

14. He must salute his Guru, after having performed his morning devotion.

15. Let him embrace his feet with crossed hands,

---

is meant, that he shall swim motionless like a stick (see Âpast. I, 1, 2, 30, with Dr. Bühler's note). According to a third explanation, which is mentioned both by Haradatta and by Devapâla in his Commentary on the Kâthaka Grihya-sûtra, the sense would be, that he is not allowed, while bathing, to rub his skin, in order to clean himself, with bathing powder and the like.

11. [1] Nand. interprets sukta, 'food turned sour,' by 'rude speeches,' because if taken in its other meaning, it would be included in the next term, paryushita, 'stale food.' However, if Nand.'s interpretation were followed, it would coincide with the last term of this enumeration, aslîla, 'rude speeches;' and its position between two articles of food renders the above interpretation more plausible.

16. The right foot with his right hand, and the left foot with his left.

17. After the salutation (abhivâdaye, 'I salute') he must mention his own name and add the word 'bhos' (Venerable Sir) at the end of his address.

18. He must not speak to his Guru while he is himself standing, or sitting, or lying, or eating, or averting his face.

19. And let him speak, if his teacher sits, standing up; if he walks, advancing towards him; if he is coming near, meeting him; if he runs, running after him;

20. If his face is averted, turning round so as to face him;

21. If he is at some distance, approaching him;

22. If he is in a reclining position, bending to him;

23. Let him not sit in a careless attitude (such as e. g. having a cloth tied round his legs and knees, while sitting on his hams) before the eyes of his teacher.

24. Neither must he pronounce his mere name (without adding to it the word *Srî* or a similar term at the beginning).

25. He must not mimic his gait, his manner, his speech, and so on.

26. Where his Guru is censured or foully belied, there let him not stay.

27. Nor must he sit on the same seat with him,

28. Unless it be on a rock [1], on a wooden bench, in a boat, or in a carriage.

---

28. [1] Thus according to Kullûka (on M. II, 204). Nand. takes the term *sîlaphalaka* as a compound denoting 'a stone seat.'

29. If his teacher's teacher is near, let him behave towards him as if he were his own teacher.

30. He must not salute his own Gurus without his teacher's leave.

31. Let him behave towards the son of his teacher, who teaches him the Veda, as towards his teacher, even though he be younger or of an equal age with himself;

32. But he must not wash his feet,

33. Nor eat the leavings of his food.

34. Thus let him acquire by heart one Veda, or two Vedas, or (all) the Vedas.

35. Thereupon, the Vedângas (that treating of phonetics and the rest)[1].

36. He who, not having studied the Veda, applies himself to another study, will degrade himself, and his progeny with him, to the state of a Sûdra.

37. From the mother is the first birth; the second, from the girding with the sacrificial string.

38. In the latter, the Sâvitrî hymn[1] is his mother, and the teacher his father.

39. It is this which entitles members of the three higher castes to the designation of ' the twice-born.'

40. Previous to his being girded with the sacrificial string, a member of these castes is similar to a Sûdra (and not allowed to study the Veda).

---

30. Nand. here interprets Guru by 'a paternal uncle and the rest.'

31. This rule refers to a son of his spiritual teacher, who teaches him one or two chapters of the Veda, while the teacher himself is gone out for bathing or some such reason. Vâ, ' or,' is added in order to include a son of the teacher, who is himself a pupil, as Manu (II, 208) says. (Nand.)

35. [1] See Max Müller, Ancient Sanskrit Literature, p. 108 seq.

38. [1] Rig-veda III, 62, 1.

41. A student shall shave all his hair, or wear it tied in one lock.

42. After having mastered the Veda, let him take leave of his teacher and bathe, after having presented him with a gift.

43. Or let him spend the remainder of his life at his teacher's house.

44. If, while he is living there, his teacher should die, let him behave to his teacher's son as towards his teacher himself;

45. Or[1] towards one of his wives, who is equal to him in caste.

46. On failure of such, let him pay homage to the fire, and live as a perpetual student.

47. A Brâhmana who passes thus without tiring (of the discharge of his duties) the time of his studentship will attain to the most exalted heavenly abode (that of Brahman) after his death, and will not be born again in this world.

48. A voluntary effusion of the semen by a twice-born youth (in sexual intercourse with a woman), during the period of his studentship, has been pronounced a transgression of the rule prescribed for students by expounders of the Vedas well acquainted with the system of duties.

49. Having loaded himself with that crime, he must go begging to seven houses, clothed only with the skin of an ass, and proclaiming his deed.

---

42. After the solemn bath (see Âsv. III, 8, 9; Gobh. III, 4; Pâr. II, 6; Sânkh. III, 1), which terminates the period of studentship, the student, who is henceforth called Snâtaka, 'one who has bathed,' is allowed to return home.

45. [1] According to Nand., the particle vâ, 'or,' is used in order to include another alternative, that of living with an old fellow-student, as directed by Gautama, III, 8.

50. Eating once a day only a meal consisting of the alms obtained at those (houses), and bathing at the three Savanas (dawn, noon, and evening), he will be absolved from guilt at the end of the year.

51. After an involuntary effusion of the semen during sleep, a twice-born student must bathe (on the next morning), worship the sun (by offerings of perfumes and the like), and mutter three times the Mantra, 'Again shall my strength return to me [1].'

52. He who for seven days omits to collect alms and to kindle the sacred fire, must perform the penance of an Avakîrnin (breaker of his vow), provided that he has not been prevented from the discharge of his duties by an illness.

53. If the sun should rise or set while a student is purposely indulging in sleep, ignoring (the precepts of law), he must fast for a day, muttering (the Gâyatrî one thousand and eight times).

XXIX.

1. He who having initiated a youth and instructed him in the Vratas[1], teaches him (one branch of) the Veda (together with its Angas, such as that relating to phonetics, and the rest) is called Âkârya (teacher).

---

51. [1] Taitt. Âran̄y. I, 30.

XXIX. 1. Âpast. I, 1, 1, 13; Gaut. I, 9. — 1–3. M. II, 140–143; Y. I, 34, 35. — 7–10. M. II, 111, 112, 114, 115. — 9, 10. See Bühler, Introd. to Digest, p. xxix.

1. The Vratas of a student are certain observances to be kept by him before he is admitted to the regular course of study of the Veda, and again before he is allowed to proceed to the study of the Mahânâmnî verses and to the other higher stages of Vedic learning. See, particularly, Sânkh. II, 11, 12, with Dr. Oldenberg's note (Ind. Stud. XV, 139).

2. He who teaches him (after he has been initiated by another) either (an entire branch of the Veda) in consideration of a fee, or part of a Veda (without taking a fee), is called Upâdhyâya (sub-teacher).

3. He who performs sacrifices (whether based upon *Sruti* or upon Sm*ri*ti) is called *Ri*tvi*g* (officiating priest).

4. He must not engage a priest for the performance of sacrifices without having ascertained (his descent, character, and conduct).

5. Neither must he admit to his teaching (one whom he does not know).

6. And he must not initiate such a one.

7. If one answers improperly, or the other asks improperly [1], that one (or both) will perish or incur hatred.

8. If by instructing a pupil neither religious merit nor wealth are acquired, and if no sufficient attention is to be obtained from him (for his teacher's words), in such soil divine knowledge must not be sown : it would perish like fine seed in barren soil.

9. The deity of sacred knowledge approached a Brâhma*n*a (and said to him), 'Preserve me, I am thy treasure, reveal me not to a scorner, nor to a wicked man, nor to one of uncontrolled passions : thus I shall be strong.

10. 'Reveal me to him, as to a keeper of thy gem, O Brâhma*n*a, whom thou shalt know to be pure, attentive, possessed of a good memory, and chaste, who will not grieve thee, nor revile thee.'

---

7. [1] A proper question is, e. g. if the pupil modestly says, 'I don't know about this, therefore I want to be instructed.' An improper question is, e. g. if he says, 'Why do you pronounce this thus wrongly?' An improper answer is an answer to an improper question. (Nand.)

XXX.

1. After having performed the Upâkarman ceremony on the full moon of the month Srâva*n*a, or of the month Bhâdra, the student must (pass over the two next days without studying, and then) study for four months and a half.

2. After that, the teacher must perform out of town the ceremony of Utsarga for those students (that have acted up to this injunction); but not for those who have failed to perform the ceremony of Upâkarman.

3. During the period (subsequent upon the ceremony of Upâkarman and) intermediate between it and the ceremony of Utsarga, the student must read the Vedângas.

4. He must interrupt his study for a day and a night on the fourteenth and eighth days of a month[1].

5. (He must interrupt his study for the next day

XXX. 1–33. Weber, Ind. Stud. X, 130–134; Nakshatras II, 322, 338–339; M. IV, 95–123; II, 71, 74; Y. I, 142–151; Âpast. I, 3, 9–11; Gaut. XVI; I, 51, 53. — 33–38. Âsv. III, 3, 3; M. II, 107; Y. I, 41–46. — 41, 42. M. II, 116. — 43–46. M. II, 117, 146–148, 144.

1–3. The annual course of Vedic studies opens with a ceremony called Upâkarman, and closes with a ceremony called Utsarga. The latter, according to the rule laid down in Sûtra 1, would fall upon the first day of the moon's increase, either in Pausha or in Mâgha. Nand. states that those students who have not performed the Upâkarman ceremony in due time must perform a penance before they can be admitted to the Utsarga; nor must those be admitted to it who have failed to go on to the study of another branch of the Veda at the ordinary time, after having absolved one.

4. [1] Nand., with reference to a passage of Hârîta, considers the use of the plural and of the particle *k*a to imply that the study must also be interrupted on the first and fifteenth days.

5. [1] This refers to the second days of the months Phâlguna, Âshâ*dh*a, and Kârttika. (Nand.)

and night) after a season of the year has begun [1], (and for three nights) after an eclipse of the moon.

6. (He must not study for a day and a night) when Indra's flag is hoisted or taken down.

7. (He must not study) when a strong wind is going.

8. (He must not study for three days) when rain, lightning, and thunder happen out of season [1].

9. (He must not study till the same hour next day) in the case of an earthquake, of the fall of a meteor, and when the horizon is preternaturally red, as if on fire.

10. (He must not study) in a village in which a corpse lies;

11. Nor during a battle;

12. Nor while dogs are barking, jackals yelling, or asses braying;

13. Nor while the sound of a musical instrument is being heard;

14. Nor while Sûdras or outcasts are near;

15. Nor in the vicinity of a temple, of a burial-ground, of a place where four ways meet, or of a high road;

16. Nor while immersed in water;

17. Nor with his foot placed upon a bench;

18. Nor while riding upon an elephant, a horse, or a camel, (or in a carriage drawn by any of those animals), or being borne in a boat, or in a carriage drawn by oxen;

19. Nor after having vomited;

---

8. [1] 'I. e. not during the rains.' (Nand.)

12. Nand. considers the term sva, 'dog,' to include all the other animals mentioned by Âpastamba, I, 3, 10, 17.

19–21. After having vomited or been purged, he shall interrupt

20. Nor after having been purged;

21. Nor during an indigestion.

22. When a five-toed animal has passed between the teacher and the pupil (the latter must interrupt his study for a day and a night).

23. When a king or a learned Brâhmana (who has mastered one Veda), or a cow, or a Brâhmana (in general) has met with an accident (he must not study).

24. After the Upâkarman (he must not study for three days).

25. And after the Utsarga (he must interrupt his study for as many days).

26. And (he must avoid to study) the hymns of the *Ri*g-veda, or those of the Ya*g*ur-veda, while the Sâman melodies are being chanted.

27. Let him not lie down to sleep again when he has begun to study in the second half of the night.

28. Let him avoid studying at times when there ought to be an intermission of study, even though a question has been put to him (by his teacher);

---

his study for a day and a night; when suffering from indigestion, till he has digested his food. (Nand.)

22. According to Nand., the interruption of study is to last for two days, when a crow, or an owl, or a wild cock, or a mouse, or a frog, and the like animals have passed; and for three days, when a dog, or an ichneumon, or a snake, or a frog (sic), or a cat has passed. He quotes Gaut. I, 59 in support of his interpretation. I have translated according to M. IV, 126; Y. I, 147.

23. In these cases the study shall not be taken up again till the accident has been appeased by propitiatory rites. If any of the persons in question has died, the interruption is to last for a day and a night, in case they were persons of little merit; but in case they should have been very virtuous, it is to last for three days. (Nand.)

28. Every lesson consists of questions put by the teacher and the pupil's answers to them.

29. Since to study on forbidden days neither benefits him in this nor in the other world.

30. To study on such days destroys the life of both teacher and pupil.

31. Therefore should a teacher, who wishes to obtain the world of Brahman, avoid improper days, and sow (on proper days) the seed of sacred knowledge on soil consisting of virtuous pupils.

32. At the beginning and at the end of the lecture let the pupil embrace his teacher's feet ;

33. And let him pronounce the sacred syllable Om.

34. Now he who studies the hymns of the *Rig*-veda (regularly), feeds the manes with clarified butter.

35. He who studies the Ya*g*us texts, (feeds them) with honey.

36. He who studies the Sâman melodies, (feeds them) with milk.

37. He who studies the Atharva-veda, (feeds them) with meat.

38. He who studies the Purâ*n*as, Itihâsas, Vedâṅgas, and the Institutes of Sacred Law, feeds them with rice.

39. He who having collected sacred knowledge, gains his substance by it in this world, will derive no benefit from it in the world to come.

---

33. Nand., quoting a passage of Yama, states the particle *ka* to imply that the pupil must touch the ground, after having pronounced the syllable Om.

38. Nand. considers the use of a Dvandva compound to imply that logic (Nyâya) and the Mîmâ*m*sâ system of philosophy are also intended in this Sûtra. Regarding the meaning of the terms Purâ*n*a and Itihâsa, see Max Müller, Ancient Sanskrit Literature, p. 40 seq.

39. This rule cannot refer to teaching for a reward, because

40. Neither will he (derive such benefit from it), who uses his knowledge in order to destroy the reputation of others (by defeating them in argument).

41. Let no one acquire sacred knowledge, without his teacher's permission, from another who is studying divine science.

42. Acquiring it in that way constitutes theft of the Veda, and will bring him into hell.

43. Let (a student) never grieve that man from whom he has obtained worldly knowledge (relating to poetry, rhetoric, and the like subjects), sacred knowledge (relating to the Vedas and Vedângas), or knowledge of the Supreme Spirit.

44. Of the natural progenitor and the teacher who imparts the Veda to him, the giver of the Veda is the more venerable father; for it is the new existence acquired by his initiation in the Veda, which will last him both in this life and the next.

45. Let him consider as a merely human existence that which he owes to his father and mother uniting from carnal desire and to his being born from his mother's womb.

46. That existence which his teacher, who knows all the Vedas, effects for him through the prescribed rites of initiation with (his divine mother) the Gâyatrî, is a true existence; that existence is exempt from age and death.

47. He who fills his ears with holy truths, who

---

that is a minor offence (upapâtaka ; see below, XXXVII, 20); nor can it refer to teaching in general, because it is lawful to gain one's substance by it; but it refers to those who recite the Veda in behalf of another, and live by doing so. (Nand.)

41. See XXVIII, 6, and the preceding note.

frees him from all pain (in this world and the next), and confers immortality (or final liberation) upon him, that man let the student consider as his (true) father and mother: gratefully acknowledging the debt he owes him, he must never grieve him.

XXXI.

1. A man has three Atigurus (or specially venerable superiors):

2. His father, his mother, and his spiritual teacher.

3. To them he must always pay obedience.

4. What they say, that he must do.

5. And he must do what is agreeable and serviceable to them.

6. Let him never do anything without their leave.

7. Those three are equal to the three Vedas (*Rig*-veda, Sâma-veda, and Ya*g*ur-veda), they are equal to the three gods (Brahman, Vish*n*u, and *S*iva), they are equal to the three worlds (of men, of gods, and of Brahman), they are equal to the three fires.

8. The father is the Gârhapatya (or household) fire, the mother is the Dakshi*n*a (or ceremonial) fire, and the spiritual teacher is the Âhavanîya (or sacrificial) fire.

9. He pays regard to all his duties, who pays regard to those three; he who shows no regard to

---

XXXI. 1–6. M. II, 225, 226, 228, 229; Âpast. I, 4, 14, 6; Gaut. II, 50, 51. — 7. M. II, 230. — 8. M. II, 231; Âpast. I, 1, 3, 44. — 9. M. II, 234. — 10. M. II, 233.

9. 'The father is said to be of the same nature as the Gârhapatya fire, because the Âhavanîya is produced from it; the mother is said to be of the same nature as the Dakshi*n*a fire, because it

them, derives no benefit from any religious observance.

10. By honouring his mother, he gains the present world; by honouring his father, the world of gods; and by paying strict obedience to his spiritual teacher, the world of Brahman.

XXXII.

1. A king, a priest, a learned Brâhma*n*a, one who stops wicked proceedings, an Upâdhyâya, a paternal uncle, a maternal grandfather, a maternal uncle, a father-in-law, an eldest brother, and[1] the parents-in-law of a son or a daughter are equal to a teacher;

2. And so are their wives, who are equal in caste to them.

3. And their mother's sister, their father's sister, and[1] their eldest sister.

4. A father-in-law, a paternal uncle, a maternal

---

has a separate origin, or because she has the sacrificial implements, such as the pestle and mortar and the like, in her charge; and the spiritual teacher is said to be of the same nature as the Âhavanîya fire, because all oblations fall to his share, as the Sm*ri*ti says (Y. I, 27), "Let him (the pupil) deliver to him (the teacher) the collected alms."' (Nand.)

XXXII. 1. M. II, 206. — 2. M. II, 210. — 3. M. II, 131. — 4. M. II, 130; Âpast. I, 4, 14, 11. — 5, 6. M. II, 210, 211; Âpast. I, 2, 7, 27; Gaut. II, 31, 32. — 7. M. II, 129. — 8, 9. M. XI, 205; Y. III, 292. — 10. Âpast. I, 1, 2, 20. — 11, 12. M. II, 201; Âpast. I, 2, 8, 15. — 13. M. II, 212; Gaut. II, 34. — 14. M. II, 216. — 15. M. II, 217; Gaut. II, 33; VI, 2. — 16. M. II, 136; Gaut. VI, 20. — 17. M. II, 135; Âpast. I, 4, 14, 25. — 18. M. II, 155.

1. [1] The particle *k*a is used here, according to Nand., in order to include a paternal grandfather and other persons mentioned in a Sm*ri*ti.

3. [1] The particle *k*a here refers, according to Nand., to the paternal grandmother and others mentioned in a Sm*ri*ti.

uncle, and a priest he must honour by rising to meet and saluting them, even though they be younger than himself.

5. The wives of Gurus (superiors), who are of a lower class than their husbands (such as Kshatriya or Vaisya or Mûrdhâvasikta wives), shall be honoured by (rising to meet and) saluting them from far; but he must not embrace their feet.

6. He should avoid to rub and anoint the limbs of Guru's wives, or to anoint their eyes, or to arrange their hair, or to wash their feet, or to do other such services for them.

7. To the wife of another, even though he does not know her, he must either say 'sister' (if she is of equal age with himself), or 'daughter' (if she is younger than himself), or 'mother' (if she is older than himself).

8. Let him not say 'thou[1]' to his Gurus (superiors).

9. If he has offended one of them (by saying 'thou' to him, or in some other manner), he must keep a fast and not eat again till the end of the day, after having obtained his forgiveness.

10. He must avoid to quarrel with his spiritual teacher and to argue with him (from emulation).

11. And he must not censure him;

---

5. Sûdra wives are exempt from this rule; he should rise to meet, but not salute them. (Nand.)

8. [1] Other insulting language, as e. g. if he says hush or pish to them, is also included in this term. The use of the particle *ka* indicates that other persons entitled to respect are also intended in this Sûtra. (Nand.)

10. 'The particle *ka* is used in order to include Brâhma*n*as in general in this prohibition.' (Nand.)

11. 'The use of the particle *ka* shows that defamatory speeches are also intended.' (Nand.)

12. Nor act so as to displease him.

13. (A pupil) must not embrace the feet of a Guru's young wife, if he has completed his twentieth year, or can distinguish virtue from vice.

14. But a young student may at pleasure prostrate himself before a young wife of his Guru, (stretching out both hands) as ordained (see XXVIII, 15), saying, 'I, N. N. (ho! salute thee).'

15. On returning from a journey he shall (once) embrace the feet of the wives of his Gurus (superiors), and daily salute them, remembering the practice of the virtuous.

16. Wealth, kindred, age, the performance of religious observances, and, fifthly, sacred knowledge are titles to respect; each subsequent one is superior to the one preceding in order.

17. A Brâhma*n*a, though only ten years old [1], and a member of the kingly caste, though a hundred years old, must be considered as father and son; and of these two, the Brâhma*n*a is the father.

18. The seniority of Brâhma*n*as is founded upon sacred knowledge; of Kshatriyas, upon valour in arms; of Vai*s*yas, upon grain and (other) wealth; of *S*ûdras, upon (priority of) birth.

XXXIII.

1. Now man has three most dangerous enemies, called carnal desire, wrath, and greed.

---

17. [1] I. e. a Brâhma*n*a for whom the ceremony of initiation has been performed. (Nand.) This proverb is also found in the Nîti-*s*âstra 155, in the Mahâbhârata II, 1385 seq., &c., and in other works. See Böhtlingk, Ind. Sprüche, 6163, 2456, &c.

XXXIII. 1. Âpast. I, 8, 23, 4, 5.

1. The mention which has been made in the preceding section, that on Â*k*âra or rules of conduct, of the breach of the vow of

2. They are specially dangerous to the order of householders, because they have (houses, wives, and other) property.

3. Man, being overcome by those (three enemies), commits crimes in the highest degree, high crimes, minor crimes, and crimes in the fourth degree;

4. Also crimes effecting loss of caste, crimes degrading to a mixed caste, and crimes rendering the perpetrator unworthy (to receive alms and the like);

5. And crimes causing defilement, and miscellaneous offences.

6. This is the threefold path to hell, destructive of self : carnal desire, wrath, and greed : therefore must a man shun those three vices.

XXXIV.

1. Sexual connection with one's mother, or daughter, or daughter-in-law are crimes in the highest degree.

2. Such criminals in the highest degree should proceed into the flames; for there is not any other way to atone for their crime.

XXXV.

1. Killing a Brâhma*n*a, drinking spirituous liquor,

chastity and the penance for it (see XXVIII, 48, 49), causes him (Vish*n*u) to discuss the law of penance (Prâya*sk*itta). This is done in the following section, to which Chapter XXXIV serves as Introduction. (Nand.) The section on Prâya*sk*itta extends as far as Chapter LVII.

6. This proverb is also found in the Bhagavad-gîtâ, XVI, 21, and in the Mahâbhârata, V, 1036. See Böhtlingk, Ind. Sprüche, 2645.

XXXV. 1. M. IX, 235; XI, 55; Y. III, 227; Âpast. I, 7, 21, 8; Gaut. XXI, 1. — 2, 3. M. XI, 181 ; Y. III, 227, 261 ; Gaut. XXI, 3. — 4. M. XI, 181.

stealing the gold of a Brâhma*n*a, and sexual connection with a Guru's wife are high crimes.

2. And social intercourse with such (criminals is also a high crime).

3. He who associates with an outcast is outcasted himself after a year;

4. And so is he who rides in the same carriage with him, or who eats in his company, or who sits on the same bench, or who lies on the same couch with him.

5. Sexual intercourse, intercourse in sacrificing, and intercourse by the mouth (with an outcast) entails immediate loss of caste.

6. Such mortal sinners are purified by a horse-sacrifice and by visiting all Tîrthas (places of pilgrimage) on earth.

XXXVI.

1. Killing a Kshatriya or Vaisya engaged in a sacrifice, or a woman in her courses, or a pregnant woman, or a woman (of the Brâhma*n*a caste) who has bathed after temporary uncleanness[1], or an embryo

---

5. 'Intercourse of marriage' means sexual connection with an outcasted man or woman, or giving a damsel in marriage to an outcasted man. 'Intercourse in sacrificing' means sacrificing for, or with, an outcast. 'Mouthly intercourse' means teaching, cr being taught by, or studying together with, an outcast. The present rule holds good in cases of voluntary intercourse only; if the intercourse was involuntary, the loss of caste does not follow till after a year. Others assert that the immediate loss of caste is entailed by particularly intimate intercourse only. (Nand.)

XXXVI. 1. M. XI, 88; Y. III, 251; Âpast. I, 9, 24, 6, 8, 9. — 2–7. M. XI, 57–59, 171, 172; Y. III, 228–233. — 2. Gaut. XXI, 10. — 5. Gaut. XXI, 1. — 7. Âpast. I, 7, 21, 9.

1. [1] The term âtreyî (atrigotrâ) has been translated here and in

of unknown sex, or one come for protection, are crimes equal to the crime of killing a Brâhmana.

2. Giving false evidence and killing a friend: these two crimes are equal to the drinking of spirituous liquor.

3. Appropriating to one's self land belonging to a Brâhmana or a deposit (belonging to a Brâhmana and not consisting of gold) are crimes equal to a theft of gold (belonging to a Brâhmana).

4. Sexual connection with the wife of a paternal uncle, of a maternal grandfather, of a maternal uncle, of a father-in-law, or of the king, are crimes equal to sexual connection with a Guru's wife;

5. And so is sexual intercourse with the father's or mother's sister and with one's own sister;

6. And sexual connection with the wife of a learned Brâhmana, or a priest, or an Upâdhyâya, or a friend;

7. And with a sister's female friend (or with one's own female friend), with a woman of one's own race, with a woman belonging to the Brâhmana caste, with a (Brâhmana) maiden (who is not yet betrothed to a man), with a low-caste woman, with a woman in her courses, with a woman come for protection,

---

other places in accordance with that interpretation which is sanctioned by the majority among the commentators of law works. Nand., on the other hand, gives the preference to the opinion of those who render it by 'a woman descended from or married to a man of the race of Atri.'

2. 'The term etau, "these," is used in order to include the forgetting of Veda texts and other crimes, which are mentioned as equal to drinking spirituous liquor by Manu (XI, 57) and Yâgña-valkya (III, 229).' (Nand.)

5. 'The particle ka in this Sûtra refers to little girls, as ordained by Manu, XI, 59.' (Nand.)

with a female ascetic, and with a woman entrusted to one's own care.

8. Such minor offenders become pure, like mortal sinners, by a horse-sacrifice and by visiting Tîrthas.

XXXVII.

1. Setting one's self up by false statements (as by saying, 'I have done this,' or the like).

2. Making statements, which will reach the ears of the king, regarding a (minor) offence committed by some one;

3. Unjustly upbraiding a Guru (as by saying, 'You have neglected such a household duty');

4. Reviling the Veda;

5. Forgetting the Veda texts, which one has studied;

6. (Abandoning) one's holy fire, or one's father, mother, son, or wife;

XXXVII. 1–34. M. XI, 56, 57, 60–67 ; Y. III, 228–230, 234–242 ; Âpast. I, 7, 21, 12–17 ; Gaut. XXI, 11. — 35. M. XI, 118 ; Y. III, 265.

1. 'But if a man who does not know all the four Vedas says, in order to procure a valuable present or some other advantage, 'I know the four Vedas,' or if he says of another, his superior in caste or sacred knowledge, in order to prevent his receiving a valuable present, 'This man is no Brâhma*n*a,' or 'He does not know anything,' in all such cases his crime is equal to the killing of a Brâhma*n*a.' (Nand.)

2. 'But giving information of a heavy crime constitutes a crime equal to the killing of a Brâhma*n*a.' (Nand.)

3. Guru means 'father' here. Heavy reproaches, as e. g. if a son says to his father, 'You have made unequal shares in dividing the patrimony,' are equal to killing a Brâhma*n*a. (Nand.)

4. 'But atheistical detracting from the authority of the Veda constitutes a crime equal to the drinking of spirituous liquor.' (Nand.)

6. 'The use of the particle *ka* indicates that distant relatives are also intended here, as Yâgñavalkya, III, 239, states.' (Nand.)

7. Eating the food of those whose food may not be eaten, or forbidden food;

8. Appropriating to one's self (grain, copper, or other) goods of another man (but not his gold);

9. Sexual intercourse with another man's wife;

10. Sacrificing for persons for whom it is forbidden to sacrifice (such as Sûdras, persons for whom the initiation has not been performed, and the like);

11. To live by a forbidden occupation (as, if a Brâhmana lives by the occupation of a Kshatriya, or of a Vaisya).

12. Receiving unlawful presents;

13. Killing a Kshatriya, or a Vaisya, or a Sûdra, or a cow;

14. Selling articles that ought not to be sold (such as salt, lac, or others);

15. For an elder brother to suffer his younger brother to marry before him;

16. For a younger brother to marry, though his elder brother is not yet married;

17. To give a girl in marriage to either of those two (categories of offenders);

18. Or to perform the nuptial ceremony for them;

19. To allow the proper time for the ceremony of initiation to pass without being initiated;

---

10. 'But sacrificing for an outcast is a high crime.' (Nand.)

12. This rule refers to receiving presents from an outcast or other person, whose gifts must not be accepted, to receiving improper gifts, such as a ram, or a black antelope, and to receiving presents at an improper place, such as Kurukshetra, or at an improper time, such as during an eclipse of the sun. The particle *k*a further refers to giving instruction to those who are not entitled to receive it, as Yama mentions. (Nand.)

20. To teach the Veda for a reward (unless it be in an emergency);

21. To be taught by one who teaches the Veda for a reward (unless it be in an emergency);

22. To be employed (by the king's order) in the working of mines of any sort (whether gold mines, or silver mines, or others, or manufactories);

23. To make large (sharp) instruments (such as instruments for piercing an elephant's ear);

24. Cutting trees, shrubs, creepers, long climbing plants (such as vines), or herbs;

25. Living by (prostituting) one's own wife;

26. Trying to overcome another by incantations (tending to kill him), or by forcible means;

27. Performing the act (of cooking) for one's own sole benefit;

28. Not to have kindled one's own sacred fire;

29. Omitting to pay one's debts to the gods, *Ri*shis, and manes (or sacrificing, study of the Veda, and propagation of one's race);

30. Studying irreligious books;

31. Atheism;

32. Subsisting by a reprehensible art (such as dancing);

33. Intercourse with women who drink spirits;

34. Thus have the crimes in the fourth degree been enumerated.

---

20. It is true that the above definition of an Upâdhyâya (XXIX, 2) implies that teaching the Veda for a fee is no reprehensible act; but that permission has reference to cases of distress only. (Nand.)

26. Nand. asserts that the particle *k*a is used here in order to include the performance of an Ahîna sacrifice and of the other sinful acts mentioned by Manu, XI, 198.

31. Atheism (nâstikatâ) consists in denying the existence of another life. (Nand.)

35. Such criminals in the fourth degree shall perform the *K*ândrâya*n*a or Parâka penances, or shall sacrifice a cow (as the case may require).

XXXVIII.

1. Causing (bodily) pain to a Brâhma*n*a;

2. Smelling at things which ought not to be smelt (such as excrements), or at spirituous liquor;

3. Dishonest dealing;

4. Sexual connection with cattle;

5. And (sexual connection) with a man (or unnatural intercourse with a woman):

6. Such are the crimes effecting loss of caste.

7. He who has knowingly committed one of the acts effecting loss of caste shall perform the Sânta-pana[1] penance; he who has done so unawares shall perform the Prâ*g*âpatya[1] penance.

XXXIX.

1. Killing domestic or wild animals are crimes degrading to a mixed caste.

2. He who has committed a crime degrading to a mixed caste shall eat barley-gruel for a month (if he has committed it knowingly), or perform the penance *Krikkh*râtik*rikkh*ra (if he has committed it unawares).

---

35. Regarding the penances called *K*ândrâya*n*a and Parâka, see below, XLVIII and XLVII, 18.

XXXVIII. 1–6. M. XI, 68.

7. [1] See XLVI, 19, 10.

XXXIX. 1. M. XI, 69.

2. Regarding the penance *Krikkh*râtik*rikkh*ra, see XLVI, 13. 'The use of the causative form kârayet indicates that he may

XL.

1. Receiving anything from a (Mle*kkh*a or other) despicable person (even though not as a present, but in the form of interest, &c.), traffic (even with articles that are not forbidden to sell), subsisting by money-lending (even without exceeding the legitimate rate of interest), telling lies (even though not in giving evidence), and serving a *Sû*dra (even though without doing servile acts for him) are crimes rendering unworthy to receive alms.

2. He who has committed a crime rendering unworthy to receive alms, is purified by the penance Taptak*rikkh*ra (in case he committed it knowingly), or by the penance *Sî*tak*rikkh*ra (in case he did it unawares), or by the penance Mahâsântapana (in case it was committed) repeatedly.

XLI.

1. Killing birds, amphibious animals, and aquatic animals (such as fish);
2. And worms or insects;
3. Eating (nutmegs or other) plants similar to intoxicating drinks (in their effect upon the system):

---

perform the penance mentioned here through a substitute, if unable to perform it himself.' (Nand.)

XL. 1. M. XI, 70.

2. Regarding the penances mentioned here, see XLVI, 11, 12, 20.

XLI. 1–4. M. XI, 71.

3. 'Or the term madyânugata means hemp and the like.' (Nand.) Kullûka (on M. XI, 71) interprets it by 'what has been brought in the same basket or vessel with spirituous liquor;' Medâtithi, quoted by the same, by 'what has been defiled by spirituous liquor.' The rendering given in the text agrees with the first interpretation proposed by Nand.

4. Such are the crimes causing defilement.

5. The penance ordained for crimes causing defilement is the Taptak*rikkh*ra penance (if they were committed unintentionally), or they shall be atoned for by the K*rikkh*râtik*rikkh*ra penance (if they were committed intentionally).

XLII.

1. Miscellaneous crimes are those which have not been mentioned before.

2. Having committed one out of the number of miscellaneous crimes, a prudent man should always perform a penance, by the advice of a Brâhma*n*a, after the higher or less degree of his guilt has been ascertained.

XLIII.

1. Now follow the hells.   (They are called :)
2. Tâmisra (darkness) ;
3. Andhatâmisra (complete darkness) ;
4. Raurava (place of howling) ;
5. Mahâraurava (place of much howling) ;
6. Kâlasûtra (thread of time or death) ;
7. Mahânaraka (great hell) ;
8. Sañ*g*îvana (restoring to life) ;
9. Av*î*ki (waveless) ;

XLIII. 1–22. M. IV, 88–90; Y. III, 222–224. — 34. M. XII, 76.

4. Nand. derives the term Raurava from 'ruru, a kind of serpent.'   But it seems preferable to connect it with the root ru, 'to howl.'

6. This hell is defined by Nand. as a kind of threshing-place, made of copper, burning hot, and measuring ten thousand Yo*g*anas.

8. In this hell those who have perished in consequence of the tortures which they had to undergo are restored to life and tortured anew. (Nand.)

10. Tâpana (burning);

11. Sampratâpana (parching);

12. Samghâtaka (pressing together);

13. Kâkola (ravens);

14. Kudmala (bud);

15. Pûtimrittika (stinking clay);

16. Lohasanku (iron-spiked);

17. *Rikî*sha (frying-pan);

18. Vishamapanthâna (rough or uneven roads);

19. Kantakasâlmali (thorny Sâlmali trees);

20. Dîpanadî (flame river);

21. Asipattravana (sword-leaved forest);

22. Lohakâraka (iron fetters);

23. In each of those (hells) successively criminals in the highest degree, who have not performed the penance (prescribed for their crime), are tormented for the time of a Kalpa.

24. Mortal sinners (who have not done penance) for a Manvantara;

25. Minor offenders, for the same period;

---

12. In this hell a large number of individuals is packed up closely in a very narrow space. (Nand.)

13. In this hell the sinners are devoured by ravens. (Nand.)

14. In this hell the sinners are put in sacks, which are tied up at the end. (Nand.)

17. In this hell the sinners are roasted. (Nand.)

20. This river, which contains hot water, is called Vaitaranî, as it is said, 'The river called Vaitaranî has a stinking odour, is full of blood, and is moving on swiftly a torrent of hot water, carrying bones and hair in its course.' (Nand.) A detailed description of the river Vaitaranî may be found in the Gâruda-purâna, p. 8 (Bombay ed., 1863).

22. 'The particle iti is added here, in order to include in the above enumeration the hells called Savisha, Mahâpatha, Kumbhî-pâka, Taptabâluka, and the rest.' (Nand.) See Y. III, 223, 224; M. XII, 76.

26. Criminals in the fourth degree, for the period of a *K*aturyuga;

27. Those who have committed a crime effecting loss of caste, for a thousand years;

28. Those who have committed a crime degrading to a mixed caste, for the same period;

29. Those likewise who have committed a crime rendering unworthy to receive alms and the like.

30. And those who have committed a crime causing defilement;

31. Those who have committed one of the miscellaneous crimes, for a great number of years;

32. All sinners who have committed (one of those nine kinds of) crimes have to suffer terrible pangs, when they have departed life and entered upon the path of Yama.

33. Being dragged hither and thither (upon even and uneven roads), by the dire ministers of Yama, they are conducted (to hell by them), with menacing gestures.

34. (There) they are devoured by dogs and jackals, by hawks, crows, herons, cranes, and other (carnivorous animals), by (bears and other) animals having fire in their mouth, and by serpents and scorpions.

35. They are scorched by blazing fire, pierced by thorns, divided into parts by saws, and tormented by thirst.

36. They are agitated by hunger and by fearful troops of tigers, and faint away at every step on account of the foul stenches proceeding from pus and from blood.

---

31. 'A great number of years' means three hundred years. (Nand.)

37. Casting wistful glances upon the food and drink of others, they receive blows from ministers (of Yama), whose faces are similar to those of crows, herons, cranes, and other horrid animals.

38. Here they are boiled in oil, and there pounded with pestles, or ground in iron or stone vessels.

39. In one place they (are made to) eat what has been vomited, or pus, or blood, or excrements, and in another place, meat of a hideous kind, smelling like pus.

40. Here, enveloped in terrible darkness, they are devoured by worms and (jackals and other) horrible animals having flames in their mouth.

41. There again they are tormented by frost, or have to step through unclean things (such as excrements), or the departed spirits eat one another, driven to distraction (by hunger).

42. In one place they are beaten with their deeds in a former existence, in another they are suspended (by trees and the like, with a rope), or shot with heaps of arrows, or cut in pieces.

43. In another place again, walking upon thorns, and their bodies being encircled by snakes, they are tormented with (grinding) machines, and dragged on by their knees.

44. Their backs, heads, and shoulders are fractured, the necks of these poor beings are not stouter than a needle, and their bodies, of a size fit for a hut only, are unable to bear torments.

45. Having thus been tormented (in the hells) and suffered most acute pain, the sinners have to

---

43. The Gâru*d*a-purâ*n*a (p. 17) also mentions that in one hell the sinners are thrown into machines like the sugar-cane.

endure further pangs in their migration through animal bodies.

XLIV.

1. Now after having suffered the torments inflicted in the hells, the evil-doers pass into animal bodies.

2. Criminals in the highest degree enter the bodies of all plants successively.

3. Mortal sinners enter the bodies of worms or insects.

4. Minor offenders enter the bodies of birds.

5. Criminals in the fourth degree enter the bodies of aquatic animals.

6. Those who have committed a crime effecting loss of caste, enter the bodies of amphibious animals.

7. Those who have committed a crime degrading to a mixed caste, enter the bodies of deer.

8. Those who have committed a crime rendering them unworthy to receive alms, enter the bodies of cattle.

9. Those who have committed a crime causing defilement, enter the bodies of (low-caste) men (such as *Kand*âlas), who may not be touched.

10. Those who have committed one of the miscellaneous crimes, enter the bodies of miscellaneous wild carnivorous animals (such as tigers).

11. One who has eaten the food of one whose food may not be eaten, or forbidden food, becomes a worm or insect.

XLIV. 1–43. M. XII, 54–67; Y. III, 207–215. — 44, 45. M. XII, 68, 69.

11. See LI, 3 seq.

12. A thief (of other property than gold), becomes a falcon.

13. One who has appropriated a broad passage, becomes a (serpent or other) animal living in holes.

14. One who has stolen grain, becomes a rat.

15. One who has stolen white copper, becomes a Ha*m*sa.

16. One who has stolen water, becomes a water-fowl.

17. One who has stolen honey, becomes a gad-fly.

18. One who has stolen milk, becomes a crow.

19. One who has stolen juice (of the sugar-cane or other plants), becomes a dog.

20. One who has stolen clarified butter, becomes an ichneumon.

21. One who has stolen meat, becomes a vulture.

22. One who has stolen fat, becomes a cormorant.

23. One who has stolen oil, becomes a cock-roach.

24. One who has stolen salt, becomes a cricket.

25. One who has stolen sour milk, becomes a crane.

26. One who has stolen silk, becomes a partridge.

27. One who has stolen linen, becomes a frog.

28. One who has stolen cotton cloth, becomes a curlew.

29. One who has stolen a cow, becomes an iguana.

30. One who has stolen sugar, becomes a Vâlguda.

---

30. 'The Vâlguda is a kind of bat.' (Nand.) The name Vâl-guda is evidently related to valgulî, 'a kind of bat,' and identical with Vâgguda (M. XII, 64) and Vâgvada (Haradatta on Gaut. XVII, 34), which, according to Dr. Bühler's plausible suggestion,

31. One who has stolen perfumes, becomes a musk-rat.

32. One who has stolen vegetables, consisting of leaves, becomes a peacock.

33. One who has stolen prepared grain, becomes a (boar called) Svâvidh (or Sedhâ).

34. One who has stolen undressed grain, becomes a porcupine.

35. One who has stolen fire, becomes a crane.

36. One who has stolen household utensils, becomes a wasp (usually called *Kara/a*).

37. One who has stolen dyed cloth, becomes a *K*akor partridge.

38. One who has stolen an elephant, becomes a tortoise.

39. One who has stolen a horse, becomes a tiger.

40. One who has stolen fruits or blossoms, becomes an ape.

41. One who has stolen a woman, becomes a bear.

42. One who has stolen a vehicle, becomes a camel.

43. One who has stolen cattle, becomes a vulture.

44. He who has taken by force any property belonging to another, or eaten food not first presented to the gods (at the Vai*s*vadeva offering), inevitably enters the body of some beast.

45. Women, who have committed similar thefts, receive the same ignominious punishment: they become females to those male animals.

---

are names of 'a large herbivorous bat, usually called the flying fox (in Gûgaratî vâgud or vâgul).' See Dr. Bühler's note on Gâut. loc. cit.

XLV.

1. Now after having undergone the torments inflicted in the hells, and having passed through the animal bodies, the sinners are born as human beings with (the following) marks (indicating their crime) :

2. A criminal in the highest degree shall have leprosy ;

3. A killer of a Brâhma*n*a, pulmonary consumption ;

4. A drinker of spirits, black teeth ;

5. A stealer of gold (belonging to a Brâhma*n*a), deformed nails ;

6. A violator of his spiritual teacher's bed, a disease of the skin ;

7. A calumniator, a stinking nose ;

8. A malignant informer, stinking breath ;

9. A stealer of grain, a limb too little ;

10. One who steals by mixing (i. e. by taking good grain and replacing the same amount of bad grain in its stead), a limb too much ;

11. A stealer of food, dyspepsia ;

12. A stealer of words [1], dumbness ;

XLV. 2–31. M. XI, 49–52 ; Y. III, 209–211. — 32, 33. M. XI, 53, 54.

2. According to a text of *S*âtâtapa, which Nand. quotes in explanation of this Sûtra, connection with the mother is punished with ' falling or incurable epilepsy,' when the organ falls of ; connection with a daughter is punished with red epilepsy ; connection with a daughter-in-law, with black leprosy ; and connection with a sister, with yellow leprosy.

12. [1] I. e. according to Kullûka and Nand., ' one who studies the Veda without permission to do so ;' or it may denote, according to Nand., ' a stealer of a book,' or ' one who fails to communicate information which he is able to give.'

13. A stealer of clothes, white leprosy;

14. A stealer of horses, lameness;

15. One who pronounces an execration against a god or a Brâhmana, dumbness;

16. A poisoner, a stammering tongue;

17. An incendiary, madness;

18. One disobedient to a Guru (father), the falling sickness;

19. The killer of a cow, blindness;

20. The stealer of a lamp, the same;

21. One who has extinguished a lamp, blindness with one eye;

22. A seller of tin, chowries, or lead, is born a dyer of cloth;

23. A seller of (horses or other) animals whose foot is not cloven, is born a hunter;

24. One who eats the food of a person born from adulterous intercourse[1], is born as a man who suffers his mouth to be abused;

25. A thief (of other property than gold), is born a bard;

26. A usurer becomes epileptic;

27. One who eats dainties alone, shall have rheumatics;

28. The breaker of a convention, a bald head;

---

19. Nand. quotes a text of Sâtâtapa, from which he infers the use of the particle tu to indicate here, that a killer of his mother shall also be born blind.

21. The particle ka, according to Nand., indicates here, that such persons shall also be afflicted with the morbid affection of the eyes called Timira, as stated by Sâtâtapa.

24. [1] Nand. says that kundâsin may also mean 'one who eats food to the amount of a kunda.' See also Dr. Bühler's note on Gaut. XV, 18.

29. The breaker of a vow of chastity, swelled legs;

30. One who deprives another of his subsistence, shall be poor;

31. One who injures another (without provocation), shall have an incurable illness.

32. Thus, according to their particular acts, are men born, marked by evil signs, sick, blind, hump-backed, halting, one-eyed;

33. Others as dwarfs, or deaf, or dumb, feeble-bodied (eunuchs, whitlows, and others).   Therefore must penances be performed by all means.

XLVI.

1. Now follow the penances.

2. Let a man fast for three days;

3. And let him perform each day the three ablutions (at dawn, noon, and sunset);

4. And let him, at every ablution, plunge into the water three times;

5. And let him mutter the Aghamarshana three times, after having plunged into the water;

6. During day-time let him be standing;

7. At night let him continue in a sitting position;

8. At the close of the ceremony let him give a milch cow (to a Brâhmana).

9. Thus[1] has the penance Aghamarshana been described.

XLVI. 10, 11, 18, 19. M. XI, 212, 213, 215, 216. — 10, 11, 13, 18–20, 22, 23. Y. III, 315–323. — 10. Âpast. I, 9, 27, 7. — 10, 11, 13. Gaut. XXIII, 2; XXVI, 1–5, 20. — 24, 25. M. XI, 224, 225.

9. [1] Nand. thinks that the word iti, ' thus,' has a double meaning

10. Let a man for three days eat in the evening only; for other three days, in the morning only; for further three days, food (given to him) unsolicited; (and let him fast entirely for three days): that is the Prâgâpatya (the penance invented by Pragâpati).

11. Let him drink for three days hot water; for other three days, hot clarified butter; and for further three days, hot milk; and let him fast for three days: that is the Taptak*rikkh*ra (hot penance).

12. Taking the same (liquids) cold is called the Sîtak*rikkh*ra (cold penance).

13. The K*rikkh*râtik*rikkh*ra (the most difficult penance) consists in subsisting on milk only for twenty-one days.

14. Eating (nothing but) ground barley mixed with water for a whole month is called the Udaka-k*rikkh*ra (water penance).

15. Eating nothing but lotus-fibres (for a whole month) is called the Mûlak*rikkh*ra (root penance).

16. Eating nothing but Bèl fruit (for a whole month) is called the Srîphalak*rikkh*ra (Bèl fruit penance).

17. Or[1] (this penance is performed) by (eating) lotus-seeds.

18. A total fast for twelve days is called Parâka.

19. Subsisting for one day on the urine and fæces of a cow, milk, sour milk, butter, and water

here, and refers to another kind of Aghamarsha*n*a penance at the same time, which is described by *S*ankha, and consists simply in fasting for three days and muttering the Aghamarsha*n*a hymn three times.

17. [1] According to Nand., the particle vâ, 'or,' here indicates another alternative, that of performing this penance with Âmalakas (Emblica Officinalis Gaertn.)

in which Ku*s*a grass has been boiled, and fasting the next day, is called Sântapana (the tormenting penance).

20. Swallowing (the same six things, viz.) cow-urine and the rest, each for one day, is called Mahâsântapana (the particularly tormenting penance).

21. Swallowing each for three days is called Atisântapana (the extremely tormenting penance).

22. Swallowing oil-cakes, foam of boiled rice, buttermilk, water, and ground barley (each for one day), with a fasting day between (every two days), is called Tulâpurusha (a man's weight).

23. Drinking water boiled with Ku*s*a grass, leaves of the Palâsa and Udumbara trees, of lotuses, of the *S*ankhapushpî plant, of the banyan tree, and of the Brahmasuvar*k*alâ plant, each (for one day), is called Par*n*akri*kkh*ra (leaves penance).

24. Let a man perform all those penances after having shorn his hair and his beard, and let him bathe at morning, noon, and evening every day, lying on a low couch, and restraining his passions,

25. And let him (while engaged in performing them) avoid to converse with women, *S*ûdras, or outcasts, and let him constantly, to the best of his ability, mutter purifying Ma*n*tras and make oblations in the fire.

XLVII.

1. Now follows the *K*ândrâya*n*a (lunar penance).

2. Let a man eat single mouthfuls (of food) unchanged in size;

XLVII. 1–10. M. XI, 217–222. — 1–3, 9. Y. III, 324, 325. — 1–4. Gaut. XXVII, 12–15.

2. 'Unchanged in size' means 'of that size precisely which the law prescribes.' Yâ*g*ñavalkya (III, 324) states that each daily

3. And let him during the moon's increase add (successively) one mouthful (every day, so as to eat one mouthful on the first day of the moon's increase, two mouthfuls on the second day, and so on; fifteen mouthfuls on the day of full moon), and during the wane of the moon let him take off one mouthful (every day, so as to eat fourteen mouthfuls on the first day of the moon's wane, thirteen mouthfuls on the second, and one mouthful on the fourteenth day of the moon's wane), and on the day of new moon let him fast entirely: thus has the barley-shaped *K*ândrâya*n*a been described.

4. Or the ant-shaped *K*ândrâya*n*a (may be performed).

5. That *K*ândrâya*n*a is called 'ant-shaped' in which the day of new moon is placed in the middle.

6. That one is called 'barley-shaped' in which the day of full moon is placed in the middle.

7. If a man eats for a month eight mouthfuls a day, it is (the penance called) Yati*k*ândrâya*n*a (an hermit's *K*ândrâya*n*a).

8. Eating (for a month) four mouthfuls each morning and evening is (the penance called) *Sî*su-*k*ândrâya*n*a (a child's *K*ândrâya*n*a).

9. Eating anyhow[1] three hundred minus sixty mouthfuls a month is the penance called Sâmânya-*k*ândrâya*n*a (general *K*ândrâya*n*a).

---

portion must have the size of a peacock's egg, and Gautama (XXVII, 10) prescribes that the size of a mouthful shall be such as not to cause a distortion of the mouth in swallowing it. (Nand.)

9. [1] 'Anyhow,' i. e. otherwise than ordained above, as e. g. eating four mouthfuls on one day, and twelve on the next day; or fasting on one day, and eating sixteen mouthfuls on the following day; or fasting for two days, and eating twenty-four mouthfuls on the third

10. After having performed this penance, in a former age, the seven holy *Ri*shis, Brahman, and Rudra acquired a splendid abode, O Earth.

XLVIII.

1. Now if a man feels his conscience charged with some guilty act (such as performing a sacrifice for, or accepting a gift from, unworthy persons, or eating excrements) committed by himself (or if his conscience tells him that he has done more evil than good, or if he thinks himself less pure than others), let him boil a handful of barley-gruel for the sake of his own spiritual welfare.

2. Let him not make the (customary) Vais*v*adeva offering after that.

3. Neither must he make the Bali offerings.

4. Let him consecrate with Mantras the barley, before it has been put to the fire, while it is being boiled, and after it has been boiled.

5. Let him watch the barley, while it is being boiled (muttering at the same time the following Mantra):

6. 'Soma, who is the highest priest among priests (gods), leader among the wise, *Ri*shi among bards, the falcon among rapacious birds, the Svadhiti tree among trees, trickles murmuring through the filter[1].'

---

day; or fasting for three days, and eating thirty-two mouthfuls on the fourth day. (Nand.)

XLVIII. 1. Gaut. XIX, 13.

2, 3. Regarding the regular oblations which have to be offered at meal times &c. to the Vis*v*edevâs and to all beings (bhûtâni), see LIX, 22, 24; LXVIII, 1–22.

4. The Mantras are given below, 17–22.

6. [1] Rig-veda IX, 96, 6. Regarding the translation of this verse, see Dr. Zimmer's remarks, Altindisches Leben, p. 207.

With these words he must fasten blades of Kusa grass (round the neck of the kettle).

7. The pulse having been boiled, he must pour it into another vessel and eat it.

8. Let him help himself to it, while muttering the Mantra, 'The gods, who have sprung up in the mind and satisfy the mind, who are gifted with great energy, and whose father is Daksha, shall protect and help us. To them be Namah (adoration), to them be Svâhâ (hail).'

9. Then, after having sipped water, let him seize the centre (of the vessel) and mutter the Mantra:

10. 'Be satisfied in our stomach, O ye waters, and ye barley-corns, after having been bathed; they shall be salubrious to us, conferring bliss, causing health, divine, causing immortality, and increasers of *Ri*ta (truth and justice).'

11. One desirous of wisdom (must perform this rite) for three days;

12. A sinner, for six days.

13. Any of the mortal sinners (killers of a Brâhma*n*a, stealers of gold, and the rest) becomes purified by swallowing it for seven days.

14. Swallowing it for twelve nights effaces even sins committed by an ancestor;

15. Swallowing it for a month, every sin (whether light or heavy, and whether committed by himself or by an ancestor).

16. And so does swallowing barley-corns dissolved in the excrements of a cow for twenty-one days (efface every sin).

17. 'Thou art barley, thou the king of grains,

8. Taittirîya Samhitâ I, 2, 3, 1. See also Vâgasaneyi Samhitâ IV, 11, &c.

thou water mixed with honey; the *Ri*shis have proclaimed thee an expeller of every kind of guilt and
an instrument of purification.

18. 'You are clarified butter and honey, O ye
barley-corns; you are water and ambrosia, O ye
barley-corns. May you efface whatever sinful acts
I have committed:

19. 'Sins committed by words, by acts, and by
evil thoughts. Avert distress and ill-fortune from
me, O ye barley-corns.

20. 'Purify food licked at by dogs or pigs, or
defiled by leavings (of food), and (purify me from
the stain) of disobedience towards mother and
father, O ye barley-corns.

21. 'Purify for me food given by a multitude of
persons, the food of a harlot, or of a *S*ûdra, food
offered at a *S*râddha, food rendered impure by the
birth of a child in the house, the food of a thief, and
food offered at a Nava*s*râddha (or new *S*râddha,
which takes place on the first, third, fifth, seventh,
ninth, and eleventh day after a person's demise).

22. 'Purify me, O ye barley-corns, from the sin
of injuring a child or of causing (a punishment) to
be inflicted on some one by the king, from theft of
gold (or other high crimes), from the violation of a
religious duty, from performing a sacrifice for an
unworthy person, and from abusing a Brâhma*n*a.'

XLIX.

1. After having fasted during the eleventh day
of the bright half of the month Mârga*s*îrsha, let a

XLIX. 1. 'He must worship Vâsudeva either with sixteen acts,
muttering one out of the sixteen verses of the Purushasûkta with
each single act, the first act being the invocation of the gods, and

man worship, on the twelfth day, the venerable Vâsudeva (Vish*n*u).

2. (He shall worship him) with flowers, incense, unguents, lamps, eatables (such as milk), and repasts given to Brâhma*n*as.

3. By performing this rite (on the twelfth day of the bright half of every month, from the month Mârgasîrsha to the month Kârttika) for one year, he is purified from every sin.

4. By performing it till he dies, he attains *S*vetadvîpa ('the white island,' the abode of Bhagavat).

5. By performing it for a year on each twelfth day of both halves of a month, he attains heaven.

6. By performing it (within the same intervals), till he dies, (he attains) the world of Vish*n*u.

7. The same (heavenly rewards are gained by him who performs this rite) on each fifteenth day (after having fasted during the fourteenth).

8. If he worships (according to the latter rite) Ke*s*ava (Vish*n*u) who has become one with Brahman, on the day of full moon, and Ke*s*ava absorbed in meditation, on the day of new moon, he will obtain a great reward.

---

the last the dismissal of the assembled Brâhma*n*as; or he must worship him with the "five offerings," perfumes, and the rest, muttering at the same time the "twelve syllables" (Om namo bhagavate vâsudevâya, "Om, adoration to the venerable Vâsudeva").' (Nand.)

2. 'He must worship him with those offerings and with burnt-oblations. The burnt-oblation, which must consist either of sesamum, or of barley, or of clarified butter, has to be accompanied by the recitation of the Purushasûkta or of the "twelve syllables."' (Nand.)

8. According to Nand., the two forms of Vish*n*u mentioned here must be considered as two separate deities, the one having to be invoked with the words 'Adoration to Brahmake*s*ava,' and the

9. If in a year on a day of full moon the moon and the planet Jupiter are seen together in the sky, it is called a great full moon.

10. Gifts, fasts, and the like are declared to be imperishable on that day. The same is the case if a conjunction with the asterism *Sravanâ* falls on the twelfth day of the bright half (of any month).

L.

1. Let a man make a hut of leaves in a forest and dwell in it;

2. And let him bathe (and perform his prayers) three times a day;

3. And[1] let him collect alms, going from one village to another, and proclaiming his own deed;

4. And[1] let him sleep upon grass:

5. This is called a Mahâvrata (great observance).

6. He who has killed a Brâhma*n*a (unintentionally) must perform it for twelve years.

7. (He who has unintentionally killed) a Kshatriya or a Vai*s*ya engaged in a sacrifice, for the same period.

other with the words 'Adoration to Yogake*s*ava.' 'A great reward' he interprets by 'a shape identical with that of Brahman.'

L. 1–6, 15. M. XI, 73; Y. III, 243; Âpast. I, 9, 24, 11–20; Gaut. XXII, 4–6. — 7–10, 12–14. M. XI, 88, 89, 129–131; Y. III, 251, 266, 267; Gaut. XXII, 12–16. — 16–24. M. XI, 109–116; Y. III, 263. — 25–41. M. XI, 132–138; Y. III, 270–274. — 30–33. Âpast. I, 9, 25, 13; Gaut. XXII, 19. — 34–36. Gaut. XXII, 23–25. — 46–50. M. XI, 141–145; Y. III, 275, 276. — 46. Âpast. I, 9, 26, 2 ; Gaut. XXII, 20, 21.

3. [1] Nand., quoting Gautama XXII, 5, takes the particle *ka*, 'and,' to imply that he should also make way for any Ârya whom he meets.

4. [1] The particle *ka* here means, according to Nand., that he ought to remain chaste, as ordained by Gautama, XXII, 4.

8. Likewise, he who has killed (unintentionally) a pregnant woman, or[1] a woman in her courses.

9. Or[1] a woman who has bathed after temporary uncleanness;

10. Or[1] a friend.

11. He who has (unintentionally) killed a king, must perform the Mahâvrata for twice the same number of years (or twenty-four years);

12. He who has (unintentionally) killed a Kshatriya (not engaged in a sacrifice, nor a king), for one quarter of that time less (or for nine years);

13. He who has (unintentionally) killed a Vaisya (not engaged in a sacrifice), for half of that time (or for six years).

14. He who has (unintentionally) killed a (virtuous) Sûdra, for half of that time again (or for three years).

15. He who is performing any of those penances, must carry (on his stick) the skull of the person slain, like a flag.

16. Let a man serve cows for a month, his hair and beard having been shorn.

17. And let him sit down to rest when they rest;

18. And[1] let him stand still when they stand still;

---

8. [1] Nand. infers from texts of Praketas, Yama, and Parâsara, that the particle vâ, 'or,' here refers to pregnant cows, and to women whose confinement is close at hand, or who are married to one who has kindled his sacred fire, or for whom all the sacred rites have been duly performed from their birth.

9. [1] Nand. refers the particle vâ, 'or,' to women of high rank and to a rival wife, or a mother, or a daughter, or a sister, or a daughter-in-law, or a wife, who is of the same caste as her husband.

10. [1] 'The particle vâ includes children here.' (Nand.)

18. [1] According to Nand., the particle ka here refers to the

19. And[1] let him give assistance to a cow that has met with an accident (such as getting into a slough, or falling into a pit).

20. And let him preserve them from (the attacks of lions and tigers and other) dangers.

21. Let him not seek shelter himself against cold (and hot winds) and similar dangers, without having previously protected the cows against them.

22. Let him wash himself with cow-urine (three times a day);

23. And[1] let him subsist upon the (five) productions of a cow:

24. This is the Govrata (cow rite), which must be performed by him who has (unintentionally) killed a cow (belonging to a Kshatriya).

25. If a man has killed an elephant (intentionally), he must give five black (nîla) bulls.

26. If he has killed (unintentionally) a horse, he must give a garment.

27. If he has (intentionally) killed an ass, he must give a bull one year old.

28. The same if he has (intentionally) killed a ram or a goat.

29. If he has (intentionally) killed a camel, he must give one Krishnala of gold.

---

precept of Parâsara, that he should drink water when the cows drink, and lie down when they lie down.

19. [1] According to Nand., the particle ka here implies another precept of Parâsara, that he should not take notice of a cow grazing or drinking water upon his own ground or that of another.

23. [1] 'The particle ka implies that he should also mutter the Gomatî hymn, as Sâtâtapa says.' (Nand.)

25. 'He is called a black bull whose colour is red, whose mouth and tail are of a yellowish-white colour, and whose hoofs and horns are white.' (Yagñapârsva, quoted by Nand.)

30. If he has (intentionally) killed a dog, he must fast for three days.

31. If he has (unintentionally) killed a mouse, or a cat, or an ichneumon, or a frog, or a *Dund*ubha snake, or a large serpent (a boa constrictor), he must fast one day, and on the next day he must give a dish of milk, sesamum, and rice mixed together to a Brâhma*n*a, and give him an iron hoe as his 'fee.'

32. If he has killed (unintentionally) an iguana, or an owl, or a crow, or a fish, he must fast for three days.

33. If he has killed (intentionally) a Ha*m*sa, or a crane, or a heron, or a cormorant, or an ape, or a falcon, or the vulture called Bhâsa, or a Brâhma*n*î duck, he must give a cow to a Brâhma*n*a.

34. If he has killed a snake, (he must give) an iron spade.

35. If he has killed emasculated (cattle or birds)[1], (he must give) a load of straw [2].

36. If he has killed (intentionally) a boar, (he must give) a Kumbha of clarified butter.

37. If he has (intentionally) killed a partridge, (he must give) a Dro*n*a of sesamum.

38. If he has (intentionally) killed a parrot, (he must give) a calf two years old.

39. If he has (intentionally) killed a curlew, (he must give) a calf three years old.

40. If he has (unintentionally) killed a wild carnivorous animal, he must give a milch cow.

---

35. [1] Thus according to Nand., who declares himself against the interpretation of sha*nd*a by 'a eunuch;' see, however, Kullûka on M. XI, 134, and Dr. Bühler's rendering of Gaut. XXII, 23.— [2] Nand. adds, 'and a Mâsha of lead;' see the passages just referred to.

41. If he has (unintentionally) killed a wild animal not carnivorous, (he must give) a heifer.

42. If he has (intentionally) killed an animal not mentioned before, he must subsist upon milk for three days.

43. If he has (unintentionally) killed a bird (not mentioned before), he must eat at night only;

44. Or (if unable to do so), he must give a silver Mâsha.

45. If he has (unintentionally) killed an aquatic animal, he must fast (for a day and a night).

46. If he has killed a thousand (small) animals having bones, or an ox-load of animals that have no bones, he must perform the same penance as for killing a Sûdra.

47. But, if he has killed animals having bones, he must (moreover) give some trifle to a Brâhmana (for each animal which he has killed); if he has killed boneless animals, he becomes purified by one stopping of the breath.

48. For cutting (unawares ?) trees yielding fruit (such as the bread-fruit or mango trees), shrubs, creeping or climbing plants, or plants yielding blossoms (such as the jasmine tree), he must mutter a Vedic text (the Gâyatrî) a hundred times.

49. For killing (unintentionally) insects bred in rice or other food, or in (sweets and) the like, or in liquids (such as molasses), or elsewhere (in water and so on), or in flowers or fruits, the penance consists in eating clarified butter.

50. If a man has wantonly cut such plants as

46, 47. Nand. thinks that the former Sloka refers to intentional, and the latter to unintentional murder of those animals.

grow by cultivation (such as rice and barley), or such as rise spontaneously in the wood (such as wild rice), he must wait on a cow and subsist upon milk for one day.

LI.

1. A drinker of spirituous liquor must abstain from all religious rites and subsist on grains separated from the husk for a year.

2. If a man has (knowingly) tasted any of the (twelve) unclean excretions of the body, or of the (twelve) intoxicating drinks, he must perform the *K*ândrâya*n*a penance.

3. Likewise, if he has (knowingly) eaten garlic, or onions, or red garlic, or any plant which has a similar flavour (to that of garlic or onions), or the meat of village pigs, of tame cocks (and other tame birds), of apes, and of cows.

4. In all those cases men belonging to a twice-born caste have to be initiated a second time, after the penance is over.

5. On their second initiation, the tonsure, the girding with the sacred string, the wearing of the staff, and the begging of alms shall be omitted.

LI. 1. M. XI, 93; Y. III, 254. — 3. M. V, 19; Y. I, 176. — 4, 5. M. XI, 151, 152; Y. III, 255; Gaut. XXIII, 2. — 6. M. V, 18; Y. I, 177; Âpast. I, 5, 17, 37; Gaut. XVII, 27. — 7–20. M. IV, 205–217; Y. I, 161–168; Âpast. I, 5, 16, 27, 29; 17, 4, 5; 18, 21–23; 19, 1, 15; II, 6, 15, 14; Gaut. XVII, 10–12, 17, 19, 21, 31. — 21. M. V, 16; Y. I, 177, 178. — 23. M. XI, 148. — 25. M. XI, 150; Gaut. XXIII, 6. — 26–42. M. V, 5–21, 24, 25; XI, 152–157; Y. I, 169–178; Âpast. I, 5, 17, 17–20, 22–26, 28, 29, 33–36; Gaut. XVII, 14, 16, 22–26, 28, 29, 32–34. — 43–46. M. XI, 158–160. — 59. M. V, 36; Y. I, 179; Âpast. I, 5, 17, 31. — 60. M. V, 38; Y. I, 180. — 61. M. V, 39. — 62. M. V, 34. — 63–78. M. V, 40–55. — 64. *S*ânkh. II, 16, 1. See also Bühler, Introd. to Digest, p. xxxi, note. — 76, 77. Y. I, 181.

6. If a man has (unawares) eaten meat of a five-toed animal, with the exception of the hare, the porcupine, the iguana, the rhinoceros, and the tortoise, he must fast for seven days.

7. If he has eaten the food of a multitude of persons, of a harlot, of a thief, or of a singer, he must subsist upon milk for seven days.

8. And [1] (if he has eaten) the food of a carpenter or of a leather manufacturer;

9. Or of a usurer, of a miser, of one who has performed the initiatory ceremony of a Soma-sacrifice, of a jailer, of an Abhisasta, or of a eunuch;

10. Or of a dissolute woman, of a hypocrite, of a physician, of a hunter, of a hard-hearted or cruel person, and of one who eats the leavings of food;

11. Or of a woman who has neither husband nor son, of a goldsmith, of an enemy, or of an outcast;

12. Or of a malignant informer, of a liar, of one who has transgressed the law, and of one who sells himself, or who sells (molasses or other) liquids and condiments;

13. Or of a public dancer, of a weaver, of an ungrateful man, or of a dyer of clothes;

14. Or (the food) of a blacksmith, of a man of the Nishâda tribe (who subsist by fishing), of a stage-player [1], of a worker in cane, or of a seller of weapons;

---

8. [1] "As shown by *ka*, "and," other persons who have a dishonourable profession, such as fishermen, have also to be understood.' (Nand.)

9. Abhisasta means 'accused of a heinous crime,' i. e. 'a person of bad repute.' (Nand.) See also Dr. Bühler's notes on Âpast. I, 9, 24, 6, and on Gaut. XVII, 17.

14. [1] This is the usual meaning of the term rangâvatârin. Nand. explains it by 'wrestlers and the like.'

15. Or of a trainer of dogs, of a distiller of spirituous liquor, of an oil manufacturer, or of a washerman ;

16. Or (the food) of a woman in her courses (whether belonging to her, or dressed for her), or of one who lives under one roof with the paramour of his wife ;

17. Or (food) which has been looked at by the killer of an embryo (of a Brâhma*n*a), or which has been touched by a woman in her courses, or nibbled by a bird [1], or touched by a dog, or smelt at by a cow ;

18. Or that which has been designedly touched with the foot, or that which has been sneezed at ;

19. Or the food of insane, or wrathful, or sick persons ;

20. Or (food that is given) in a disrespectful manner, or the meat (of animals killed) for no sacred purpose.

21. After having (unawares) eaten the flesh of any sort of fish, excepting the Pâ*th*îna, Rohita, Râ*g*îva, Si*m*hatu*nd*a, and *S*akula fishes, he must fast for three days.

22. Likewise, after having (unawares) eaten the flesh of (any other) aquatic animal (such as the alligator, or the Gangetic porpoise).

23. After having (knowingly) drunk water from a vessel in which spirituous liquor had been kept, he must drink for seven days milk boiled together with the *S*ankhapushpî plant.

---

17. [1] Nand. considers the term patatrin to refer to crows only in this place. Kullûka (on M. IV, 208) interprets it by 'crows and the like.' See also Gaut. XVII, 10.

20. See Dr. Bühler's notes on Gaut. XVII, 19, 31.

24. After having (knowingly drunk water) from a vessel in which an intoxicating beverage had been kept, (he must drink the same) for five days.

25. A Soma-sacrificer, who has (unawares) smelt the breath of a man who had been drinking spirituous liquor, must plunge into water, (suppress his breath) and mutter the Aghamarshana three times, and eat clarified butter afterwards.

26. For eating (designedly) the flesh of an ass, of a camel, or of a crow [1], he must perform the *K*ândrâya*n*a penance.

27. Likewise, for eating (knowingly) the flesh of an unknown (beast or bird), meat kept in a slaughter-house, and [1] dried meat.

28. For eating (unawares) the flesh of carnivorous beasts (tigers and others), or birds (hawks and others), he must perform the Taptak*rikkh*ra.

29. For (knowingly) eating a sparrow, or (the heron called) Plava, or a Brâhma*n*î ´duck, or a Ha*m*sa, or the (wild cock called) Ra*gg*udâla, or a Sârasa crane, or a Dâtyûha, or a male or female parrot, or a crane, or a heron, or a cuckoo, or a wagtail, he must fast for three days. _

30. Likewise, for eating (unawares the flesh of) animals whose hoof is not cloven (such as horses),

---

26. Nand. argues from a passage of Pra*k*etas, that the flesh of the following other animals, dogs, jackals, cocks, boars, carnivorous animals in general, Gangetic porpoises, apes, elephants, horses, tame hogs, cows, and human beings, is also implied here. But if that were the case, Sûtra 26 would be partly a mere repetition of, and partly opposed to, the rules laid down in Sûtras 33 and 22.

27. [1] Nand. infers from a passage of the Brâhma-purâ*n*a, that the use of the particle *k*a further implies a prohibition to eat the flesh on the back, or flesh which had been interred in the ground, or covered with earth, fried meat, and the flesh of the uterus.

or of animals having a double row of teeth (such as the Rohita deer).

31. For eating (unawares) the flesh of any bird, excepting the francoline partridge, the Kâpiñgala, the (quail called) Lâvaka, the peahen, and the peacock, (he must fast) for a day and a night.

32. For eating (knowingly) insects (ants and others), he must drink for one day (water in which the plant) Brahmasuvarkalâ (has been boiled).

33. For eating (unawares) the flesh of dogs, he must perform the same penance [1].

34. For eating (unawares the mushroom called) *Kh*attrâka, or (the mushroom called) Kavaka, he must perform the Sântapana penance.

35. For eating (unawares) stale food, other than a mess prepared with barley (such as cakes), or with wheat (such as gruel), or with milk (boiled with rice, or mixed with coagulated milk, or otherwise dressed), and dishes sprinkled with fat (such as clarified butter), sour gruel, and sweetmeats, he must fast (for one day).

36. Likewise, (for eating unawares) the juice flowing from an incision in a tree, (plants raised in) unclean substances (such as excrements and the like), and the red exudation of trees.

37. Also, (for eating unawares) the root of the water-lily; (and for eating) rice boiled with sesamum, or with beans, Sa*m*yâva [1], rice boiled in milk with sugar, pastry, *S*ashkulî (cakes), or food destined for

---

33. [1] 'And he must perform the Sântapana penance mentioned in the next Sûtra, as the use of the particle *k*a implies.' (Nand.)

37. [1] Nand. interprets this term by utkarikâ, which, according to Wilson, is a sort of sweetmeat made with milk, treacle, and clarified butter. Kullûka (on M. V, 7) has a somewhat different interpretation.

the gods, if those dishes have not been announced to the gods first; and (for eating) food destined for burnt-oblations.

38. Also, for tasting the milk of any animal, save the milk of cows, goats, and buffalos (and for tasting any eatables made of such milk)[1].

39. Also, (for tasting the milk) of those animals (cows and the rest) within ten days after their giving birth to a young one.

40. And (for tasting) the milk of a cow whose milk flows of itself, of one that has just taken the bull[1], or of one whose calf is dead[2].

41. And (for tasting the milk of a cow) that has been feeding upon ordures.

42. And (for tasting) any such food as has turned sour (but not that which is sour by nature, like sorrel), except sour milk (and what is made with it).

43. A student, who partakes (unawares) of a Srâddha repast, must fast for three days.

44. And he must remain in water for a whole day (afterwards).

45. If he eats honey or meat (at any time), he must perform the Prâgâpatya penance.

46. If any one eats (unawares) the leavings of the

38. [1] Nand. infers from the use of the particle *ka* that the same penance is ordained for tasting any other production of those animals, as e.g. their excrements.

40. [1] Sandhinî means 'a cow that has just taken the bull,' or 'a female animal that gives milk once a day,' or 'a cow that is milked by the calf of another cow.' (Nand.) Haradatta (see Âpast. I, 5, 17, 23; Gaut. XVII, 25) interprets it by 'an animal giving milk while big with young.' For other interpretations, see the Petersburg Dictionary. — [2] 'The particle *ka* indicates that animals bearing twins have also to be included in this prohibition.' (Nand.) See Gaut. loc. cit.

food of a cat, of a crow, of an ichneumon, or of a rat, he must drink water in which the Brahmasuvar*k*alâ plant has been boiled.

47. For eating (unawares) what has been left by a dog, he must fast for one day, and drink Pañ*k*agavya (afterwards).

48. For tasting (knowingly) the excrements of five-toed animals (excepting human excrements), he must (fast) for seven days (and drink Pañ*k*agavya on the eighth).

49. If one (not a student) eats (unawares) of a *S*râddha repast consisting of raw food, he must subsist on milk for seven days.

50. If a Brâhma*n*a eats what has been left by a *S*ûdra, (he must also subsist on milk) for seven days.

51. If he eats what has been left by a Vai*s*ya, (he must subsist upon milk) for five days.

52. If he eats what has been left by a Kshatriya, (he must subsist upon milk) for three days.

53. If he eats what has been left by another Brâhma*n*a, (he must subsist upon milk) for one day.

54. If a Kshatriya eats what has been left by a *S*ûdra, (he must undergo the same penance) for five days.

55. If he eats what has been left by a Vai*s*ya, (he must undergo it) for three days;

56. And so must a Vai*s*ya, if he eats what has been left by a *S*ûdra.

---

50. Nand. explains that he should drink Pañ*k*agavya alternately with milk. This explanation extends to the following Sûtras also (up to Sûtra 56). He further argues from another Sm*ri*ti text that the term *S*ûdra means '*S*ûdras and women' here.

57. For (knowingly) eating (undressed) food, which has been left by 'a *Kand*âla (or *Svapa*ka or other member of the seven lowest castes), he must fast for three days.

58. For (unawares) eating dressed food (left by such), the Parâka penance is ordained.

59. Let no Brâhma*n*a ever eat (the flesh of) beasts which has not been consecrated with Mantras; but if it has been consecrated with Mantras, he may eat it, following the eternal rule (laid down in the Veda).

60. As many hairs as the beast has, which he has slain in this world, for so many days will the killer of a beast for other purposes than a (*S*rauta or Smârta) sacrifice, suffer terrible pangs in this world and in the next [1].

61. It is for sacrifices that beasts have been created by the Self-existent (Brahman) himself. Sacrificing causes the whole universe to prosper; therefore is the slaughter (of beasts) for a sacrifice no slaughter.

62. The sin of him who kills deer for the sake of gain, is not so great (and visited less heavily) in the world to come, than the sin of him who eats meat which has not been offered to the gods.

63. Plants, cattle, trees, amphibious animals, and birds, which have been destroyed for the purposes of sacrifice, obtain exaltation in another existence (in which they are born as Gandharvas, or other beings of a high rank).

---

60. [1] My translation follows Nand. It is, however, doubtful, whether the reading is correct; see Manu V, 38.

62. This is because the former kills animals in order to support his family, whereas the latter eats meat merely in order to tickle his palate. (Nand.)

64. When honouring a guest, at a sacrifice, or when worshipping the manes, or the gods, a man may slay cattle, but not otherwise on any account.

65. That twice-born man who, knowing the exact truth (promulgated) in the Veda, slays cattle for the sacrifices (ordained in the Veda), will convey himself and the cattle (slain by him) to a blissful abode.

66. A self-controlled[1] man of a twice-born caste, whether he be a householder, or be dwelling with his spiritual teacher, or in the forest, must never slay an animal in opposition to the precepts of the Veda, even in cases of distress.

67. That slaughter which is in accordance with the precepts of the Veda, and has been fixed for this world of movable and immovable creatures, should be considered as no slaughter at all; because it is from the Veda that law shines forth.

68. He who hurts animals that do not hurt any one, merely in order to afford pleasure to himself, will never obtain happiness, whether living or dead[1].

69. He who gives no living creature intentionally the pain of confining or killing (or hurting) it, from benevolence towards all (creatures), will enjoy everlasting happiness.

70. Whatever he thinks of, whatever he strives for, and whatever he desires in his heart, all that is easily obtained by him who does not injure any created being.

71. Meat cannot be obtained without injuring an

---

66. [1] Nand. interprets the term âtmavân by samnyâsî, 'an ascetic, or member of the fourth order,' apparently because the first three orders are mentioned in this Sloka. I have followed Kullûka's interpretation (on M.V, 43).

68. [1] 'But it is no sin to kill tigers or other beasts of prey.' (Nand.)

animal, and the murder of animals excludes the murderer from heaven, therefore must meat be avoided.

72. Reflecting upon the origin of flesh [1] and upon the (sin of) hurting or confining animated creatures, he must abstain from animal food of any kind.

73. He who transgresses not the law and eats not flesh like a Pisâ*k*a, is beloved by men and remains free from disease.

74. He who gives his consent to the killing of an animal, he who cuts it up, he who kills it, the purchaser and the seller, he who prepares it, he who serves it up, and he who eats it, all these are denominated slaughterers of an animal.

75. There is no greater sinner than he who, without giving their share to the manes and to the gods, wants to increase his own flesh with the flesh of another creature.

76. Those two, he who performs a horse-sacrifice annually for a hundred years and he who does not eat meat, shall both obtain the same recompense for their virtue.

77. By eating (wild rice or other) sacred fruits or roots, and by living upon such grains as are the food of hermits, a man does not reap so high a reward as by avoiding meat.

78. (An eater of flesh must say within himself), 'Me he (mâ*m* sa) will eat in the next world, whose

---

72. [1] The human soul is enveloped in six sheaths, three of which come from the father, and three from the mother. The three that come from the mother are skin, flesh, and blood. Now flesh is said in the *S*ruti to be derived from the menstrual discharge, and the latter is one of the species of forbidden food. (Nand.)

flesh I am tasting here.' This, say the learned, is the derivation of the word flesh (mâ*m*sa).

LII.

1. He who has stolen the gold (of a Brâhma*n*a), must bring a club to the king, proclaiming his deed.

2. Whether the king kills him with it, or dismisses him unhurt, he is purified.

3. Or (in case he committed the theft unawares), he must perform the Mahâvrata [1] for twelve years.

4. He who appropriates (knowingly) a deposit, (must perform the same penance.)

5. He who steals (knowingly) grain or valuable objects [1], (or prepared food belonging to a Brâhma*n*a,) (must perform) the K*rikkh*ra [2] for a year.

6. For stealing male or female slaves (not belonging to a Brâhma*n*a, and for seizing) a well or pool (actually containing water), or a field, the *K*ândrâya*n*a (penance must be performed).

7. (For stealing) articles of small value (such as tin or lead, not exceeding twenty-five Pa*n*as in value), the Sântapana (penance must be performed).

8. (For stealing) sweetmeats, (rice or other) food,

LII. 1, 2. M. VIII, 314–316; XI, 100–101; Y. III, 257; Âpast. I, 9, 25, 4–5; Gaut. XII, 43, 44. — 3. M. XI, 102. — 5–13. M. XI, 163–169.

3. [1] See L, 1–5.

5. [1] By dhana, 'valuable objects,' the objects mentioned below (in 10), copper and the rest, are meant. (Nand.) — [2] Nand. does not explain the meaning of K*rikkh*ra, which is a general term for 'a heavy penance.' It probably denotes the Prâ*g*âpatya penance here, as in a number of other law texts (e. g. below, LIV, 26), and in the corresponding text of Manu in particular. See Kullûka on M. XI, 163.

8–13. Nand. explains that these Sûtras refer to a small amount of those articles which are mentioned in them.

(milk or other) drinks, a bed, a seat, flowers, roots, or fruit, drinking Pañkagavya (is ordained as penance).

9. (For stealing) grass, firewood, trees, rice in the husk, sugar, clothes, skins, or flesh, the thief must fast for three days.

10. (For stealing knowingly) precious stones, pearls or coral, copper, silver, iron, or white copper, he must eat grain separated from the husk for twelve days.

11. For stealing (unawares) cotton, silk, wool or other (stuffs), he must subsist for three days upon milk.

12. For stealing two-hoofed or one-hoofed animals, he must fast for three days.

13. For stealing birds, or perfumes, or medicinal herbs, or cords, or basket-work, he must fast for one day.

14. Though a thief may have restored to the owner the stolen property (either openly or) in some indirect manner[1], he must still perform a penance, in order to purify himself from guilt.

15. Whatever a man takes from others, unchecked (by the dictates of religion), of that will he be bereft in every future birth.

16. Because life, religious merit, and pleasure depend upon wealth, therefore let a man take care not to injure the wealth (of others by robbing them) by any means.

17. Among those two, he who injures animal life, and he who injures wealth, the one who injures wealth shall incur the heavier penalty.

---

14. [1] 'As under pretext of handing over to him the dowry of a wife.' (Nand.)

LIII.

1. One who has (unawares) had illicit sexual intercourse[1], must perform the Prâgâpatya penance for a year, according to the rule of the Mahâvrata, clad in a garment of bark, and living in a forest.

2. The same (penance is ordained) for sexual intercourse with the wife of another man (who belongs to his own caste, but is no Guru of his).

3. For intercourse with a cow, the Govrata (must be performed).

4. For intercourse with a man, for unnatural crimes with a woman, (for wasting his manhood) in the air, (for intercourse with a woman) in water, by day, or in a go-cart[1], he must bathe dressed in his clothes.

5. By intercourse (knowingly) with a *Kand*âla woman[1], he becomes her equal in caste.

6. For intercourse unawares with such, he must perform the *K*ândrâya*n*a twice.

7. For intercourse (knowingly) with cattle (other) than cows) or with a public prostitute, (he must perform) the Prâgâpatya penance.

8. A woman who has committed adultery once,

LIII. 1–8. M. XI, 106, 171–177. — 4. Y. III, 291. — 9. M. XI, 179.

1. [1] The crime intended here is explained by Nand. as being illicit intercourse with a step-mother, who belongs to the *S*ûdra caste.

3. See L, 16–24.

4. [1] 'Or in a cart drawn by asses or by other beasts of draught, as the particle *k*a implies.' (Nand.)

5. [1] 'Or with a woman of an equally degraded caste, such as the *S*vapa*k*a caste and others.' (Nand.)

8. See Sûtra 2.

must perform that penance which has been prescribed for an adulterer.

9. That guilt which a Brâhma*n*a incurs by intercourse with a *Kand*âla woman one night, he can only remove by subsisting upon alms, and constantly repeating (the Gâyatrî) for three years.

LIV.

1. If a man associates with one guilty of a crime, he must perform the same penance as he.

2. A Brâhma*n*a who has drunk water from a well in which a five-toed animal has perished, or which has been defiled in the highest degree, must fast for three days.

3. A Kshatriya (must fast) for two days (in the same case).

4. A Vai*s*ya (must fast) for one day (and one night).

5. A *S*ûdra (must fast) for a night only.

6. And all (the former, but not a *S*ûdra) must drink Pañ*k*agavya, when their penance has been completed.

7. If a *S*ûdra drinks Pañ*k*agavya, or if a Brâhma*n*a drinks spirituous liquor, they both go to the hell called Mahâraurava [1].

LIV. 1. M. XI, 182. — 10. M. XI, 203. — 11. M. II, 220; Âpast. II, 5, 12, 22; Gaut. XXIII, 21. — 12. M. XI, 200; Y. III, 277; Gaut. XXIII, 7. — 23. M. XI, 202; Y. III, 291. — 24. M. XI, 195; Y. III, 290. — 25. M. XI, 198; Y. III, 289. — 26. M. XI, 192. — 27. M. XI, 193. — 28. M. XI, 294. — 29. M. XI, 204. — 30. M. XI, 209; Y. III, 293. — 31. M. XI, 190. — 32. M. XI, 191; Y. III, 299. — 34. M. XI, 210; Y. III, 294.

7. [1] See XLIII, 5. Nand. infers from an anonymous Sm*ri*ti passage, that the first part of this Sûtra refers not only to *S*ûdras, but to women also, and not only to the drinking of Pañ*k*agavya,

8. If a man has not connection with his wife in the natural season, unless it be on the days of the full and new moon, or because she is ill, he must fast for three days.

9. A false witness [1] must perform the penance ordained for killing a Brâhmana.

10. He who has (unawares) voided excrements without water (being near), must bathe in his clothes, pronounce the 'great words [1],' and offer a burnt-oblation [2].

11. One who has been surprised asleep by the sun rising or setting, must bathe in his clothes and mutter the Gâyatrî one hundred and eight times.

12. He who has been bitten by a dog, a jackal, a tame pig, an ass, an ape, a crow, or a public prostitute, shall approach a river and (standing in it, shall) stop his breath sixteen times.

13. One who forgets the Vedic texts which he has studied, or who forsakes the sacred fires, must subsist upon alms for a year, bathing at the tree Savanas (morning, noon, and evening), sleeping upon the ground, and eating one meal a day.

14. For setting one's self up by false statements, and for falsely accusing or abusing a Guru, he must subsist upon milk for a month.

15. An atheist, one who leads the life of a member of the Kandâla or of other low castes that

---

but also to the offering of burnt-oblations and the muttering of prayers.

9. [1] According to Nand., this particular species of criminals is only quoted as an instance of anupâtakinah (criminals in the third degree, see XXXVI), who are all intended in this Sûtra.

10. [1] See LV, 10. — [2] 'The particle ka implies that he must touch a cow besides, as Manu directs (XI, 203).' (Nand.)

14. See XXXVII, 1, 3.

dwell outside the village (Bâhyas)[1], an ungrateful man, one who buys or sells with false weights, and one who deprives Brâhma*n*as of their livelihood (by robbing them of a grant made to them by the king or private persons, or by other bad practices), all those persons[2] must subsist upon alms for a year.

16. An unmarried elder brother whose younger brother is married, a younger brother married before the elder, an unmarried elder sister whose younger sister is married, the relative who gives such a damsel in marriage, and the priest who officiates at such a marriage, must perform the *K*ândrâya*n*a.

17. He who sells living beings, land, religious merit (obtained by a sacrifice or o herwise), or Soma, must perform the Taptak*rikkh*ra.

18. He who sells fresh ginger[1], (edible) plants (such as rice or barley), perfumes, flowers, fruits, roots, skins, canes, (winnowing baskets or fans and the like) made of split bamboo, chaff, potsherds, hair, ashes, bone, cow-milk or curds, oil-cakes, sesamum, or oil, must perform the Prâ*g*âpatya.

19. He who sells the fruit of the *S*leshmâtaka tree, lac, bees-wax, shells, mother-of-pearl, tin, lead, iron, copper, or (sacrificial) vessels made of the horn of the rhinoceros, must perform the *K*ândrâya*n*a.

20. He who sells dyed cloth, tin[1], precious

---

15. [1] 'Or nâstikav*ri*tti means "one who receives his substance from an atheist."' See also Gaut. XV, 16. — [2] 'The use of the particle *k*a implies that calumniators are also intended.' (Nand.)

17. See XLVI, 11.

18. [1] The term ârdra, which Nand. interprets by ârdrakam, might also be connected with the following word, and both together be translated by 'fresh plants.' See Y. III, 38.

20. [1] Tin, perfumes, and, of the articles enumerated in Sûtra 21,

stones, perfumes, sugar, honey, liquids or condiments (other than sugar, salt, and the like), or wool, must fast for three days.

21. He who sells meat, salt, lac, or milk, must perform the *K*ândrâya*n*a.

22. And[1] all those persons (mentioned in Sûtras 17–21) must be initiated a second time.

23. He who has been riding (voluntarily) upon a camel[1], or upon an ass, and he who has (purposely) bathed, or slept, or eaten, quite naked, must stop his breath three times.

24. By muttering attentively the Gâyatrî three thousand times, (by dwelling) upon the pasture of cows, (and) by subsisting on milk for a month, he becomes free from the sin of accepting unlawful presents.

25. He who has (knowingly) offered a sacrifice for an unworthy person (such as a low-caste person, or an outcast), he who has performed the funeral rites for a stranger, he who has practised magic rites (in order to destroy an enemy), and he who has performed a sacrifice of the kind called Ahîna[1], (all those persons) may rid themselves of their

---

lac, and milk have already been mentioned in Sûtras 18 and 19. Nand. tries to remove the difficulty in the second case, by stating the perfumes mentioned here to be perfumes of a different kind, and in the fourth case, by asserting that the milk of female buffalos, &c. is meant in Sûtra 21. But he interprets the two other terms as given above. Probably the passage is interpolated.

22. [1] Nand. infers from the use of the particle *ka* that this rule applies equally to the persons mentioned in the next Sûtra.

23. [1] 'The use of the particle vâ, "or," implies that riding upon a cow, and other such animals, is also intended here.' (Nand.)

25. [1] This kind of sacrifice is defined by Nand. as one connected with repeated drinking of the Soma juice, and lasting from two to twelve days. Medhâtithi (on Manu XI, 198) simply defines

sins by performing three K*rikkh*ra (Prâgâpatya) penances.

26. Those twice-born men, by whom the Gâyatri has not been repeated (and the other initiatory ceremonies performed), as the law directs, must be made to perform three (Prâgâpatya) penances and must be initiated according to custom.

27. Those twice-born men who are anxious to make an atonement for having committed an illegal act[1], or for having neglected the study of the Veda, must be made to perform the same penance.

28. Those Brâhma*n*as who have acquired property by base acts (such as living by the occupations of a lower caste, or accepting unlawful presents) become free from sin by relinquishing it, and by muttering (Veda texts) and practising austerities.

29. For omitting one of the regular acts enjoined in the revealed (and traditional) law, and for a breach of the rules laid down for a Snâtaka[1], a fast is ordained as atonement.

---

it as a sacrifice extending over two days or more; Kullûka (ibid.) states that it lasts three days or more, and that it is said in the Veda to cause impurity. See also Weber, Ind. Stud. X, 355.

26. The recitation and repetition of the Gâyatrî is one of the chief elements of the ceremony of initiation. The words with which the pupil must address his teacher on this occasion are given by Nand.; they are quoted from Âsv. I, 21, 4, and Sânkh. II, 5, 10–11. See also Gaut. I, 46, with Dr. Bühler's note.

27. [1] 'I.e. Brâhma*n*as and others who have gained their livelihood (in times of distress) by such occupations as are lawful for other castes only, and who, when the times of distress are over, wish to atone for those actions.' (Nand.)

29. [1] Regarding the meaning of this term, see above, XXVIII, 42, note. The rules to be observed by a Snâtaka are given in Chapter LXXI.

30. For attacking a Brâhma*n*a (by raising a stick or a weapon against him), the K*rikkh*ra (Prâgâ-patya) penance must be performed; for striking him, the Atik*rikkh*ra; and for fetching blood from him, the K*rikkh*râtik*rikkh*ra.

31. With sinners, who have not expiated their crime, let a man not transact business of any kind. But a man who knows the law must not blame (or shun) those who have expiated it.

32. Let him not, however, live (or have any intercourse) with those who have killed children, or with ungrateful persons, or with those who have slain one come for protection, or a woman, even though such sinners may have obtained their abso-lution, as directed by the law.

33. (An old man) who has passed his eightieth year, a youth under the age of sixteen, women, and sick persons have only to perform half of every penance [1].

34. In order to remove those sins for which no particular mode of expiation has been mentioned, penances must be prescribed, which shall be in accordance with the ability of the offender, and with the heaviness of his offence.

LV.

1. Now follow the penances for secret sins.

---

30. For the Atik*rikkh*ra penan*ç*e, see M. XI, 214.

33. [1] Nand. adds, that a youth under the age of sixteen, who has not been initiated, and old women, as well as girls who have not yet attained maturity, must only perform a quarter of it, as directed in a Sm*ri*ti.

LV. 1. M. XI, 248; Y. III, 301; Gaut. XXIV, 1. — 2, 3. M. XI, 249, 260; Y. III, 302; Gaut. XXIV, 10. — 4. Gaut. XXIV,

2. The killer of a Brâhma*n*a is purified, if, having approached a river (and bathed in it), he restrains his breath sixteen times, and takes only one meal, consisting of food fit for offerings, each day, for a month.

3. At the end of this rite he must give a milch cow.

4. By performing the same rite and by muttering (while standing in the water) the Aghamarsha*n*a [1] (instead of stopping his breath), a drinker of spirituous liquor [2] becomes free from sin.

5. (By performing the same rite and) muttering the Gâyatrî one thousand and ten times (each day), a stealer of gold becomes free from guilt.

6. One who has connection with a Guru's wife [1] (becomes free from sin) by fasting for three days and muttering the Purushasûkta [2] and (at the same time) offering a burnt-oblation.

7. Even as the horse-sacrifice, the king of sacrifices, removes all sin, the hymn of Aghamarsha*n*a likewise removes all sin.

8. Let a twice-born man stop his breath, in order to rid himself of all sin; all sins committed by a

---

10. — 6. M. XI, 252; Y. III, 305. — 7. M. XI, 260. — 10–21. M. II, 76–87.

2. Nand. infers from a text of Manu (XI, 249), that this rule refers to one who has killed a Brâhma*n*a intentionally.

3. This rule, Nand. infers from a passage of Yâ*g*ñavalkya (III, 305), applies also to the penances mentioned in the following Sûtra.

4. [1] Rig-veda X, 190. — [2] 'I. e. one who has knowingly drunk it, the penance for drinking it unknowingly being stated by Yâ*g*ñavalkya (III, 304).' (Nand.)

5, 6. [1] Nand. infers from M. XI, 251, 252, that these two Sûtras also refer to penances for crimes intentionally committed. — [2] Rig-veda X, 90.

twice-born man may be removed by repeated Prânâyâmas.

9. It is called a Prânâyâma, if a man, stopping the breath (which comes from the mouth and from the nostrils), recites the Gâyatrî three times, together with the Vyâhritis ('words')[1], with the sacred syllable Om, and with the (text called) Siras[2].

10. The lord of creatures (Brahman) has milked out from the three Vedas the letter A, the letter U, and the letter M (of which the sacred syllable Om is composed), and (the three sacred words) Bhûh, Bhuvah, Svah (earth, the atmosphere, and heaven).

11. The lord of creatures, the supreme deity, has also milked out from the three Vedas successively the three verses of the sacred stanza which begins with the word 'tad,' and is called Sâvitrî (or Gâyatrî).

12. By muttering, every morning and evening, that syllable and that stanza, preceded by the three 'words,' a Brâhmana will obtain that religious merit which the (study of the) Veda confers, just as if he had actually studied the Veda.

13. By repeating those three (Om, the 'words,' and the Gâyatrî every day) for a month out of the village, a thousand times, a twice-born man is purified even from a mortal sin, as a snake (is freed) from its withered skin.

14. Any member of the Brâhmana, Kshatriya, or Vaisya castes, who does not know those three texts,

---

9. [1] The three Vyâhritis, 'words,' or Mahâvyâhritis, 'great words,' are quoted in the next Sloka. — [2] It begins with the words, 'O ye waters, who are splendour and ambrosia.' (Nand., and Mitâksharâ on Y. I, 23.)

or fails to recite them in the proper season, meets with reproach among the virtuous.

15. The three imperishable 'great words,' preceded by the syllable Om, and the Gâyatrî consisting of three divisions, have to be recognised as the mouth (or beginning) of the Veda[1].

16. He who repeats that stanza (preceded by the syllable Om and the three 'words') carefully every day for three years, will be absorbed in the highest Brahman after death, move as freely as air, and become as pure as air.

17. The monosyllable (Om) is the highest Brahman, the stoppings of the breath are the best of austerities, but nothing is more exalted than the Gâyatrî; (declaring the) truth is better than silence.

18. All religious acts ordained in the Veda, (whether) consisting in burnt-oblations or sacrifices (or alms-giving or other pious observances), perish (after the merit obtained by them has been exhausted); but the syllable Om (akshara) must be known to be imperishable (akshara), as it is identical with Brahman, the lord of creatures.

19. The act of reciting (the syllable Om, the words,' and the Gâyatrî) is ten times better than the (Gyotish*t*oma or other) sacrifices prescribed (by the Veda); it is a hundred times better when muttered in a low voice; it is a thousand times better when repeated mentally only.

20. The four Pâkayag*ñ*as[1] (small or domestic

---

15. [1] To explain this, Nand. quotes a passage of Âsvalâyana (Gri*h*ya-sûtra III, 2, 3, where, however, part only of this quotation is found) to the effect that the study of the Veda has to be begun by pronouncing Om, the 'words,' and the Gâyatrî.

20. [1] 'The four Pâkayag*ñ*as are the offerings to gods, goblins (or "all beings"), manes, and men, together with the offering to

offerings), together with the sacrifices prescribed
(in the Veda), though all united, are not equal to a
sixteenth part of the sacrifice performed by reciting
(those sacred prayers).

21. A Brâhma*n*a may beyond doubt obtain final
emancipation by solely repeating (those prayers),
whether he perform any other religious observance
or no; one who is benevolent towards all creatures
(and does not slay them for sacrifices) is justly
called a Brâhma*n*a (or one united to Brahman).

LVI.

1. Now then [1] follow the purifying Mantras from
all the Vedas.

Brahman.' (Nand.; see LIX, 20-25.) Kullûka, on the contrary
(on M. II, 86), refers the term Pâkayag*ñ*a to the four first only out
of those five offerings, and this interpretation, besides being more
simple than Nand.'s, is preferable for several other reasons. First,
the ' offering to Brahman' includes the daily recitation of the Gâyatrî, which is mentioned here as opposed to the four Pâkayag*ñ*as.
Secondly, the number of four Pâkayag*ñ*as is equally given in the
Kâ*th*aka G*ri*hya-sûtra; and Devapâla, in his Commentary on that
work, gives a definition of them, which agrees in the main with
Kullûka's. ' Four' Pâkayag*ñ*as are mentioned in the G*ri*hya-sûtras
of Kau*s*ika, Pâraskara, and *S*âṅkhâyana also. See Weber, Ind.
Stud. X, 48. Thirdly, the Pâkayag*ñ*as are brought in here as
opposed to the Vidhiyag*ñ*as or ' sacrifices prescribed by the Veda.'
This is probably because the latter are offered in the triad of sacred
fires, whereas the term Pâkayag*ñ*a, in its narrower use, denotes the
oblations offered in the domestic fire. Hence, it might come to
include the ' offering to men,' i. e. the feeding of a guest, but certainly not the study of the Veda.

LVI. M. XI, 250-260; Y. III, 302-305; Gaut. XIX, 12;
XXIV.

1. [1] 'Now then,' i.e. the previous chapter containing an enumeration of secret sins, an enumeration of the purifying Mantras,
by which they may be expiated, follows next. (Nand.)

2. By muttering them, or reciting them at a burnt-oblation, the twice-born are purified from their sins. (They are as follows :)

3. The Aghamarsha*n*a ;   4. The Devak*ri*ta ; 5. The *S*uddhavatîs ;   6. The Taratsamandîya ;   7. The Kûshmâ*nd*îs ;   8. The Pâvamânîs ;   9. The Durgâsâvitrî ;   10. The Atîsha*n*gas ;   11. The Padastobhas ;   12. The Vyâh*ri*ti Sâmans ;   13. The Bhâru*nd*as ;   14. The *K*andrasâman ;   15. The

---

3. Rig-veda X, 190, 1.   (This and the following references are based upo*n* Nand.'s statements.)

4. Vâ*g*asaneyi Sa*m*hitâ VIII, 13.

5. Rig-veda VIII, 84, 7–9.   6. Rig-veda IX, 58.

7. Vâ*g*as. Sa*m*h. XX, 14–16 (Taitt. Âra*n*y. X, 3–5).

8. The term Pâvamânya*h* in its most common use denotes the ninth book of the Rig-veda, but Nand. here refers it to Taitt. Brâhm. I, 4, 8.

9. Rig-veda I, 99, 1.

10. Sâma-veda II, 47–49.   Regarding this and the following Sâmans see also Benfey, Ind. Stud. III, 199 seq., Burnell's Index to the Ârsheya Brâhma*n*a, and S. Goldschmidt's remarks in his edition of the Âra*n*yaka Sa*m*hitâ, Transactions of the Berlin Academy, 1868, p. 246 seq.

11. Sâma-veda II, 578–580.

12. 'The Vyâh*ri*ti Sâmans, i. e. bhû*h* and the four others.' (Nand.) The four others are, bhuva*h*, sva*h*, satyam, pu*r*usha*h*.   See Ûhya-gâna III, 2, 10, in Satyavrata Sâmâ*s*ramî's edition of the Sâma-veda Sa*m*hitâ.

13. 'Bhâru*nd*a is the name of certain Sâmans, twenty-one in number, which begin with the words, yat te k*ri*shna*h* *s*akuna (Rig-veda X, 16, 6).   They are contained in the Âra*n*yagâna.' (Nand.)   The reading of the last word is doubtful.   At all events, the verse quoted by Nand. does not occur in the Âra*n*yagâna.   It may be that the Sâmans called Ekavi*m*satyanugâna are meant, which are found in that work, though they do not contain the verse referred to.

14. Sâma-veda I, 147.

15. Âra*n*yaka Sa*m*hitâ IV, 33, 34, in Goldschmidt's edition,= Rig-veda X, 90, 1, 4.

two Sâmans called Purushavrata ; 16. The Abliṅga ;
17. The Bârhaspatya ; 18. The Gosûkta ; 19. The
Âsvasûkta ; 20. The two Sâmans called *K*andra-
sûkta ; 21. The *S*atarudriya ; 22. The Atharva*s*iras ; 23. The Trisupar*n*a ; 24. The Mahâvrata ; 25. The Nârâya*n*îya ; 26. And the Purushasûkta ;

27. The three Â*g*yadohas [1], the Rathantara [2], the
Agnivrata [3], the Vâmadevya [4], and the B*ri*hatsâ-
man [5], properly chanted, purify man from sin ; and
if he wishes he may obtain through them recol-
lection·of his existence in a former life.

LVII.

1. Now [1] (the following persons) must be avoided:

---

16. Sâma-veda II, 1187.   17. Sâma-veda, I, 91.
18. Sâma-veda I, 122.
19. The same text as in the preceding Sûtra.
20. Sâma-veda I, 350. Nand. infers from a passage of Vâsish*th*a
(XXVIII, 12) that *k*a refers to Sâma-veda II, 812, and I, 153.
21. Kâ*th*aka XVII, 11–16, &c.
22. 'The text beginning with the words, brahmâ devânâ*m*
prathama*h* sambabhûva, "Brahman rose first among the gods."'
(Nand.) The Atharva*s*ira Upanishad has the words, very near
the beginning, aham eka*h* prathamam âsît. See the Calcutta
edition.
23. Taitt. Âra*n*y. X, 48–50.   24. Sâma-veda I, 91.
25. Taitt. Âra*n*y. X passim.
26. Rig-veda X, 90, 1. Nand. infers from a passage of Vâsish*th*a
(XXVIII, 13) that *k*a refers to Rig-veda X, 71, and I, 90, 6–8.
27. [1] Sâma-veda I, 67. — [2] Sâma-veda I, 233. — [3] Sâma-veda I,
27. — [4] Sâma-veda I, 169. — [5] Sâma-veda I, 234.
LVII. 1, 2. M. II, 39; Y. I, 38. — 3. M. XI, 182–185; Y.III,
295; Âpast. I, 10, 28, 6–8; Gaut. XX, 1. — 4. Âpast. I, 1, 2, 5. —
6, 7. M. IV, 186. — 8. M. IV, 190. — 9. M. IV, 186; Y. I, 213.
— 10. M. IV, 247, 250; Y. I, 214; Âpast. I, 6, 18, 1 ; I, 6, 19,
11 ; Gaut. XVII, 3. — 11, 12. M. IV, 248, 249; Âpast. I, 6, 19.

2. Vrâtyas (i. e. those for whom the ceremony of initiation has not been performed);

3. Outcasts;

4. Descendants within the third degree[1] of an outcast mother or father, if they (or their outcast ancestors) have not been purified (by a penance).

5. (As a rule) the food of all such persons must not be eaten, nor gifts be accepted from them[1].

6. He must avoid accepting repeated gifts from those whose presents must not be accepted[1].

7. By accepting such gifts, Brâhmaṇas lose their divine lustre.

8. And he who, not knowing the law regarding acceptance of gifts, accepts (illicit) gifts, sinks to hell together with the giver.

9. He who, being worthy to receive gifts, does not accept them, obtains that world which is destined for the liberal-minded (after death).

10. Firewood, water, roots, fruits, protection, meat, honey, a bed, a seat, a house, flowers, sour

---

14. — 13. M. IV, 251; Y. I, 216; Gaut. XVII, 4. — 14. M. IV, 213; Y. I, 215. — 15, 16. M. IV, 252, 253. — 16. Y. I, 166; Gaut. XVII, 6.

1. [1] 'There are two classes of sinners, the repentant and the unrepenting. The penances to be performed by the former having been enumerated, he goes on in the present chapter to state that the latter must be avoided.' (Nand.)

3. See XXXV, 1–5.

4. [1] Nand. refers the term 'in the third degree' to the three ascendants of the parents. The same infers from a passage of Gautama (XX, 1) that the particle ka is used in order to include a murderer of a king also.

5. [1] Nand. infers from another text of Gautama (XX, 8) that it is also forbidden to converse with them.

6. [1] 'It is no sin then, in one who is in distress, to accept a present once from them.' (Nand.)   See 14.

milk, and vegetables he must not disdain to accept when they are offered to him.

11. Even if an offender (but not a mortal sinner) has beckoned and offered alms to him, which had been brought previously for the purpose, the lord of creatures has declared that they may be accepted from him.

12. Neither will the manes eat (his funeral oblations offered to them) for fifteen years, nor will the fire convey his burnt-offerings (to the gods) if he rejects such alms.

13. If he wishes to provide for his (parents or other) Gurus or for (his wife or other) such persons as he is bound to maintain, or if he wants to worship the manes or the gods, he may accept gifts from any one; but he must not satisfy himself with them.

14. But even in those cases, and though he be worthy to receive presents, let him not accept them from a dissolute woman, from a eunuch, from an outcast, or from an enemy.

15. And if his parents are dead, or if he is living apart from them in a house of his own, he must never, while seeking to obtain food for himself, accept alms from any other persons but those who are of respectable descent (and belong to a twice-born caste).

16. One who ploughs the ground for half the crop (and gives the other half 'to the king or a private person, who is the owner), a friend of the family, a (house-)slave, a herdsman, a barber, and

---

11. 'The use of the particle *ka* implies that Kusa grass &c. is likewise intended, as Yâgñavalkya (I, 214) says.' (Nand.)

16. The reason of this rule, according to Nand., lies in this, that

one who announces himself (with the words 'I am your slave'): the food of all such may be eaten, although they are *Sûdras*.

LVIII.

1. The property of householders is of three kinds:

2. White, mottled, and black.

3. By those obsequies which a man performs with white property, he causes (his departed ancestor) to be born again as a god.

4. By performing them with mottled property, he causes him to be born as a man.

5. By performing them with black property, he causes him to be born as an animal.

6. What has been acquired by the mode of livelihood of their own caste, by members of any caste, is called 'white.'

7. What has been acquired by the mode of livelihood of the caste next below in order to their own, is called 'mottled.'

8. What has been acquired by the mode of livelihood of a caste by two or more degrees lower than their own, is called 'black.'

9. What has been inherited, friendly gifts, and

---

all the castes mentioned in this Sûtra are not properly *Sûdras*, but the offspring of unions between parents of a different caste, herdsmen being, according to Parâ*s*ara, the offspring of a Kshatriya with a *Sûdra* damsel, &c.   The same considers the use of the particle *k*a to imply that potters are also intended.   See Gaut. XVII, 6.

LVIII. 1, 2. Nârada 3, 46. — 9–12. Nârada 3, 53, 47–49, 51.

1. As the obligations of a householder, which will be discussed further on (in LIX), cannot be fulfilled without a certain amount of wealth, he discusses in the present chapter the origin of wealth. (Nand.)

the dowry of a wife, that is called white property,
for members of any caste indiscriminately.

10. What has been acquired as a bribe, as a fee
(for crossing a river and the like, or for a bride,
&c.), or by the sale of forbidden articles (such as
lac, or salt), or as a return for a benefit conferred,
is denoted 'mottled wealth.'

11. What has been acquired by servile attend-
ance [1], by gambling, by thieving, by begging, by
deceit (as if a man says that he wants a present for
another and takes it himself, or by forging gold or
other metals), by robbery, or by fraud (as if a man
shows one thing to a purchaser and delivers another
to him instead), is called 'black property.'

12. Whatever a man may do (in this world) with
anything (he has, whether white, mottled, or black
property) he will get his reward accordingly; both
in the next world and in this.

LIX.

1. A householder must perform the Pâkayagñas [1]

11. [1] Nand. interprets the term pârsvika by ' moving a chowrie to
and fro before one's master, while standing by his side.'

LIX. 1. M. IV, 67 ; Gaut. V, 7–9. — 1, 2. M. IV, 25 ; Y. I, 97. —
3, 4. Âsv. I, 9 ; I, 10 ; Gobh. I, 3, 5–9 ; Pâr. I, 9 ; I, 12 ; Sânkh.
I, 3. — 2, 4–9. Gaut. VIII, 19, 20. — 4–9. M. IV, 25, 26 ; XI, 7, 8 ;
Y. I, 124, 125. — 5–7. Âsv. I, 11 ; Gobh. III, 8 ; Pâr. III, 1 ;
III, 8 ; Sânkh. III, 8. — 10. M. XI, 27 ; Y. I, 126. — 11. M. XI,
24 ; Y. I, 127. — 12. M. XI, 25 ; Y. I, 127. — 13. M. III, 84, 90,
&c. (see below, LXVII). — 14, 15, 18. See the references given
below (ad LXVII). — 19, 20. M. III, 68, 69. — 21–25. M. III,
70 ; Y. I, 102 ; Âpast. I, 4, 12, 16 ; I, 4, 13, 1 ; Gaut. V, 3, 9 ;
Âsv. III, 1, 1–3 ; Pâr. II, 9, 1. — 26. M. III, 72. — 27–30. M. III,
77, 78, 80, 81.

1. [1] The term Pâkayagña is used in a more restricted sense here
than above (LV, 20). Nand. interprets it by ' Vaisvadeva, Sthâ-

(small or domestic offerings) in the fire kindled at the time of marriage [2].

2. He must offer the Agnihotra (or daily oblations of clarified butter) every morning and evening (in the Tretâ fires).

3. He must offer burnt-oblations to the gods (in case the Agnihotra cannot be performed).

4. Let him offer the two Darsapur*n*amâsas on the days of conjunction and opposition of the sun and moon.

5. Once in each half of the year, (at the two solstices, let him offer) the Pa*s*ubandha (animal sacrifice).

6. In autumn and summer let him offer the Âgraya*n*a (oblation of first-fruits);

---

lîpâka, *S*rava*n*âkarman, and similar sacrifices,' i. e. all the sacrifices which have to be performed in the one household fire, as opposed to those for which a Tretâ or triad of sacred fires is required (see Stenzler, note on Âsv. I, 1, 2). Gautama (VIII, 18) enumerates seven Pâkaya*gñ*as, among which, however, the Vai*s*vadeva is not included. The Vai*s*vadeva is described in LXVII. Regarding the other Pâkaya*gñ*as, see the G*ri*hya-sûtras. — [2] 'Or in the fire kindled at the division of the family estate, or in the fire kindled on his becoming master of the house.' (Nand.) See *S*ânkh. I, 1, 3–5.

2. The three Tretâ fires have been enumerated above (XXXI, 8). Regarding the Agnihotra and the sacrifices mentioned in 4–8, see Weber, Ind. Stud. X, 328–337, 343–349, 352–396.

4. 'One who has performed the ceremony of Agnyâdhâna (kindling the sacred fires) must perform these two offerings in the Tretâ fires, one who has not done so, in the household or nuptial fire.' (Nand.) This remark applies equally to the sacrifices mentioned in 5–7.

6. 'If the Âgraya*n*a is offered in the household fire, it must consist of a Sthâlîpâka (cooked offering of grain).' (Nand) See the G*ri*hya-sûtras above cited. Nand. further explains that in autumn the first-fruits of rice, and in summer the firstlings of

7. Or when rice and barley are ripening (in winter and spring).

8. He who has a sufficient supply of food for more than three years (shall perform the Soma-sacrifice) [1].

9. (He shall perform) the Soma-sacrifice once a year (in spring).

10. If he has not wealth (sufficient to defray the expenses of the Pasubandha, Soma, *K*âturmâsya, and other *S*rauta sacrifices), he shall perform the Ish*t*i Vais*v*ânarî.

11. Let him not make an offering of food obtained as alms from a *S*ûdra.

12. If he has begged articles for a sacrifice (and obtained them), let him employ them all for that purpose (and never for himself).

13. Every evening and morning let him offer up the Vais*v*adeva ;

14. And [1] let him give alms to an ascetic (afterwards).

15. For giving alms and showing due honour to the recipient (by pouring water on his hands both before and afterwards) he obtains the same reward as for giving a cow.

---

barley, or, according to Âpastamba, of Ve*n*uyava, have to be offered, and he infers from another text of the same author that the particle *k*a here refers to an oblation of *S*yâmâka grain, which has to be offered in the rainy season. The two passages in question are not found in Âpastamba's Dharma-sûtra, but Weber, loc. cit., quotes them from Kâtyâyana.

8. [1] According to Nand., the Soma-sacrifices here referred to are of the kâmya species (offered in order to obtain the gratification of a special desire).

14. [1] Nand. infers from the use of the particle *k*a, and from a text of Parâ*s*ara, that an injunction to give alms to a student is also intended here.

16. If there is no ascetic (or other person worthy to receive alms), he must give a mouthful to cows;

17. Or he must cast it into fire.

18. If there is food in the house, he must not reject a mendicant, (who arrives) after he has taken his meal himself.

19. A householder has five places where animals are liable to be destroyed: his wooden mortar, his slab to grind wheat or condiments upon, his fireplace, his water-pot, and his broom.

20. For the sake of expiating offences committed (by ignorantly destroying life) in those places, he must perform the (five) sacrifices addressed to the Veda, to the gods, to all created beings (or 'to the goblins'), to the manes, and to men.

21. Privately reciting (and teaching) the Veda is the sacrifice addressed to the Veda.

22. The regular burnt-oblation (Vaisvadeva) is the sacrifice addressed to the gods.

23. The Pitritarpana (refreshing the manes with food and water) is the sacrifice addressed to the manes.

24. The Bali-offering is the sacrifice addressed to all creatures (or 'to the goblins').

25. The sacrifice addressed to men consists in honouring a guest.

26. He who does not give their share to these five, the gods, his guests, (his wife and children and others,) whom he is bound to maintain, his manes, and himself, is not alive, though he breathes.

---

18. 'The expression, "if there is food in the house," indicates that he is not bound to cook a fresh meal for his guest.' (Nand.)

27. These (three), the student, the hermit, and the ascetic, derive their existence from the order of householders; therefore must a householder not treat them with disdain, when they have arrived (at his house at the proper time for begging alms).

28. The householder offers sacrifices, the householder practises austerities, the householder distributes gifts; therefore is the order of householders the first of all.

29. The *Ri*shis [1], the manes, the gods, all creatures (dogs, &c.), and guests beg householders for support; therefore is the order of householders the best of all.

30. If a householder is intent upon pursuing the three objects of life (virtue, love, and wealth), upon constantly distributing presents of food, upon worshipping the gods, upon honouring the Brâhma*n*as, upon discharging his duty of privately reciting (and teaching) the Veda, and upon refreshing the manes (with oblations of balls of rice, water, and the like), he will attain the world of Indra.

LX.

1. In (the last watch of the night, which is called)

27. Nand. refers the term bhikshu, which has been rendered by 'ascetic,' i.e. a member of the fourth order, to the six sorts of beggars enumerated by Parâ*s*ara. But as the first three orders are mentioned in this *S*loka, it is certainly more natural to translate the term as has been done above.

29. [1] Nand. thinks that hermits or members of the third order are meant by this term. But it seems preferable to refer it to the *Ri*shi authors of the Veda, to whom the first of the five sacrifices, the study of the Veda, is more immediately addressed. See Âpast. I, 4, 13, 1; Gaut. V, 3.

LX. 1. M. IV, 92; Y. I, 115. — 1, 2. M. IV, 50; Y. I, 16; Âpast.

the hour sacred to Brahman, let him rise and void his excrements.

2. By night (let him void them) facing the south, by day and during either twilight (let him void them) facing the north.

3. (He must) not (void them) on earth which has not been previously covered (with grass and the like);

4. Nor on a ploughed field;

5. Nor in the shade of a tree (fit to be used for sacrifices);

6. Nor on barren soil;   7. Nor on a spot abounding in fresh grass;   8. Nor where there are worms or insects;   9. Nor in a ditch (or hole, or upon the roots of a tree);   10. Nor on an ant-hill;   11. Nor on a path;   12. Nor on a public road;   13. Nor in a place previously defiled by another person;   14. Nor in a garden;   15. Nor in the vicinity of a garden or of (a reservoir of) water;   16. Nor on ashes;   17. Nor on coal;   18. Nor on

---

I, 11, 31, 1; Gaut. IX, 41–43. — 3. M. IV, 49; Âpast. I, 11, 30. 15; Gaut. IX, 38. — 4. M. IV, 46; Âpast. I, 11, 30, 18. — 5. Âpast. loc. cit. 16; Gaut. IX, 40. — 8–10. M. IV, 46, 47. — 11, 12. M. IV, 45; Âpast. loc. cit. 18; Gaut. IX, 40. — 11, 19. Y. I, 134. — 15, 21. M. IV, 46, 56; Y. I, 134, 137; Âpast. loc. cit. 18. — 16, 18. M. IV, 45; Gaut. IX, 40. — 22. M. IV, 48; Y. I, 134; Âpast. 20. — 23–26. M. IV, 49; V, 136, 137. — 23. Âpast. 15; Gaut. IX, 37. — 24. Y. I, 17. Chapters LX–LXIV treat of the daily duties of a householder. (Nand.)

6. Nand. infers from the use of the particle *k*a, that the following places (mentioned by Manu IV, 46, according to Nand.'s reading, which differs from the traditional one) are also included in this prohibition: a river, a mountain, the ruins of a temple, and the top of a mountain.

17. Nand. infers from the use of the particle *k*a, and from a text of Yama, that chaff and potsherds are also intended here.

cow-dung;   19. Nor in a fold for cattle; 20. Nor in the air; 21. Nor in water;

22. Nor facing the wind, or fire, or the moon, or the sun, or a woman, or a (father or other) Guru, or a Brâhma*n*a;

23. Nor without having enveloped his head;

24. Having cleaned his hindparts with a clod of earth, or with a brick, (or with wood or grass,) and seizing his organ (with his left, after having removed his garment), he must rise and clean himself with water and earth (previously) fetched for the purpose, so as to remove the smell and the filth.

25. The organ must once be cleaned with earth, the hindparts three times, the one hand (the left) ten times, both hands together seven times, and both feet together three times.

.26. Such is the purification ordained for householders; it is double for students; treble for hermits; and quadruple for ascetics.

LXI.

1. A householder must not use[1] Palâsa-wood for cleaning his teeth.

2. Nor (must he use the twigs of) the *S*leshmân-

---

20. 'I. e. in an apartment on the roof or in any other such place.' (Nand.)

LXI. 1. Âpast. I, 11, 32, 9; Gaut. IX, 44.

1. [1]Literally 'eat,' adyât.   In 16 and 17 the synonymous verbs bhaksh and a*s* are used.   Nevertheless it can hardly be doubted that both of the two modes of cleaning the teeth, which appear to have been customary, are indicated in this chapter: the one consisting in brushing them with little sticks or twigs provided with a brush (see 16), the other in chewing twigs.   Unfortunately the reading of Nand.'s gloss on the term sakûr*k*a in 16 is uncertain.

2. Regarding the Vibhîtaka tree, see Dr. Bühler's Kashmir Report, p. 8.

taka (or *S*elu) plant, nor of the soap plant, nor of the Vibhîtaka (or Kalidruma) tree, nor of the Dhava plant, nor of the Dhâmani tree (for that purpose).

3. Nor (the twigs of) the Bandhûka (or Bandhu-*g*îvaka) plant, nor of the Nirgu*nd*î shrub, nor of the *S*igru, Tilva, and Tinduka trees.

4. Nor (the twigs of) the Kovidâra (Yugapat-traka), *S*amî, Pîlu (Gu*d*aphala), Pippala (holy fig-tree), In*g*uda, or Guggula trees;

5. Nor (the twigs of) the Pâribhâdraka (*S*akra-pâdapa), or tamarind, or Mo*k*aka, or *S*emul trees, nor those of the hemp plant;

6. Nor sweet plants (such as liquorice sticks);

7. Nor sour plants (such as Âmlikâs);

8. Nor twigs that have withered on the stem;

9. Nor perforated (or otherwise faulty) wood;

10. Nor stinking wood;

11. Nor smooth wood;

12. He must not (use the sticks) facing the south or west.

13. He must use them facing the north or east;

14. He may use (the twigs of) the banyan or A*s*ana trees, or of the Arka plant, or of the Kha-dira, or Karañ*g*a, or Badara (jujube), or *S*al, or Nimb trees, or of the Arimeda shrub, or of the Apâ-mârga or Malatî plants, or of the Kakubha or Bèl trees;

15. Or of the Kashâya tree, or of the Tikta or Ka*t*uka plants.

16. Before sunrise let him silently clean his teeth with a stick, which must be as thick as the top of the little finger, provided with one end that may be chewed (or 'with a brush'), and twelve An*g*ulas long.

17. Having washed [1] and used the stick for cleaning the teeth, he must take care to leave it in a clean place ; he must never make use of it on the day of new moon (or on the day of full moon).

LXII.

1. The part at the root of the little finger of a twice-born man is called the Tîrtha sacred to Pragâpati.

2. The part at the root of the thumb is called the Tîrtha sacred to Brahman.

3. The part at the tops of the fingers is called the Tîrtha sacred to the gods.

4. The part at the root of the forefinger is called the Tîrtha sacred to the manes.

5. Let him sip water, which has not been put to the fire and is free from foam (and bubbles), which has not been poured out by a Sûdra (or other uninitiated person), or by a man who has one hand only, and which has no saline flavour [1] ; and (let him sip it) in a clean place, duly seated, placing (his right hand) between his knees, facing the east or the north (or the north-east), attentively regarding the water, and in a cheerful mood.

6. Let him sip water thrice with the Tîrtha sacred

---

17. [1] It must be washed both before and after using it. (Nand.)

LXII. 1–4. M. II, 59 ; Y. I, 19. — 5–8. M. II, 60, 61 ; Y. I, 20 ; Âpast. I, 5, 16, 1–7 ; Gaut. I, 36. — 9. M. II, 62 ; Y. I, 21.

1. Nand. observes that this chapter and the preceding one follow in order upon Chapter LX, because the purificatory rite described at the end of the latter is immediately followed by the Âkamana (sipping of water), and then by the Dantadhâvana (cleaning the teeth), both of which acts, however, have to be performed on other occasions also, as after a meal, &c.

5. [1] The term kshâra, 'saline flavour,' includes bad or spoiled water of any kind, according to Nand.

to Brahman (or with the Tîrthas sacred to the gods and to Pragâpati respectively).

7. Let him wipe his lips twice (with the root of his thumb).

8. Let him touch the cavities (above his navel)[1], his head, and his breast with water.

9. By water which reaches either their heart, or their throat, or their palate respectively, members of the three twice-born castes are purified each in his turn; a woman and a Sûdra are purified by water which has once touched their palate.

LXIII.

1. In order to obtain wealth and for the sake of security he shall apply to a lord.

2. He must not travel alone; 3. Nor with wicked companions; 4. Nor with Sûdras; 5. Nor with enemies; 6. Nor too early in the morning; 7. Nor too late in the evening; 8. Nor in the twilight; [9. Nor at noon; 10. Nor near water;] 11. Nor in too great a hurry; 12. Nor at night;

---

8. [1] See XXIII, 51.

LXIII. 1. M. IV, 33; Gaut. IX, 63. — 2–9. M. IV, 140, 55, 60. — 13–17, 19, 21. M. IV, 67, 131, 57. — 24, 25. M. IV, 78; Y. I, 139; Âpast. II, 8, 20, 11; Gaut. IX, 15. — 26–28. Sânkh. IV, 12, 15; M. IV, 39; Y. I, 133; Gaut. IX, 66. — 40. M. IV, 130. — 41. M. IV, 132. — 42. M. IV, 38; Gaut. IX, 52. — 43. M. IV, 38; Gobh. III, 5, 11. — 46. Âsv. III, 9, 6; M. IV, 77; Y. I, 139; Âpast. I, 11, 32, 26; Gaut. IX, 32. — 47. Âpast. I, 11, 32, 27; Gaut. IX, 33. — 49. Gobh. III, 5, 13; Pâr. II, 7, 6; Sânkh. IV, 12, 28. — 51. M. IV, 138, 139; Y. I, 117; Âpast. II, 5, 11, 5–7; Gaut. VI, 24, 25.

1. 'A lord' (îsvara) means a king or another rich man, in his own country, or in another country. (Nand.)   See also Dr. Bühler's note on Gaut. IX, 63, where the same Sûtra occurs.

9, 10. Sûtras 9 and 10 are wanting in Dr. Bühler's MS.

13. Nor (let him travel) without cessation with (horses or other) beasts of draught that are quite young, diseased, or (otherwise) afflicted;

14. Nor with such as are deficient in limb; 15. Nor with weak ones; 16. Nor with young bulls; 17. Nor with untrained animals.

18. He must not appease his hunger and allay his thirst without having first given grass and water to the animals.

19. He must not stop at a place where four ways meet; 20. Nor at night at the root of a tree; 21. Nor in an empty house; 22. Nor upon a meadow; 23. Nor in a stable;

24. Nor (must he stand) on hair, on the husks of grain, on potsherds, on bones, on ashes, or coal;

25. Nor on seeds of the cotton plant.

26. When he passes by a place where four ways meet, let him turn his right side towards it.

27. And let him do the same in passing by the image of a deity;

28. And in passing by well-known large trees.

29. After having seen a fire, or a Brâhma*n*a (with his turban on), or a public prostitute, or a jar filled (with water), or a looking-glass, or an umbrella, or a flag, or a banner[1], or a Bèl tree, or a lid (or platter), or a palace built in the shape of a certain diagram (or in the form of a quadrangle without a western gate)[2];

---

29. [1] 'More precisely the term patâkâ signifies "a staff, by which a piece of cloth torn in the middle is fastened."' (Nand.)— [2] 'The particle *ka* is added at the end of this enumeration in order to include in it perfumes, lamps, and other objects mentioned in a Sm*ri*ti.' (Nand.)

30. Or a fan, or a chowrie, or a horse, or an elephant, or a goat, or a cow (having a calf), or sour milk, or milk, or honey, or white mustard;

31. Or a lutĕ, or sandal-wood, or a weapon, or fresh cow-dung, or fruit, or a flower, or a fresh pot-herb, or Goro*k*anâ, or blades of Dûrvâ grass;

32. Or a turban, or ornaments, or jewels, or gold, or silver, or clothes, or a seat, or a vehicle, or (raw) meat;

33. Or a golden vase, or cultivated land which is being carried away (by a stream), or a single (bull or other) piece of cattle tied with a rope, or an unmarried damsel (clad in white), or a (boiled) fish, (let him turn his right side towards them and) go on.

34. Having seen one intoxicated, or insane, or deformed, he must turn back;

35. (Also, if he has seen) one who has vomited, or one who has been purged, or one who has had his head shorn, or one who wears all his hair tied in one knot, or a dwarf;

---

30. 'The particle *ka*, which is added at the end of this Sûtra, refers to a king, his ministers, his domestic priest, &c., as indicated in a Sm*ri*ti passage.' (Nand.)

31. Nand. infers from another Sm*ri*ti passage that *ka* here refers to a crow and to a *S*ûdra or workman with his tools.

32. Nand. here refers *ka* to shells and other objects mentioned in a Sm*ri*ti.

33. Nand. here refers *ka* to a dead body and other objects enumerated in a Sm*ri*ti.

34. The enumeration of auspicious objects in Sûtras 29–33 is followed by an enumeration of inauspicious objects in Sûtras 34–38. (Nand.)

35. The particle *ka* refers to enemies, outcasts, and others mentioned in a Sm*ri*ti. (Nand.)

36. Or (if he has seen) one wearing a dress (of a reddish-yellow colour) dyed with Kashâya [1], or an ascetic, or one smeared [2] (with ashes) [3];

37. Or (if he has seen) oil, or sugar, or dry cow-dung, or fire-wood, or grass (other than Kusa or Dûrvâ grass), or Palâsa (and other leaves, other than betel leaves), ashes, or coal [1];

38. Or (if he has seen) salt, or a eunuch, or (the spirituous liquor called) Âsava, or an impotent man, or cotton cloth, or a rope, or an iron chain for the feet, or a person with dishevelled hair.

39. (If he sees), while about to begin a journey, a lute, or sandal-wood, or fresh pot-herbs, or a turban, or an ornament, or an unmarried damsel, he must praise them [1].

---

36. [1] Nand. refers kâshâyin, 'wearing a dress dyed with Kashâya,' to 'persons who wear the marks of an order to which they do not belong.' But this interpretation is evidently wrong. Among the sects that wear a dress dyed with Kashâya, Buddhists are the most prominent, but it must not be overlooked that there are other important sects also, as e. g. the Svâminârâyanîs of the present day, who wear such dresses. — [2] The term malina, 'smeared,' no doubt refers to a Saiva sect. Nand. interprets it by 'Kâpâlikas and the like;' but more probably the Pâsupatas are meant. — [3] The particle ka further refers to the humpbacked, deaf, and blind, to barren women, and to naked and hungry persons, as stated in a Smriti. (Nand.)

37. [1] Nand. refers the particle ka in this Sûtra to hares, naked mendicants, snakes, iguanas, lizards, skins, and other inauspicious objects and persons enumerated in a Smriti.

38. Nand. argues from a passage of Nârada (not found in his Institutes), that the particle ka here refers to persons mounted upon an ass, camel, or buffalo, and others.

39. [1] Nand. mentions two explanations of this Sûtra: 1. he must eulogise the above objects or persons if he sees them; 2. he must gladden persons, who have those objects or persons with them, with presents and the like.

40. He must not (knowingly) step on (or step over, or stand on) the shade of the image of a deity, of a (learned) Brâhma*n*a, of a spiritual teacher, of a brown (bull or other animal), or of one by whom the initiatory ceremony at a Soma-sacrifice has been performed.

41. Nor (must he step) on anything spat out or vomited, nor on blood, nor on fæces or urine, nor on water used for ablutions.

42. He must not step over a rope to which a calf (or a cow) is tied.

43. He must not walk quickly in the rain.

44. He must not cross a river without need;

45. Nor without having previously offered an oblation of water to the gods and to the manes;

46. Nor (swimming) with his arms;

47. Nor in a leaky vessel.

48. He must not stand on the bank (of a river).

49. He must not gaze into a pool.

50. He must not cross it (by swimming through it, or in any other way).

51. Way must be made for an aged man, for one carrying a burden, for a king, for a Snâtaka (of any of the three kinds [1]), for a woman, for a sick person, for a bridegroom, and for one riding in a carriage. Among those, should they all meet, a king must be

---

41. According to Nand., the particle vâ, ' or,' is added at the end of this Sûtra, in order to include an officiating priest and others mentioned by Yâ*g*ñavalkya I, 152.

51. [1] The Snâtaka (see XXVIII, 42, note) is of three kinds: 1. the Vidyâsnâtaka, who has studied the Vedas; 2. the Vratasnâtaka, who has performed the Vratas or vowed observances of a student; 3. the Ubhayasnâtaka, who has completed both the Vedas and the Vratas. (Nand.) See the Gr*i*hya-sûtras.

honoured by the rest (excepting the Snâtaka); but the king himself must show honour to a Snâtaka.

LXIV.

1. He must not bathe in another man's pool;

2. In cases of distress (if there is no other water at hand) he may bathe (in another man's pool), after having offered up five (or seven, or four) lumps of clay and (three jars with) water.

3. (He must not bathe) during an indigestion;

4. Nor while he is afflicted (with a fever or other illness);

5. Nor without his clothes; 6. Nor at night; 7. Unless it be during an eclipse; 8. Nor in the twilight.

9. He must bathe early in the morning, when he beholds the east reddening with the rays of the (rising) sun.

10. After having bathed, he must not shake his head (in order to remove the water from his hair);

11. And he must not dry his limbs (with his hand or with a cloth);

12. Nor must he touch any oily substance.

LXIV. 1. M. IV, 201. — 1, 2. Y. I, 159. — 3, 4. M. IV, 129. — 5. M. IV, 45; Gaut. IX, 61; Âsv. III, 9, 6; Pâr. II, 7, 6; Sânkh. IV, 12, 31. — 6. M. IV, 129. — 12. M. IV, 83. — 13. Sânkh. IV, 12, 32. — 15. Gaut. IX, 16. — 16. M. IV, 263; Y. I, 159. — 24. M. IV, 152; Y. I, 100. — 27. Y. I, 196.

5. The term nagna, literally 'naked,' has to be taken in its widest sense here. According to Bhrigu and Gobhila it includes, besides one wholly undressed, 'one without his upper garment, one who has dirty clothes on, one clad in lower garments of silk only, one who wears double clothing or even a greater number of clothes, one who wears a small piece of cloth over the pudenda only,' &c. (Nand.) See also M. IV, 129.

13. He must not put on again the garment which he wore before, without its having been washed.

14. After having bathed, he must cover his head with a turban[1] and put on two garments[2] washed (by himself).

15. He must not converse, (after having bathed,) with barbarians, low-caste persons, or outcasts.

16. He must bathe in cascades, ponds dug by the gods, and lakes.

17. Stagnant water is more pure (and purifies more effectually) than water taken out (of a well or the like); the water of a spring is more pure than that of a tank; the water of a river is more pure than the former; water collected by (Vasish*th*a or some other) devout sage[1] is even more pure; but the water of the Ganges is the purest of all.

18. After having removed the dirt by means of earth and water[1], and after having dived under water and returned (to the bank of the river), he must address the bathing-place with the three Mantras (beginning with the words), 'Ye waters are[2],' with the four Mantras (beginning with the words),

---

14. [1] Ush*n*îsha, 'a turban,' here denotes a bandage used for drying the head, which is wrapped round the head and closely tied together. — [2] I. e. an upper and an under garment. (Nand.)

16. The term devakhâta, 'ponds dug by the gods,' refers to Pushkara and other holy bathing-places. (Nand.)   See below LXXXV.

17. [1] Nand. cites Vasish*th*aprâ*k*î and Vi*s*vâmitraprâ*k*î as instances of holy bathing-places of this description.

18. [1] Nand. refers this and the following Sûtras to a midday bath, because a verse, which he quotes, forbids the use of earth (in order to clean one's self with it) in the morning bath. But it seems to follow from 35 and 42, that all the rules given in this chapter refer to that bath, which must be taken at sunrise every day. — [2] Rig-

'The golden-coloured (waters) [3],' and with (the one Mantra beginning with the words), 'Carry away (all) that, O ye waters [4].'

19. Then he must dive under water and mutter the Aghamarsha*n*a three times;

20. Or (he must mutter three times the Mantra which begins with the words), 'That most exalted step of Vish*n*u;'

21. Or the Drupadâ Sâvitrî (which begins with the words, 'Like one released from a post');

22. Or the Anuvâka (which begins with the words), 'They get their minds ready;'

23. Or the Purushasûkta.

24. After having bathed, he must feed the gods and the manes, while standing in the water with his wet clothes on.

25. If (being unable to remain in water after having bathed) he has changed his dress, (he must feed the gods and the manes,) after having crossed the bathing-place (and reached the bank).

26. (But) he must not wring his bathing-dress till he has satisfied the gods and the manes.

27. After having bathed [1] and sipped water, he must sip water (once more) according to the rule.

28. He must offer (sixteen) flowers to Purusha,

---

veda X, 9, 1–3, &c. — [3] Taitt. Sa*m*h. V, 6, 1, 1–2, &c. — [4] Rig-veda I, 23, 22, &c.

20. Rig-veda I, 22, 20, &c.

21. Taitt. Brâhm. II, 4, 4, 9; 6, 6, 3; cf. Vâ*g*asan. Sa*m*h. XX, 20; Atharva-veda VI, 115, 3.

22. Rig-veda V, 81, &c.

24. 'The use of the particle *k*a indicates that he must anoint himself after having bathed.' (Nand.)

27. [1] This expression refers back to the whole proceeding described above, up to the wringing of the bathing-dress. (Nand.)

while muttering the Purushasûkta, one with each verse.

29. Afterwards (he must offer) a libation of water.

30. He must first offer one to the gods with the Tîrtha sacred to the gods.

31. Then he must offer another to the manes with the Tîrtha sacred to the manes.

32. In offering the latter he must first of all feed (the manes of) his next of kin (such as his father, mother, maternal grandfather, uncles, brothers, &c.)

33. After that (he must feed) his relatives (such as a sister's son, a father-in-law, a brother-in-law, &c.) and distant kinsmen (such as the sons of his father's sisters and of his mother's sisters).

34. Then (he must feed) his (deceased) friends.

35. According to the above rule he must bathe every day.

36. After having bathed, he must mutter as many purifying Mantras as possible.

37. And he must mutter the Gâyatrî even more often (than other Mantras);

38. And the Purushasûkta.

39. There is nothing more sublime than those two (prayers).

40. One who has bathed is thereby entitled to perform the offerings to the Visvedevâs and to the manes, to mutter sacred texts, and to exercise the duty of hospitality, as prescribed by law.

30, 31. See LXII, 3, 4.

37, 38. 'Or the meaning of these two Sûtras is, that the Gâyatrî and the Purushasûkta always have to be muttered besides the other Mantras.' (Nand.)

40. Nand. refers the term vidhinodite to a separate duty, that

41. Distress and misfortune, bad dreams and evil thoughts are taken from him even who only sprinkles himself with water (no matter from where it comes): that is the law.

42. He who regularly takes the prescribed bath (every morning), does not experience the tortures of Yama's hell. By the regular bath criminals even obtain their absolution.

LXV.

1. Now then, after having duly bathed, and duly washed his hands and feet, and duly sipped water, he must worship Bhagavat Vâsudeva (Vish*n*u), who is without beginning and end, before an idol or on the sacrificial ground.

2. Having called up in his mind (Vish*n*u to life, with the Mantra)[1], 'The two A*s*vins possess life, may they (give you life),' and having invited (Vish*n*u) with the Anuvâka (beginning with the words), 'They get their minds ready[2],' he must worship him with his knees, his hands, and his head[3].

---

of worshipping the gods; the particle *ka* to the propitiation of the planets by sacrifices and other such duties; and the particle tathâ to optional acts, such as the gift of a cow to a Brâhma*n*a, and the like. But this is certainly a too extensive interpretation of the text.

LXV, LXVI. These two chapters treat of the worship of Vish*n*u. (Nand.)

LXV. 1. The fittest place for worshipping Vish*n*u is upon a *S*âlagrâma (ammonite) stone. (Nand.)

2. [1] Kâ*th*aka XI, 7. The rendering of this Mantra is conjectural, as the reading is uncertain. Nand. states expressly that it is quoted from the Kâ*th*aka. — [2] See LXIV, 22. — [3] 'The particle *ka* indicates that he must also worship Vish*n*u in his mind, and with his speech, by saying, 'Om, adoration to Bhagavat Vâsudeva.' (Nand.)

3. With the three Mantras (beginning with the words), 'Ye waters are,' he must (fetch and) announce the Arghya (or water for washing the hands).

4. With the four Mantras (beginning with the words), 'The golden-coloured,' (he must fetch and announce) the water for washing the feet;

5. With (the one Mantra, beginning with the words), 'May the waters of the plain propitiate us,' the water which is to be sipped;

6. With (the one Mantra, beginning with the words), 'Carry away (all) that, O ye waters,' the water destined for the bath;

7. With (the four Mantras, beginning with the words, 'Proud) of the chariot, of the poles, the hero,' unguents and ornaments;

8. With (the one Mantra, beginning with the words), 'A youth, splendidly arrayed,' a garment;

9. With (the one Mantra, beginning with the word), 'Blooming,' a flower;

10. With (the one Mantra, beginning with the

3, 4. See LXIV, 18.

5. This Mantra is found Atharva-veda I, 6, 4; XIX, 2, 2; Taitt. Âra*n*y. VI, 4, 1. Nand. states that it is ka*th*asâkhîya, from the *S*âkhâ of the Ka*th*as; but I have not found it in the Berlin MS. of the Kâ*th*aka, the only complete MS. in existence of that work.

6. See LXIV, 18.

7. This Mantra also belongs to the Ka*th*a school, according to Nand. It is not found in the MS. of the Kâ*th*aka, but it occurs in the Taitt. Brâhm. II, 7, 7, 2. The above translation is in part according to Sâya*n*a's Commentary on the Taitt. Brâhm.

8. Rig-veda III, 8, 4, &c.

9. Taitt. Sa*m*h. IV, 2, 6, 1; Kâ*th*. XVI, 13; Atharva-veda VIII, 7, 27. Nand. says that it is a Taittirîya Mantra.

10. Kâ*th*. II, 7; Vâgas. Sa*m*h. I, 8 (cf. Mahîdhara's Commentary). Nand. says that it is a Taittirîya Yagus.

words), 'Thou art murderous (dhûr), slay (dhûrva) (the slayer),' incense (dhûpa) ;

11. With (the one Mantra, beginning with the words), 'Thou art splendour and light,' a lamp ;

12. With (the one Mantra, beginning with the words, 'I have praised) Dadhikrâvan,' a Madhuparka (honey-mixture) ;

13. With the eight Mantras (beginning with the word), ' Hira*n*yagarbha,' an offering of (other) eatables.

14. A chowrie, a fan, a looking-glass[1], an umbrella, a (palanquin or other) vehicle, and a (throne or other) seat, all these objects he must announce (and place before) the god (Vish*n*u), muttering the Gâyatrî (at the same time).

15. After having thus worshipped him, he must mutter the Purushasûk*t*a. After that, he who wishes to obtain eternal bliss must make oblations of clarified butter, while reciting the same hymn.

LXVI.

1. He must not make an oblation to the gods or to the manes with water collected at night.

2. He must not give any other fragrant substance than sandal, or musk, or (fragrant) wood (of the odoriferous Devadâru tree), or camphor, or saffron, or the wood of the *G*âtîphala tree ;

3. Nor a garment dyed with indigo ;

---

11. Vâ*g*as. Sa*m*h. XXII, 1. Nand. states that this Mantra belongs to the *S*âkhâ of the Ka*th*as ; but I have not met with it in the Kâ*th*aka.

12. Rig-veda IV, 39, 6, &c.

13. Rig-veda X, 121, 1–8 ; Kâ*th*. XL, 1, &c.

14. [1] Thus the term mâtrâ is interpreted by Nand.

4. Nor an ornament made of factitious jewels or gold;

5. Nor (a flower) having a nasty odour;

6. Nor one that has no odour at all;

7. Nor one grown upon a thorny plant.

8. But he may give even a flower grown upon a thorny plant, if it is white and sweet-smelling.

9. He may give even a red flower, if it is saffron, or a water-flower (such as the red lotus).

10. (He must) not (give) any animal substance (such as claws or horns) for the incense.

11. (He must) not (give) anything but clarified butter or oil for the lamp.

12. (He must) not (give) forbidden food at the offering of eatables;

13. Nor the milk of goats or female buffalos, though it is lawful food (otherwise);

14. Nor the flesh of five-toed animals, of fishes, and of boars.

15. Fully prepared for the sacrifice and pure, he must announce (and offer up to Vish*n*u) all the oblations, with his mind fixed upon the deity, with a cheerful heart, and free from precipitation or anger.

LXVII.

1. After having swept the place around the (kitchen) fire, sprinkled it with water all around,

---

9. The particle *k*a indicates that fragrant oleander and the like is also permitted. (Nand.)

13. See LI, 38.

14. This prohibition refers to those species of five-toed animals, fish, and boars, whose flesh is not in general forbidden. (Nand.) See LI, 3, 6, 21.

LXVII. 1–32. Âsv. I, 2; Gobh. I, 4; Pâr. I, 12; II, 9; *S*ânkh. II,

strewed (Ku*s*a grass) all around, and sprinkled (the latter) with water all around, he must take out of all dishes the uppermost part and offer it:

2. To Vâsudeva, to Sankarsha*n*a, to Pradyumna, to Aniruddha, to Purusha, to Satya, to A*k*yuta, to Vâsudeva.

3. Afterwards (he must offer twelve burnt-oblations) to Agni, to Soma, to Mitra, to Varu*n*a, to Indra, to Indra and Agni united, to the Vi*s*vedevâs, to Pra*g*âpati, to Anumati, to Dhanvantari, to Vâstoshpati, and to Agni Svish*t*ak*ri*t (the god of the fire who causes the proper performance of the sacrifice).

4. Then let him make a Bali-offering with that which has been left of the dishes.

5. To (the serpent demons) Taksha and Upataksha,

6. (Strewing the two Balis) on both sides of the fire, to the east of it (on the north-eastern side first, and on the south-eastern side afterwards).

14; M. III, 84–94; Y. II, 103–108; Âpast. II, 2, 3; II, 2, 4, 1–13; Gaut. V, 10–18. — 33–46. Â*s*v. I, 24; Gobh. IV, 10; Pâr. II, 9, 12–16; I, 3; *S*ânkh. II, 15–17; M. III, 99, 100, 102, 103, 111–118; Y. I, 107–113; Âpast. II, 2, 4, 11–20; II, 3; II, 4; Gaut. V, 21–45. Regarding the parallel passages of the Kâ*th*aka and Mânava G*ri*hya-sûtras, see the Introduction. This chapter treats of the Vaisvadeva sacrifice. (Nand.)

1. Nand. infers from a text of *S*aunaka, that the particle atha points to the recitation of the Purushasûkta as an initiatory ceremony.

2. Regarding this Sûtra, see the Introduction. The oblations to be offered are eight in number, one for each invocation.

3. Devapâla, in his Commentary on the corresponding section of the Kâ*th*aka G*ri*hya-sûtra, states that the deities to whom burnt-oblations are offered (Sûtra 3) shall be invoked with the word svâhâ, 'hail!' and those for whom Bali-offerings are strewed upon the ground, with the word nama*h*, 'adoration.'

6–8. These three Sûtras have been translated in accordance

7. (Then let him offer other seven Balis) to all (the seven Ish*t*akâs or goddesses of the bricks of the altar, also to the east of the fire, while pronouncing the Mantras), 'Thy name is Ambâ; thy name is Dulâ; thy name is Nitatnî (Nitatnir); thy name is *K*upu*n*îkâ (and so on).'

8. (He must offer four Balis with the Mantras), 'O Nandinî; O Subhagâ; O Suma*n*galî; O Bhadra*n*karî,' (placing the Balis) in the corners (beginning with the south-eastern corner and proceeding) towards the south.

9. (He must place two Balis), addressed to *S*rî Hira*n*yakesî and to the trees, near the firm pillar [1].

10. (He must place two Balis), addressed to Dharma and Adharma and to M*ri*tyu, near the door.

11. (He must place one Bali), addressed to Varu*n*a, in the water-jar.

12. (With the words, 'Adoration be) to Vish*n*u,' (he must place one Bali) in the mortar.

13. (With the words, 'Adoration be) to the Maruts,' (he must place one Bali) on the mill-stone.

14. (In the apartment) on the roof (let him place two Balis) addressed to Vai*s*râva*n*a (Kubera) the king, and to all created beings.

15. (With the words, 'Adoration be) to Indra and to Indra's ministers,' (he must place two Balis) in the eastern part (of the house).

with Devapâla's readings and his remarks on them. Nand. wrongly refers the four names mentioned in 7 to the four quarters of the globe. The Mantra quoted in 7 is found complete in the Kâ*th*aka, XL, 4, and, in a modified form, in the Taitt. Sa*m*h. IV, 4, 5, 1.

9. [1] 'I. e. the pillar which supports the house.' (Nand.) It appears from an analogous passage of the Mânava Gr*i*hya-sûtra, that a pillar in the middle of the house is meant.

16. (With the words, 'Adoration be) to Yama and to Yama's ministers,' (he must place two Balis) in the southern part.

17. (With the words, 'Adoration be) to Varu*n*a and to Varu*n*a's ministers,' (he must place two Balis) in the western part.

18. (With the words, 'Adoration be) to Soma and to Soma's ministers,' (let him place two Balis) in the northern part.

19. (With the words, 'Adoration be) to Brahman and to Brahman's ministers,' (let him place two Balis) in the centre (of the house).

20. (Let him throw) in the air (a Bali) addressed to Âkâ*s*a (the air).

21. (With the words, 'Adoration be) to the goblins roaming by day,' (let him place a Bali) on the sacrificial ground.

22. (With the words, 'Adoration be to the goblins) roaming by night,' (let him offer a Bali in the same place at the Vai*s*vadeva which takes place) at night.

23. Afterwards he must offer upon blades of Ku*s*a grass, having the points turned towards the south, balls of rice to his father, to his grandfather, and to his great-grandfather, to his mother, to his grandmother, and to his great-grandmother, proclaiming at the same time their name and race (and adding the word Svadhâ, 'reverence').

24. Along with the balls of rice let him give ointments, flowers, incense, eatables, and the like.

25. After having fetched a jar with water, let him

---

24. 'And the like' means betel and the sacrificial fee for the Brâhma*n*as.' (Nand.)

25. This has to be done with the words, svastitva*m* brûhi, 'say

cause a Brâhma*n*a to say the benediction (and give him the jar).

26. (The share) of dogs, crows, and *S*vapa*k*as let him strew upon the earth.

27. And let him give (a mouthful of food as) alms.

28. By honouring guests he obtains the highest reward.

29. Let him assiduously honour a guest who arrives in the evening (after the Vai*s*vadeva is over).

30. Let him not suffer a guest to stay at his house unfed.

31. As the Brâhma*n*as are lords over all other castes, and as a husband is lord over his wives, a guest is the lord of a householder.

32. By honouring a guest he obtains heaven.

33. (One who has arrived as) a guest and is obliged to turn home disappointed in his expectations, takes away from the man, to whose house he has come, his religious merit, and throws his own guilt upon him.

34. A Brâhma*n*a who stays for one night only as a guest, is called atithi (a guest); because he does not stay for a long time, therefore is he termed atithi.

---

the benediction.' (Nand.) The benediction, according to Deva-pâla, consists of the Purushasûkta, the Kanikrada (Vâ*g*as. Sa*m*h. XIII, 48), and other Mantras.

27. According to Nand., who argues from a passage of Bau*dh*â-yana, the particle *k*a implies that he should feed Brâhma*n*as also.

33. This proverb is also found in the Mahâbhârata XII, 6995, in the Hitopade*s*a I, 56 (64 ed. Johnson), and in the Mârka*nd*eya-purâ*n*a XXIX, 31. See Böhtlingk, Ind. Sprüche, 134.

34. Atithi in this derivation is supposed to mean 'one who does not stay for a whole tithi or lunar day.'

35. Let him not consider a Brâhmana fellow-villager or an acquaintance as his guest, though he has come to the house where his wife and his fires are.

36. But if a Kshatriya has come to his house in the way of a guest, let him hospitably entertain him also, to his heart's desire[1], after the Brâhmana guests have eaten.

37. Should a Vaisya or a Sûdra come to his house as guests, he must even give food to them (at the same time and) with his servants, and treat them with kindness (but not like guests in the proper sense of the term).

38. To (members of) other castes (such as Mûrdhâvasiktas) and to friends (or relatives or) other such persons, who have come to his house out of attachment, let him offer such food as happens to be there, to the best of his power, at the time when his wife takes her meal.

39. One recently married (but not yet delivered to her husband), an unmarried damsel, a sick woman, and a pregnant woman: to these let him give food unhesitatingly, even before his guests.

40. The foolish man who eats first himself, without having offered food to those (persons that have been mentioned), is not aware that he will himself be food (after death) for dogs and vultures.

41. After the Brâhmanas, (the Kshatriyas who have come as guests), the friends and relatives, (the parents and others) whom he is bound to maintain,

---

36. [1] This is Kullûka's rendering of the term kâmam (on M. III, 111). According to Nand., it means that he is at liberty to feed such guests or no.

38. The wife takes her meal when the husband has eaten. (Nand.)

(and the servants) have made their repast, let man and wife eat the leavings themselves.

42. Having shown honour to the gods, to the manes, to men, to those whom he is bound to maintain, and to the household deities (as well as to dogs, crows, and the rest), let a householder enjoy that which has been left.

43. He who cooks food for himself only, eats nothing but sin : for that alone is considered as fit food for the virtuous, which is left, after the (customary) oblations have been offered.

44. By the daily recitation of the Veda, by the Agnihotra, by sacrificing, and by austerity, a householder does not obtain such excellent places of abode (after death) as by honouring a guest.

45. Whether he arrives in the evening or in the morning, he must offer a seat and water to his guest, and food, to the best of his ability, after having shown him marks of honour as the law directs [1].

46. By giving (to a guest) shelter, a bed, ointments for his feet, and a lamp : for each of these gifts singly he reaps the same reward as for the gift of a cow.

LXVIII.

1. He must not eat during an eclipse of the moon or of the sun.

---

45. [1] For the rules regarding the reception of a guest, see Âsv. I, 24, and the other Grihya-sûtras ; M. III, 119 seq., and the other Dharmasâstras.

LXVIII. 12. M. IV, 55. — 14. M. IV, 45 ; Y. I, 131 ; Âpast. II, 8, 19, 18. — 19. M. IV, 74. — 20. M. IV, 65. — 21. M. IV, 63 ; Gaut. IX, 56. — 23. M. IV, 74. — 26. M. III, 106 ; Âpast. II, 4, 8, 4. — 27. M. IV, 62 ; Âpast. II, 8, 18, 1 ; II, 8, 20, 10 ; Gaut. IX, 58. — 29. M. IV, 75. — 34. M. IV, 76. — 37. M. IV, 37 ; Y.

2. He shall eat, after having previously bathed, when the eclipse is over.

3. If (the sun or moon) have set before the eclipse was over, he must bathe, and on the next day he may eat again, after having seen (the sun or moon rise).

4. A cow or a Brâhmana having met with a calamity, he must not eat on that day.

5. If the king has met with an accident, (he must not eat on that day).

6. An Agnihotrin, who is absent on a journey, must eat at that time of the day when the Agnihotra is supposed to be over.

7. He may also eat at that time of the day when the Vaisvadeva is supposed to be over.

8. On the days of new and full moon (he may eat at that time) when he supposes the sacrifice customary on those days to have been performed.

I, 135. — 38. M. IV, 82. — 40. Âpast. I, 11, 31, 1. — 42, 43. M. II, 54 ; Y. I, 31 ; Gaut. IX, 59. — 46. Sânkh. IV, 11, 10 ; M. IV, 43 ; Y. I, 131 ; Gaut. IX, 32. — 47. M. IV, 63 ; Y. I, 138 ; Âpast. II, 1, 1, 3 ; Gaut. IX, 9. — 48. M. IV, 62. — 49. M. IV, 65 ; Gaut. XVII, 13. 'The injunctions regarding meals having been given in the previous chapter, he now proceeds to propound some prohibitions concerning the same subject.' (Nand.)

2, 3. Nand. states that in both of these Sûtras it has to be understood, that the bath occasioned by the eclipse must be followed by the ordinary bath, which precedes every meal.

6. An Agnihotrin is one who daily performs the Agnihotra. Regarding the Agnihotra and the times for its performance, see LIX, 2.

7. The term Vaisvadeva includes not only the oblation to the Visvedevâs (LXVII, 3), but also the Bali-offerings and the entertainment of a guest, &c., as prescribed in LXVII, 4 seq. (Nand.)

8. According to Nand., the use of the particle ka implies, that this rule applies equally to the first days of the moon's increase and wane.

9. He must not eat during an indigestion;

10. Nor at midnight;   11. Nor at noon;

12. Nor in the twilight;

13. Nor dressed in wet clothes;

14. Nor without his upper garment;

15. Nor naked;

16. Nor in water (nor in a boat);

17. Nor lying stretched out on the back;

18. Nor sitting on a broken stool;

19. Nor reclining on a couch;

20. Nor from a broken dish;

21. Nor having placed the food on his lap;

22. Nor (having placed the food) upon the ground;

23. Nor from the palm of his hand.

24. That food which has been seasoned with salt (after having been cooked) he must not eat.

25. He must not abuse children (eating in the same row with him).

26. (He must) not (eat) dainties alone.

27. (He must) not (eat) substances from which the fat has been extracted.

28. Nor (must he eat) roasted grain in the day-time.

29. At night (he must not eat) anything mixed with sesamum-seeds.

---

9. According to Nand., the use of the particle *ka* implies a prohibition to eat again, after having partaken of a *S*râddha meal.

15. See note on LXIV, 5.

24. Nand., quoting a passage of Vâsish*tha* (XIV, 28), states the use of the particle *ka* to imply, that food twice cooked and food cooked in a frying-pan should also be avoided.

27. This rule refers to skimmed milk and to a dough made of ground sesamum, from which the oil has been extracted. (Nand.)

30. Nor (must he eat at night) sour milk or ground barley.

31. Nor (must he eat) the leaves of the mountain ebony, or of the banyan, or of the holy fig-tree, or of the hemp plant.

32. (He must) not (eat) without having first given to eat (to the gods and to the Brâhma*n*as);

33. Nor without having made a burnt-offering first ;

34. Nor without having sprinkled his feet ;

35. Nor without having sprinkled his hands and his face ;

36. While having the remains of food on his mouth or hands, he must not take clarified butter.

37. Nor must he look at the moon, or at the sun, or at the stars (while unclean).

38. Nor must he touch his head (while unclean).

39. Nor must he recite the Veda (while unclean).

40. He must eat facing the east ;

41. Or facing the south ;

42. And after having honoured his food [1] ;

43. And cheerfully, adorned with a garland of flowers, and anointed with unguents.

---

42. [1] Nand. describes the ceremony of ' honouring one's food' as follows : ' He must first sprinkle the food, while reciting the Gâyatrî and the Vyâh*ri*tis (see LV, 10). Then he must sprinkle water all around it, with the Mantra, " Forsooth, I sprinkle righteousness around thee." After that he must sip water with the Mantra, " Thou art an imperishable basis " (Taitt. Âra*n*y. X, 32, rendered according to Sâya*n*a's Commentary), and offer up five oblations to Prâ*n*a, &c. (see Dr. Bühler's note on Âpast. II, 1, 1, 2). Finally he must eat in silence, without blaming the food, and taking care to leave some remnant of it in the dish, and sip water again, with the Mantra, " Thou art an imperishable covering "' (Taitt. Âra*n*y. X, 35, according to Sâya*n*a).

44.   He must not eat up his food completely;

45.   Unless it consist of sour milk, or honey, or (clarified) butter, or milk, or ground barley, or meat, or sweetmeats.

46.   He must not eat together with his wife, nor in the open air, nor standing, nor in the presence of many (hungry spectators), nor must many eat in the presence of one (hungry spectator).

47.   Let him never eat in an empty house, in a house where the sacred fires are preserved, or in a temple dedicated to the gods.   Neither must he drink water out of his joined hands, or satiate himself to repletion.

48.   Let him not take a third meal (over and above the two regular meals in the mornings and evenings), nor let him ever take unwholesome food. He must eat neither too early, nor too late, and he must take no food in the evening, after having fully satiated himself in the morning.

49.   He must not eat bad food (whether injurious to health or otherwise reprehensible), nor from a bad dish (which is similar to the dishes used by barbarians, or which has been defiled by a wicked man eating from it), nor lying on the ground, nor with his feet raised upon a bench, nor sitting on his hams with a cloth tied round his legs and knees.

---

46. Nand. thinks that this rule refers to those wives only who belong to a lower caste than their husbands.

48. 'Too early' means before sunrise; 'too late' means immediately before sunset. (Nand.)

LXIX.

1. He must not have connection with his wife on the eighth, or fourteenth, or fifteenth day of the half-month.

2. And (he must avoid connubial intercourse) after having partaken of a Srâddha;

3. And after having given (a Srâddha);

4. And after having been invited to a Srâddha;

5. And while performing a vow of abstinence (such as that to be kept on the day before a Srâddha, or the fast to be observed on the eleventh day of the half-month);

6. And one who has performed the initiatory ceremony of a Soma-sacrifice;

7. And in a temple, in a burial-ground, and in an empty house;

8. And at the root of a tree (or shrub);

9. And in the day-time; 10. And in the twilight;

11. And with one unclean (or in her courses);

12. And while he is unclean himself; 13. And with one anointed with unguents; 14. And being anointed himself; 15. And with one sick; 16. And while he is sick himself.

17. He must not have connection, if he wishes to enjoy a long life, with a woman who has a limb too little, nor with one who has a limb too much, nor with one older than himself, nor with a pregnant woman.

LXIX. 1. M. IV, 128; Y. I, 79. — 9. Âpast. II, 1, 1, 16. — 15. Gaut. IX, 28. The subject of daily duties being absolved, he now goes on to state (in Chapters LXIX, LXX) the rules that must be observed during the night. (Nand.)

4. The invitations to a Srâddha are issued on the day before it is to take place. (Nand.)

LXX.

1.   He must not sleep with his feet wet;

2.   Nor facing the north or the west;

3.   Nor naked;   4. Nor on wet (fresh) bamboo;

5.   Nor in the open air;

6.   Nor on a bedstead made of Palâsa-wood;

7.   Nor on one made of the wood of five trees;

8.   Nor on one made of the wood of a tree which has been split by an elephant;

9.   Nor on a bedstead made of the wood of a tree that has been kindled by lightning;

10.   Nor on a broken bedstead;

11.   Nor on one made of scorched wood;

12.   Nor on one made of the wood of a tree that used to be watered with a jar;

13.   Nor in a burial-ground, nor in an empty house, nor in a temple;

14.   Nor with people who are restless of limb;

15.   Nor with women;

16.   Nor on grain, nor (in a stable of) cows, nor (on the couch of any of his) Gurus, nor on the fire-place, nor (in a building dedicated to the) gods.

17.   He must not sleep while the remnants of

LXX. 1. M. IV, 76. — 2. Y. I, 136. — 3. Âsv. III, 9, 6; M. IV, 75; Gaut. IX, 60. — 13. M. IV, 57. — 17. Sânkh. IV, 11, 17; Âpast. I. 1, 2, 24 ; Gaut. II, 13.

7. Nand. mentions three explanations of this term: 1. a bedstead made of five pieces of wood (or of the wood of five trees); 2. a bedstead made of any of the five kinds of wood enumerated in the Vishnu-purâna; 3. a bedstead made of any of the five kinds of wood enumerated in Sûtras 8–12. The second explanation is inadmissible, because part of the species of wood mentioned in the passage of the Vishnu-purâna referred to is identical with those enumerated in Sûtras 8–12.

food are on his hands or face, nor in the day-time, nor in the twilight, nor upon ashes, nor in a place soiled (by excrements and the like), nor in a wet place, nor on the top of a mountain.

LXXI.

1. Now[1] he must not contemn any one (whether of equal rank, or of higher or lower rank than himself).

LXXI. 1. M. IV, 135; Y. I, 153. — 2. M. IV, 141. — 3. Gaut. II, 17. — 4. Gobh. III, 5, 29. — 4–6. M. IV, 17, 18; Y. I, 129, 123. — 8. M. IV, 19. — 9. M. IV, 34; Âpast. I, 11, 30, 13; Gaut. IX, 3. — 11. Gobh. III, 5, 15. — 13–16. M. IV, 36; Y. I, 133. — 14. Sânkh. IV, 11, 21. — 17–21. M. IV, 37. — 17, 18. Pâr. II, 7, 6; Sânkh. IV, 11, 2; Âpast. I, 11, 31, 20. — 23. Pâr. II, 7, 8; M. IV, 38. — 25. M. IV, 43. — 26. Âsv. III, 9, 6; Sânkh. IV, 11, 1; M. IV, 53; Y. I, 135; Gaut. IX, 48. — 32–35. M. IV, 56, 53; Y. I, 137. — 36, 37. M. IV, 54, 53; Y. I, 137. — 39. M. IV, 65. — 40. Âpast. II, 8, 20, 11; Gaut. IX, 32. — 42, 43. M. IV, 70; Âpast. I, 11, 32, 28; Gaut. IX, 51. — 44. M. IV, 69. — 45. M. IV, 74; Y. I, 138; Gaut. II, 17. — 46. M. IV, 69. — 47. M. IV, 66; Gaut. IX, 4, 5. — 48–52. M. IV, 80. — 53. Sânkh. IV, 12, 18; M. IV, 82. — 54. M. IV, 250; Y. I, 214. — 55. M. IV, 55. — 56. M. IV, 57; Y. I, 138. — 58. M. IV, 57; Sânkh. IV, 11, 6. — 59. Sânkh. IV, 11, 6; Gaut. IX, 16. — 60. M. IV, 58. — 61, 62. Âpast. I, 11, 31, 9, 10. — 62. Pâr. II, 7, 14; M. IV, 59; Y. I, 140; Gaut. IX, 23. — 63–68. M. IV, 60, 61. — 69–71. M. IV, 63, 64. — 70. Pâr. II, 7, 3. — 72–74. M. IV, 138; Y. I, 132. — 75. Y. I, 153. — 76. M. IV, 137; Y. I, 153. — 77. M. IV, 94. — 79. M. IV, 144. — 80, 81. M. IV, 164. — 82. M. VIII, 299. — 83. M. IV, 135; Y. I, 153. — 84, 85. M. IV, 176; Y. I, 156. — 86. M. IV, 150. — 87. M. IV, 2, 246; Gaut. IX, 73. — 90. M. IV, 155; Y. I, 154. — 91, 92. M. IV, 156, 158.

1. [1] This chapter treats of the duties of a Snâtaka (see XXVIII, 42, note). The particle atha, 'now,' however, signifies that some of these duties are common to the Snâtaka and to the householder, whose special duties have been treated in the previous chapters. (Nand.)

2. He must not mock those who have a limb too little or a limb too much, who are ignorant, or who are poor.

3. He must not serve low people.

4. Let him not engage in work that may keep him from repeating (or teaching) the Veda.

5. Let him wear such a dress as becomes his age,

6. And his sacred knowledge, his descent, his means, and his country.

7. He must not be overbearing.

8. He must constantly consult the holy laws and other (salutary precepts relating to the acquisition of wealth, wisdom, and freedom from disease).

9. He must not wear a worn-out or filthy dress, if he has means (enough to procure a new one).

10. (Even though he lacks firewood or the like necessaries) he must not say to another man, 'I have got none.'

11. He must not wear a garland of flowers which has no smell at all, or an offensive smell, or which is red.

12. Let him wear a garland of water-flowers even though they be red.

13. And (he must wear) a staff made of bamboo;

14. And a jar with water;

15. And a sacrificial string made of cotton thread;

16. And two golden ear-rings.

---

2. The particle *ka* refers to ugly persons and the rest, enumerated by Manu IV, 141. (Nand.)

8. The use of the particle *ka* implies, according to Nand., that his frame of mind and his speech should also be in conformity with his age, &c., as ordained by Manu IV, 18.

13–16. Nand., arguing from texts of Baudhâyana and of Manu (IV, 36), takes the use of the particle *ka* in Sûtras 13 and 14 to

17. He must not look at the rising sun;

18. Nor at the setting (sun);

19. Nor (must he look at the sun) shining through an awning of cloth (under which he is lying).

20. Nor at the sun reflected in a looking-glass or in water;

21. Nor at the midday sun;

22. Nor at the face of any of his Gurus while he is angry;

23. Nor at his own image reflected in oil or in water;

24. Nor reflected in a dirty looking-glass;

25. Nor at his wife eating;

26. Nor at a naked woman;

27. Nor at a man in the act of discharging urine (or voiding excrements);

28. Nor at an elephant (or other dangerous animal) broken loose from the rope that ties him;

29. Nor at a fight between bulls (or elephants or buffalos) or the like animals, while he is himself standing in a (crowd or any other) place, from which it would be difficult for him to effect his escape;

30. Nor at one insane;

---

imply that a Snâtaka must wear three garments, an under garment, an upper garment, and a mantle, and in Sûtra 16, that he must carry about him a bushel of Ku*s*a grass.

19. This rule appears to refer, likewise, to the custom of suspending, by a tree or a post, an upper garment or a piece of cloth, in order to ward off the rays of the sun.

20. The particle *ka* here is used, according to Nand., in order to include 'the sun, while it is eclipsed,' as mentioned by Manu IV, 37.

29. 'As shown by *k*a, a place where arrows, spears, or other missiles are falling down, is also intended here.' (Nand.)

31. Nor at one intoxicated;

32. He must not throw any impure substances into the fire;

33. Nor blood;   34. Nor poison;

35. Neither (must he throw any of those substances) into water.

36. He must not step over a fire.

37. He must not warm his feet (by the fire).

38. He must not wipe (the dirt from his feet) with blades of Kusa grass.

39. He must not wash (his feet) in a vessel of white copper.

40. He must not (wash) one foot with the other.

41. He must not scratch the ground (with a piece of wood or the like).

42. He must not crush clods of earth.

43. He must not cut grass.

44. He must not tear his nails or the hairs (of his beard or others) with his teeth.

45. He must avoid gambling;

46. And the heat of the sun just risen.

47. He must not wear a garment, or shoes, or a garland, or a sacrificial string which had before been worn by another.

48. He must not give advice to a Sûdra;

49. Nor (must he give him) the leavings of his food, nor the residue of an oblation (unless he is his own servant);

---

46. Besides the above interpretation of the term bâlâtapa, which is proposed by Kullûka also (on M. IV, 69), Nand. mentions two others: 1. the heat of that time of the day when the cows are collected for milking; 2. the heat of the autumn season. The particle *ka*, according to Nand., is used in order to include the smoke of a burning corpse and the other forbidden objects mentioned by Manu IV, 69.

50. Nor (must he give him) sesamum ;

51. Nor (must he point out) the sacred law to him ;

52. Nor (must he prescribe) a penance (for him for atonement of a sin).

53. He must not scratch his head or his belly with both hands joined.

54. He must not reject sour milk or the Sumanas flower (when offered to him).

55. He must not take off his garland (from his head) himself (but he may cause another to do so).

56. Let him not rouse (a superior) from sleep.

57. He must not (by harsh speeches and the like) render disaffected one who is well affected towards him.

58. He must not speak to a woman in her courses ;

59. Nor to barbarians or low-caste persons.

60. When a sacred fire, or an idol, or a Brâhmana is near, he must stretch forth his right hand (from his upper garment).

61. If he sees a cow trespassing upon another man's field, he must not announce it (to the owner of that field).

62. And if he sees a calf sucking (at the udder of a cow, he must not announce it to the owner of the latter).

63. He must not endeavour to please overbearing men (by flattering their pretensions).

64. He must not dwell in a kingdom governed by a Sûdra king ;

---

54. Nand. states that this rule does not contain a vain repetition of the rule laid down above (LVII, 10), as the latter refers to householders and the former to Snâtakas.

65.   Nor in one abounding with wicked people ;

66.   And he must not live (in a kingdom) in which there are no physicians ;

67.   Nor in one afflicted (with a disease or other calamity).

68.   And (he must not stay) long on a mountain.

69.   He must not (walk or otherwise) exert himself without a purpose.

70.   He must not dance or sing.

71.   He must not make a noise by slapping (his left arm, after having placed it upon his right shoulder, with his right hand).

72.   He must not make vulgar speeches.

73.   He must not tell an untruth.

74.   He must not say disagreeable things.

75.   He must not strike any one upon a vital part.

76.   He must not despise himself if he wishes to enjoy long life.

77.   He must often repeat his prayers at each twilight (if he wishes to live long).

78.   He must not play with (venomous) serpents or with weapons.

79.   He must not touch the cavities of his body without a cause.

80.   He must not raise a stick against another man.

81.   One who deserves punishment he must strike in order to punish him.

82.   (He must strike) him upon his back with a shoot of bamboo or with a rope.

---

75. 'Others' take this Sutra to mean, that he must not make public another man's misconduct. (Nand.)   This interpretation is proposed by Vigñânesvara, on Yâgñavalkya I, 153.

79. See XXIII, 51.

83. He must take care not to revile a god, a Brâhma*n*a, the Sâstras, or the high-minded (*Ri*shis).

84. And (he must avoid) gain and pleasure repugnant to duty.

85. (He must avoid) even lawful acts which may give offence to mankind.

86. On the days of new and full moon let him make a propitiatory offering.

87. He must not cut even grass (on those two days).

88. He must adorn himself (with garlands, sandal, and the like).

89. Thus he must observe established customs.

90. Those customs, which have been explicitly ordained in revealed and in traditional texts, and which are practised by the virtuous, must always be observed by a righteous man with subdued passions.

91. By adhering to established usage he attains to old age; this is the way to obtain that state in the next life which he desires, and imperishable riches, this is the way to destroy the effect of (bodily) marks foreboding future misfortunes.

92. He who observes the usages established among the virtuous, who is a believer in revelation, and free from ill-will, lives a hundred years, even

---

84. '"Or repugnant to the final liberation," as the use of the particle *k*a implies.' (Nand.)　See Manu VI, 37.

85. The use of the particle *k*a, Nand. argues from Manu IV, 176, implies that acts which may cause future pain should also be avoided.

88. The use of the particle *k*a, according to Nand., implies that he must also observe auspicious rites and established customs, as ordained by Manu IV, 145. The latter injunction is, however, expressly given in the next Sûtra.

though he does not possess any external marks of prosperity.

LXXII.

1. He must persist in keeping his mind and his organs of sense under restraint.

2. Restraint of the mind implies restraint of the senses.

3. One who has acquired complete command over himself, gains this world and the next.

4. One who has no command over himself, reaps no fruit from any of his acts (whether worldly or tending to the acquisition of spiritual merit).

5. Self-restraint is the best instrument of purification; self-restraint is the best of auspicious objects; by self-restraint he obtains anything he may desire in his heart.

6. The man who rides (as it were) in a chariot drawn by his five senses and directed by his mind (as the charioteer), who keeps it on the path of the virtuous, can never be overcome by his enemies (lust, wrath, and greed), unless the horses (unrestrained by the charioteer) run away with the chariot.

7. As the waters (of all streams) are stored up (and reabsorbed) in the ocean, which, though being filled with them, remains unmoved and tranquil, even so that man, in whose mind the passions are stored up (and dissolved), obtains perfect calmness: but not he who strives after the gratification of his desires.

LXXII. 7 = Bhagavad-gîtâ II, 70. This chapter treats of duties which are common to all the four orders. (Nand.)

LXXIII.

1. One desirous of celebrating a *S*râddha must invite the Brâhma*n*as on the day before (it is to take place).

2. On the next day, in the forenoon, if it falls in the bright half of the month, and in the afternoon, if it falls in the dark half of the month, the Brâhma*n*as, who must have duly bathed and duly sipped water, must be placed by him, in the order of their seniority[1] (or) of their sacred knowledge, upon seats covered with Ku*s*a grass.

3. (He must entertain) two (Brâhma*n*as) facing the east at the *S*râddha of the gods (Vi*s*vedevâs), and three facing the north at the *S*râddha of the manes;

4. Or one only at each *S*râddha.

5. After having (worshipped the Vi*s*vedevâs and) offered a burnt-oblation: during the recitation of the first Pañ*k*aka (pentad) at a *S*râddha repast con-

---

LXXIII. 1–32. Â*sv*. II, 5, 11–14; IV, 7; Gobh. IV, 2–4; Pâr. III, 10, 48–55; *S*â*n*kh. IV, 1; M. III, 125, 204–259; Y. I, 225–248; Âpast. II, 7, 17, 11–19; Gaut. XV. Regarding the corresponding section of the Kâ*th*aka Gr*i*hya-sûtra, see Introduction. This chapter opens the section on *S*râddhas (funeral oblations), which consists of thirteen chapters (LXXIII–LXXXV. Nand.)

. 1. The Ekoddish*t*a and Sapi*nd*îkara*n*a *S*râddhas have been described above, XXI. The rules given in the present chapter refer to all the remaining kinds of *S*râddhas. See 5–9, LXXIV, LXXVI–LXXVIII. ·

2. [1] At the *S*râddha of the manes the oldest Brâhma*n*a represents the great-grandfather; the one next to him in age, the grandfather; the youngest of the three, the father of the sacrificer. (Nand.)

5–9. The three Pañ*k*akas referred to in Sûtras 5–9 are respectively vv. 1–5, 6–10, and 11–15 of Kâ*th*aka XXXIX, 10. (Nand.) The great majority of the Mantras quoted in Sûtras 11–26 have

sisting of undressed grain or performed for the gratification of a special desire[1];

6. At a Srâddha repast consisting of meat, during the recitation of the second Pañkaka;

7. At a new moon (Srâddha), during the recitation of the last Pañkaka;

8. On the Ashtakâs (or eighth days) of the (three) dark halves subsequent to the full moon day of the month Âgrahâyana (or Mârgasîrsha)[1], during the recitation of the first, second, and last Pañkakas respectively;

9. Likewise, on the Anvashtakâs (or ninth days of the dark halves of those months);

10. He must invite the manes, after having received permission to do so from the Brâhmanas[1].

11. Having driven away the Yâtudhânas by strewing grains of sesamum and by reciting the two

---

not been traced in the Berlin MS. of the Kâthaka, nor indeed in any other Samhitâ of the Veda, but there can be no doubt that they belong to the school of the Kathas, as nearly all are quoted by their Pratîkas in the Kâthaka Grihya-sûtra, and given at full in Devapâla's Commentary on the latter. The above renderings of the Pratîkas rest upon Devapâla's interpretations. That the rules in 5 seq. teach the performance of a Srâddha according to the rites of the Katha school, is confirmed by Nand. in his remarks on 5 seq. and 9 seq.

5. [1] See LXXVIII.

8. The days referred to are the eighth days of the dark halves of the months Mârgasîrsha, Pausha, and Mâgha.

9. 'And on the Srâddhas taking place on the seventh day of the dark half, as ka indicates.' (Nand.) This statement does not, however, deserve much credit, as such Srâddhas are neither mentioned in our work nor in the Kâthaka Grihya-sûtra.

10. [1] 'The permission of the Brâhmanas has to be asked with the Mantra, "I shall invite (the manes);" and their answer must be, "Invite them." ' (Nand.)

11. The Yâtudhânas are a class of demons supposed to disturb

Mantras (the first of which begins with the words), 'May the Asuras go away;'

12. He must invite the manes (with the four Mantras), 'Come near, O ye manes,' '(Conduct) them all (here), O Agni,' 'May my (ancestors) come near,' 'This is your (share), O ye manes.' Then let him prepare the water for washing the feet with scented water, which has been mixed up with Kusa grass and sesamum, while reciting (the three Mantras), 'Those standing [1],' 'Speech is imperishable,' and 'What my mother (has sinned) [1],' and offer it (to the Brâhmanas); let him prepare the Arghya (or water mixed with Dûrvâ grass, flowers, &c.) and offer it to them; let him offer to the Brâhmanas, to the best of his power, Kusa grass, sesamum, clothes, flowers, ornaments, incense, and lamps; let him take food sprinkled with clarified butter; let him look them in the face with the Mantra, 'O ye Âdityas, Rudras, and Vasus;' let him say, 'I will offer an oblation in the fire,' and if the Brâhmanas say, 'Offer an oblation,' let him offer three burnt-oblations [2].'

13. After having consecrated the offerings with the Mantras, 'They, who are my ancestors,' 'This is your (share), O ye manes,' and 'This offering,' he must pour (what is left of) the food into such vessels as happen to be there, or (into golden ones at the offering addressed to the Visvedevâs and) into silver

---

the effect of a Srâddha. The second Mantra, according to Devapâla, is from the Rig-veda, X, 15, 1.

12. [1] These two Mantras are also quoted, with slight variations, by Sânkhâyana III, 13, 5.— [2] The three burnt-oblations have to be accompanied by the recitation of the three Mantras, 'To Soma accompanied by the manes svadhâ namah; to Yama Angiras svadhâ namah; to Agni who takes the offerings addressed to the manes svadhâ namah.' (Nand.)

ones (at the offering addressed to the manes), and offer it first to the two Brâhma*n*as facing the east (who have been invited to the *S*râddha of the gods).

14. Afterwards he must offer it to the (three) Brâhma*n*as facing the north (who represent his three ancestors, addressing himself) to his father, grandfather, and great-grandfather, (and calling out) their name and race.

15. While the Brâhma*n*as are eating the food, let him mutter (the three Mantras), 'Whatever (trickles down) through my fault,' 'With days and nights[1],' and 'Whatever (limb) of yours, Agni.'

16. And (let him mutter) the Itihâsa (Epics), Purâ*n*a (Legends), and Dharma*s*âstra (Institutes of the Sacred Law).

17. Near the leavings let him deposit upon blades of Ku*s*a grass with the ends turned towards the south one ball of rice for his father, while saying, 'Earth is (like) a spoon, imperishable (satisfaction).'

18. With the Mantra, 'Air is (like) a spoon, imperishable (satisfaction,' let him deposit) a second ball for his grandfather.

19. With the Mantra, 'Heaven is (like) a spoon, imperishable (satisfaction,' let him deposit) a third ball for his great-grandfather.

20. With the Mantra, 'Those ancestors who

---

14. The formula of this invocation, according to Nand., is this, 'To NN., my ancestor, of the Gotra NN., who is like a Vasu, (I offer) this food, svadhâ nama*h*.' The use of the particle *k*a, according to the same, implies that the maternal grandfather and the other maternal ancestors must also be addressed, as ordained below (LXXV, 7).

15. [1] A similar Mantra is quoted, *S*âṅkh. III, 13, 5.

have died,' let him place a garment (upon the balls).

21. With the Mantra, 'Give us sons, O ye manes.' (let him place) food upon them.

22. With the Mantra, 'Enjoy it, O ye manes, partake of it, each according to his share[1],' let him wipe off the grease from his hands with the ends of the blades.

23. With the Mantra, '(Ye waters) imparting vigour[1],' let him sprinkle the balls to the right with the wet (remainder of the food), and offer the Argha[2], flowers, incense, unguents, and rice, and other victuals and dainties to the Brâhma*n*as.

24. And (he must offer them) a jar with water. which has been mixed up with honey, clarified butter, sesamum, and (ointments, oil, and the like).

25. The Brâhma*n*as having eaten and being satisfied, let him sprinkle the food (as much as has been left by them) and the grass with the Mantra, 'Mayest thou not fail me,' and strew the food near the leavings; and having asked them, 'Are you satisfied? Is (the *S*râddha) finished,' he must first give water for sipping to the Brâhma*n*as facing the north, and then to those facing the east: and he must sprinkle the place where the *S*râddha has been offered (with water, with the Mantra), 'Well sprinkled.' All these rites he must perform while holding blades of sacred grass in his hand.

26. Afterwards he must, while turning his face towards the Brâhma*n*as facing the east, circumambu-

---

22. [1] Vâ*g*asan. Sa*m*h. II, 31; Kâ*th*. IX, 6.
23. [1] Vâ*g*asan. Sa*m*h. II, 34. — [2] The Arg*h*a is a respectful offering, the ingredients of which vary.

late them from left to right, with the Mantra, 'What a crow (may have eaten of my offering),' and turn back again; he must honour them with sacrificial fees, to the best of his power, saying, 'May you be satisfied,' and on their answering, 'We are satisfied,' he must address them with the Mantra, ' The gods and the manes.'

27. After having given (to all) water (with the Mantra, 'May the food and water and whatever else I gave you be) imperishable,' (and) calling out their name and race, and having added the Mantra, 'May the Vi*s*vedevâs be satisfied,' he must ask, with folded hands, and with an attentive and cheerful mind, the following (benediction) from the Brâhma*n*as facing the east:

28. ' May the liberal-minded in our race increase in number, and may the (study of the) Vedas and our progeny (also increase). May faith not depart from us, and may we have plenty to bestow on the poor.'

29. They shall answer, ' Thus let it be.'

30. (The second half of the benediction shall be as follows), 'May we have plenty of food, and may we receive guests. May others come to beg of us, and may not we be obliged to beg of any one.'

31. After having received this double benediction (through the Brâhma*n*as saying, ' Thus let it be '),

32. He must dismiss the Brâhma*n*as, with the Mantra, ' With all food[1],' after having honoured them according to custom, accompanied them (as far as the limits of his estate), and taken his leave of them.

---

32. [1] Rig-veda VII, 38, 8.

LXXIV.

1. After having worshipped, on each Ash*t*akâ, the gods and performed, with vegetables, meat, and cakes respectively, a *S*râddha (according to the rules given in the last chapter), he must, on each Anvash-*t*akâ[1], worship the gods and offer a burnt-oblation in the same way as on the Ash*t*akâs (i. e. reciting the same three Pañ*k*akas successively), and entertain Brâhma*n*as in the same way as (directed) before (in the preceding chapter), in honour of his mother, his paternal grandmother, and his paternal great-grand-mother, honour them with presents, accompany them (as far as the limits of his estate), and dismiss them[2].

2. Then he must dig (six) trenches.

3. On the border of these trenches, to the north-east of them, he must light fires and place balls of rice.

4. On the border of three of the trenches (he must place balls) for the men, and on the border of the other three (he must place balls) for the women.

LXXIV. 1–8. Â*sv.* II, 5; Gobh. IV, 2; Pâr. III, 3, 10–12; *S*ânkh. III, 13, 6; M. IV, 150. Regarding the corresponding section of the Kâ*th*aka Gr*i*hya-sûtra, see the Introduction.

1. [1] See LXXIII, 8, 9; LXXVI, 1. — [2] Nand. considers the use of the particle *k*a to imply that the father together with the other paternal ancestors, and the maternal grandfather along with the other maternal ancestors, should also be invoked, which would make in all nine ancestors to be invoked. The first part of this observation appears to be correct, but the maternal grandfather and the rest are neither referred to in the following Sûtras, nor in the Kâ*th*aka Gr*i*hya-sûtra.

2. Nand. gives it as his opinion, that nine trenches should be made, three of which are to be for the maternal grandfather, &c. But Sûtra 4 refers to three trenches for the men only, and the Kâ*th*aka Gr*i*hya-sûtra expressly mentions the number of six trenches.

5. He must fill the three trenches for the men with water mixed with food.

6. (He must fill) the three trenches for the women with milk mixed with food.

7. (And he must fill up) each triad of trenches singly with sour milk, meat, and milk.

8. After having filled (the trenches), he must mutter the Mantra, 'May this (food) be imperishable for ye men and for ye women.'

LXXV.

1. He who makes a Srâddha-offering while his father is alive, must offer it to those persons to whom his father offers (his Srâddhas).

2. (If he offers a Srâddha) while both his father and grandfather are alive, (he must offer it to those persons) to whom his grandfather (offers his Srâddhas).

3. While his father, grandfather, and great-grandfather are alive, he must offer no Srâddha at all.

4. He whose father is dead (but whose grandfather is alive), must first of all offer a ball of rice to his father, after that, two balls to the two ancestors coming before his grandfather (or to his great-grandfather and to his fourth ascendant).

5. He whose father and grandfather are dead (but whose great-grandfather is alive), must first offer two balls to those two, and then offer one ball to the grandfather of his grandfather.

---

7. Nand. renders this Sûtra differently, in accordance with his own theory regarding the number of the trenches.

LXXV. 1. M. III, 220. — 4. M. III, 221. — 7. Y. I, 228.

6. He whose grandfather is dead (but whose father and great-grandfather are alive), must give one ball to his grandfather and two balls to the father and grandfather of his great-grandfather.

7. An intelligent man must offer Sraddhas to his maternal grandfather, and to the father and grandfather of him, in the same way (as to his paternal ancestors), duly modifying the Mantras. But the Sraddhas addressed to other relatives, (uncles, brothers, and the like, must be performed) without Mantras.

LXXVI.

1. The (twelve) days of new moon, the three Ashtakâs, the three Anvashtakâs, a Mâgha day (i.e. 'day on which the moon enters the lunar asterism Maghâ'), which falls on the thirteenth of the dark half of the month Praushthapada, and the two seasons when rice and barley grow ripe (or autumn and spring):

---

7. The Mantras are those quoted above, in Chapters LXXIII and LXXIV. They have to be modified, i.e. the names of the maternal ancestors must be put in, and the verb &c. of the sentence be altered accordingly. (Nand.)

LXXVI. 1. M. III, 122, 273, 281; IV, 150; Y. I, 217, 260; Gaut. XV, 2; Âpast. II, 7, 16, 4–6.

1. Nand. infers from a passage of Âsvalâyana (Grihya-sûtra II, 4, 3) that Srâddhas to be offered on the day before each Ashtakâ are also intended here. See, however, note on LXXIII, 9. The same proposes two explanations of the term Mâghî : 1. It has to be separated from the following words, and refers directly to the day of full moon in the month Mâgha, and indirectly to the days of full moon in Âshâdha, Kârttika, and Vaisâkha as well, as indicated in a passage of the Brâhma-purâna. 2. It has to be connected with the clause following it. This latter interpretation, on which the rendering given above is based, is supported by Manu (III, 273, 274),

2. Thus have the regular times for a *S*râddha been declared by the lord of creatures. He who fails to perform a *S*râddha on those days, goes to hell.

LXXVII.

1. The sun's passage from one sign of the zodiac to another ;

2. The two equinoctial points ;

3. The two solstitial points particularly ;

4. The (Yoga) Vyatîpâta ;

5. The constellation under which (the sacrificer himself, or his wife, or his son) is born ;

6. A time of rejoicing (as, when a son has been born, or another happy event happened) :

7. These occasions for a *S*râddha the lord of creatures has pronounced optional; a *S*râddha which is performed on these occasions gives infinite satisfaction (to the manes).

8. No *S*râddha must be performed in the twilight or at night by an intelligent man. A *S*râddha may be performed at those times also when an eclipse (of the sun or of the moon) takes place.

9. For a *S*râddha which is offered them at the time of an eclipse satisfies the manes, as long as the moon and the stars exist, and procures immense advantages and the satisfaction of all his desires to the sacrificer.

Yâg*ñ*avalkya (I, 260), according to the interpretations of Kullûka and Vig*ñ*âne*s*vara, and to the Vish*n*u-sûtra itself (LXXVIII, 52).

LXXVII. 1–6, 9. Y. I, 217, 218. — 6. Â*s*v. IV, 7, 1 ; Sânkh. IV, 4. — 8. M. III, 280 ; Âpast. II, 7, 17, 23, 25.

4. This is the seventeenth among the twenty-seven Yogas or astrological divisions of the zodiac. (Nand.)

7. The meaning is, that the *S*râddhas mentioned in this chapter are naimittika, 'occasional.' (Nand.)

LXXVIII.

1. By performing a *S*râddha on Sunday he procures everlasting freedom from disease.

2. (By performing a *S*râddha) on Monday he becomes beloved [1].

3. (By performing it) on Tuesday (he procures) success in battle.

4. (By performing it) on Wednesday (he enjoys) all his desires.

5. (By performing it) on Thursday (he acquires) such religious knowledge as he desires.

6. (By performing it) on Friday (he acquires) wealth.

7. (By performing it) on Saturday (he procures) longevity.

8. (By performing it under the Nakshatra or constellation) K*ri*ttikâs (he gains) heaven.

LXXVIII. 8–35. M. III, 277; Y. I, 264–267. — 36–50. M. III, 276; Y. I, 261–263; Âpast. II, 7, 16, 8–22; Gaut. XV, 4. — 52, 53. M. III, 273, 274. Regarding Sûtras 1–7, see the Introduction.

1. Nand. states that the *S*râddhas mentioned in this chapter are of the kâmya sort, i.e. 'offered for the gratification of a special desire.'

2. [1] This is Nand.'s interpretation of the term saubhâgyam. It might also be taken in its usual acceptation, as meaning 'happiness.'

8–35. Those names of the twenty-eight Nakshatras or lunar asterisms, which I have included in parentheses, are from Nand.'s Commentary. Most of the objects which are said to be gained by the *S*râddhas mentioned in Sûtras 8–35 are connected etymologically, or through their import, with the names of the particular Nakshatras under which they are performed. Thus the term push*t*i, 'prosperity,' in Sûtra 13, is etymologically connected with Pushya; the term mitra, 'friend,' in 22, is connected with Maitra; the term râ*g*yam, 'royalty,' in 23, is connected with *S*âkra, the name of that Nakshatra being derived from *S*akra, a name of Indra, the king of the gods, &c.

9. (By performing it under the constellation) Rohi*n*î (he obtains) progeny.

10. (By performing it under the constellation) Saumya (or M*ri*ga*s*iras he procures) the superhuman power of a pious Brâhma*n*a.

11. (By performing it under the constellation) Raudra (or Ârdrâ he reaps) the fruit of his labours.

12. (By performing it under the constellation) Punarvasu (he procures) land.

13. (By performing it under the constellation) Pushya (or Tishya he procures) prosperity.

14. (By performing it under the constellation) Sârpa (or Â*s*leshâs he obtains) beauty.

15. (By performing it under the constellation) Paitrya (or Maghâ he enjoys) all his desires.

16. (By performing it under the constellation) Bhâgya (or Pûrvaphâlgunî) he becomes beloved[1].

17. (By performing it under the constellation) Âryama*n*a (or Uttaraphâlgunî he procures) wealth.

18. (By performing it under the constellation) Hasta (he acquires) superiority among his kindred.

19. (By performing it under the constellation) Tvâsh*t*ra (or *K*itrâ he procures) handsome sons.

20. (By performing it under the constellation) Svâti (he procures) success in trade.

21. (By performing it under the constellation) Vi*s*âkhâs (he acquires) gold.

22. (By performing it under the constellation) Maitra (or Anurâdhâ he procures) friends.

23. (By performing it under the constellation) *S*âkra (or *G*yvesh*th*â he procures) royalty.

24. (By performing it under the constellation) Mûla (he procures good results in) agriculture.

---

16. [1] See 2, note.

25. (By performing it under the constellation) Âpya (or Pûrvâshâ*dh*âs he procures) success in sea-voyages.

26. (By performing it under the constellation) Vai*s*vadeva (or Uttarâshâ*dh*âs he enjoys) all his desires.

27. (By performing it under the constellation) Abhi*g*it (he procures) superiority.

28. (By performing it under the constellation) *S*rava*n*a (he enjoys) all his desires.

29. (By performing it under the constellation) Vâsava (or Dhanish*th*âs he procures success in preparing) salt [1].

30. (By performing it under the constellation) Vâru*n*a (or *S*atabhishâ he obtains) freedom from disease.

31. (By performing it under the constellation) Â*g*a (or Pûrvabhâdrapadâ he obtains) copper vessels.

32. (By performing it under the constellation) Âhirbudhnya (or Uttarabhâdrapadâ he obtains) a house.

33. (By performing it under the constellation) Paush*n*a (or Revatî he acquires) cows.

34. (By performing it under the constellation) Â*s*vina (or A*s*vinî he obtains) a horse.

35. (By performing it under the constellation) Yâmya (or Bhara*n*î he procures) longevity.

36. (By offering it) on the first day of a lunar fortnight (he procures) a house and handsome wives.

---

29. [1] Lava*n*am means either 'salt' or 'beauty' or 'medicinal herbs and fruits.' (Nand.)

37. (By offering it) on the second day (he procures) a beautiful daughter (and sons-in-law).

38. (By offering it) on the third day (he enjoys) all his desires.

39. (By offering it) on the fourth day (he procures) cattle.

40. (By offering it) on the fifth day (he procures) handsome sons.

41. (By offering it) on the sixth day (he obtains) success in gaming.

42. (By offering it) on the seventh day (he procures good results in) agriculture.

43. (By offering it) on the eighth day (he procures success in) trade.

44. (By offering it) on the ninth day (he procures) cattle [1].

45. (By offering it) on the tenth day (he procures) horses.

46. (By offering it) on the eleventh day (he procures) sons endowed with the superhuman power of a pious Brâhma*n*a.

47. (By offering it) on the twelfth day (he procures) gold and silver.

48. (By offering it) on the thirteenth day he becomes beloved.

49. (By offering it) on the fifteenth day (he enjoys) all his desires.

---

44. [1] Nand. infers from a passage of Yâgñavalkya (I, 266) that the term 'cattle' here refers to horses and other one-hoofed animals. See, however, the next Sûtra.

48. The term saubhâgyam is stated by Nand. (with reference to Y. I, 264) to denote 'superiority among his kindred,' in this Sûtra. But there is no cogent reason for deviating here from that interpretation of the term which he proposes in his Commentary on Sûtras 2 and 16. See above.

50. For *Srâddhas* for those who have been killed in battle the fourteenth day is ordained.

51. There are two stanzas on this subject recited by the manes :

52. 'May that excellent man be born to our race, whosoever he may be, who attentively offers a *Srâddha* in the rainy season[1] on the thirteenth of the dark half,

53. 'With milk profusely mixed with honey; and (he who offers such *Srâddhas*) during the whole month Kârttika and (in the afternoon) when the shadow of an elephant falls towards the east.'

LXXIX.

1. He must not perform a *Srâddha* with water collected at night.

2. On failure of Ku*s*a grass he must employ Kâ*s*a or Dûrvâ grass instead.

3. Instead of a garment (he may give) cotton thread.

4. He must avoid (giving) the fringe of cloth, though it be of cloth not yet used.

5. And (he must not give) flowers having a nasty odour, or no odour at all, the blossoms of thorny plants, and red flowers.

---

52. [1] The term prâv*ri*tkâle, 'in the rainy season,' probably refers to one month only of the rainy season, the month Bhâdrapada or Praush*th*apada. See above, LXXVI, 1, and M. III, 273, 274, with Kullûka's Commentary; Y. I, 260, with Vig*ñ*âne*s*vara's Comment.

LXXIX. 8, 16. M. III, 226, 227, 235, 257; Âpast. II, 8, 19, 19–22. — 19–21. M. III, 229.

5. The use of the particle *k*a implies, according to Nand., who quotes a text in support of his assertion, that the leaves of the Kadamba, Bèl, Ketaka, and Bakula trees, as well as those of the Barbara plant and of the thorn-apple tree, are also included in this prohibition.

6. He may give white and sweet-smelling flowers, even though grown on thorny plants, and aquatic flowers, even though they be red.

7. He must not give marrow or fat instead of a lamp.

8. He may give clarified butter or sesamum-oil.

9. He must not give (the nails or horns) of animals instead of the incense of all kinds (prescribed for a Srâddha).

10. He may give bdellium mixed up with honey and clarified butter.

11. He may give sandal, saffron, camphor, aloe wood, or Padmaka wood instead of an ointment.

12. He must not salt (the dishes) publicly (after they have been cooked).

13. He must not give clarified butter, condiments, or the like (i. e. sour milk, milk, &c.) with his hands.

14. He must use metallic vessels ;

15. Especially vessels made of silver.

16. He must place (on the sacrificial ground) vessels made of the horn of the rhinoceros, blankets made of the hair of the mountain-goat, the skin of a black antelope, sesamum, white mustard, unbroken grains, (silver and copper vessels and other) purificatory objects, and (a goat and other animals or objects), by which the demons are kept aloof.

---

7. 'Or mustard-oil or any other such substance, as *ka* indicates.' (Nand.)

8. 'Or the juice of plants, as mentioned by Sankha, on account of vâ.' (Nand.)

13. He must give those liquids with a spoon or similar implement. (Nand.)

16. According to Nand., the particle *ka* refers to other purificatory things, viz. the following seven, ' milk, water from the Ganges, honey, silken cloth, a grandson, blankets made of the hair of the

17. He must avoid to use pepper, (the onion called) Mukundaka, (the pot-herb called) Bhûstrina, (the leaves, blossoms, or roots of) the Sigru tree, mustard-seeds, (the plant) Nirgundî, (the fruit or leaves of) the Sâl tree, the plant Suvarkalâ, the (pumpkin-gourd called) Kûshmânda, the bottle-gourd, the egg-plant, (the plants or pot-herbs called) Pâlakyâ, Upotakî, and Tandulîyaka, the herbs of the safflower, the Pindâluka (root), and the milk of female buffalos.

18. And (he must not use the bean called) Râga-mâsha, (the lentil called) Masûra, stale food, and factitious salt.

19. Let him avoid wrath.

20. He must not shed a tear.

21. He must not be in a hurry.

22. In offering the clarified butter and other (liquids, such as condiments, sour milk, milk, and the like) he must use metallic vessels, vessels made of the horn of the rhinoceros, and vessels made of the wood of the Phalgu tree.

23. There is a Sloka on this subject :

24. 'That which has been offered in vessels made of gold, or of silver, or of the horn of the rhinoceros, or of copper, or of Phalgu wood, becomes imperishable (and brings infinite reward to the sacrificer).'

---

mountain-goat, and sesamum.' The last two are, however, already contained in the above enumeration.

17. The term 'buffalo's milk' includes here, according to a text quoted by Nand., the milk of sheep, of antelopes, of camels, and of all one-hoofed animals.

18. 'As shown by ka, chick-peas and other grains and herbs mentioned in a Smriti must also be avoided.' (Nand.)

19. 'This rule applies both to the sacrificer and to the guests at a Srâddha.' (Nand.)

LXXX.

1. Sesamum, rice, barley, beans, water, roots, fruits, vegetables, Syâmâka grain, millet, wild rice, kidney-beans, and wheat satisfy (the manes) for a month;

2. The flesh of fishes (excepting those species that are forbidden), for two months;

3. The flesh of the common deer, for three months;

4. The flesh of sheep, for four months;

5. The flesh of birds (of those kinds that may be eaten), for five months;

6. The flesh of goats, for six months;

7. The flesh of the spotted deer, for seven months;

8. The flesh of the spotted antelope, for eight months;

9. Beef, for nine months;

10. Buffalo's meat, for ten months;

11. The meat of a hornless goat, for eleven months;

12. The milk of a cow, or preparations from it, for a year.

13. On this subject there exists a stanza, which the manes utter:

14. '(The pot-herb) Kâlasâka (sacred basil), (the prawn) Mahâsalka, and the flesh of the (crane called) Vârdhrînasa [1], (and of) a rhinoceros having no horn, is food which we always accept.'

LXXX. 1–14. M. III, 267–272; Y. I, 257–259; Âpast. II, 7, 16, 23–II, 7, 17, 3; II, 8, 18, 13; Gaut. XV, 15.

14. [1] This is the first of the two interpretations which Nand. proposes of the term Vârdhrînasa. It is supported by Âpastamba's

LXXXI.

1. He must not place the food upon a chair.

2. He must not touch it with his foot.

3. He must not sneeze upon it.

4. He must drive the Yâtudhânas away by means of sesamum or mustard-seeds.

5. Let him perform the *S*râddha in an enclosed place.

6. He must not look at a woman in her courses;

7. Nor at a dog; 8. Nor at a tame pig;

9. Nor at a tame cock.

10. Let him strive to perform the *S*râddha in sight of a goat.

11. The Brâhma*n*as must eat in silence.

12. They must not eat with their heads covered;

13. Nor with shoes on their feet;

14. Nor with their feet placed upon a stool.

15. Let not men with a limb too little, or with a limb too much, look at a *S*râddha;

16. Nor *S*ûdras; 17. Nor outcasts.

---

commentator, Haradatta, and by Âpastamba himself (I, 5, 17, 36). Nand.'s second interpretation, 'an old white goat,' is probably wrong, although it is supported by the authority of Kullûka and Vig*ñ*âne*s*vara.

LXXXI. 2, 6–9, 11–13, 15, 16, 19. M. III, 229, 236–242. — 4, 5. Gaut. XV, 25, 26. — 7, 16, 17. Âpast. II, 7, 17, 20; Gaut. XV, 24. — 18. M. III, 243. — 20. M. III, 237. — 21–23. M. III, 244–246.

4. Nand. quotes the following Mantra, which has to be recited on this occasion, 'The Asuras, the Râkshasas, and the Pi*s*â*k*as have been driven away.' A similar Mantra occurs in the Vâg*g*asan. Sa*m*h. II, 29.

5. '*K*a indicates that it must be a place inclining to the south, as stated in a Sm*ri*ti.' (Nand.)

6. This and the following Sûtras refer both to the host at a *S*râddha and to the guests invited by him. (Nand.)

18. If at the time of a Srâddha a Brâhmana or an ascetic (has come to his house), he must feed him, if (the invited) Brâhmanas permit it.

19. The Brâhmanas must not declare the qualities of the sacrificial dishes, even though asked to do so by their host.

20. As long as the dishes remain warm, as long as (the Brâhmanas) eat in silence, as long as the qualities of the sacrificial food are not declared by them, so long the manes enjoy it.

21. Having brought together (the remainder of) all the sorts of substantial food and (of the vegetables and) the like, he must sprinkle it with water, and place it before the Brâhmanas, who have taken their meal, strewing it on the ground.

22. The leavings (that have remained in the dishes) and what has been strewn (in the manner just mentioned) upon the blades of Kusa grass (spread on the ground) is the share of such (Brâhmanas) as have died before they were initiated, and of husbands who have deserted wives descended from good families.

23. What has dropped on the ground from the dishes, at a sacrifice addressed to the manes, they declare to be the share of servants, provided they be not dishonest or depraved.

LXXXII.

1. At a (Srâddha) offering to the Visvedevâs let him not enquire (into the qualities or descent of) a Brâhmana (whom he means to invite).

LXXXII. 1, 2. M. III, 149. — 3–29. M. III, 150–166; Y. I, 222–224; Âpast. II, 7, 17, 21; Gaut. XV, 16–18.

2. But at a (*Sr*âddha offering) to the manes he must enquire as closely as possible (into the qualities and descent of a Brâhma*n*a, whom he means to invite).

3. He must not invite (to a *Sr*âddha) such as have a limb too little, or a limb too much;

4. Nor such as follow an occupation forbidden (by the Veda or by the traditional law) [1].

5. Nor those who act (deceitfully) like cats;

6. Nor those wearing the insignia of some particular order, without having a claim to them;

7. Nor astrologers;

8. Nor Brâhma*n*as who subsist upon the offerings made to an idol which they attend;

9. Nor physicians;

10. Nor sons of an unmarried woman;

11. Nor sons of the son of an unmarried woman;

12. Nor those who sacrifice for a multitude of persons;

13. Nor those who offer sacrifices for a whole village;

14. Nor those who offer sacrifices for *S*ûdras;

15. Nor those who offer sacrifices for those for whom it is forbidden to sacrifice (such as outcasts and others);

16. Nor those for whom the ceremony of initiation has not been performed;

17. Nor those who sacrifice for such;

---

4. [1] The particle *k*a, according to Nand., in this Sûtra, refers to other categories, mentioned by Atri, viz. persons belonging to the same Gotra, or descended from the same *R*i*sh*i ancestors as the sacrificer, and unknown persons.

8. '*K*a indicates here that thieves and wicked persons are also intended, as stated in a Sm*ri*ti.' (Nand.)

18. Nor those who do work on holidays ;

19. Nor malignant informers ;

20. Nor those who teach (the Veda) for a fee ;

21. Nor those who have been taught (the Veda) for a fee ;

22. Nor those who subsist on food given to them by a *S*ûdra ;

23. Nor those who have intercourse with an outcast ;

24. Nor those who neglect their daily study of the Veda ;

25. Nor those who neglect their morning and evening prayers ;

26. Nor those who are in the king's service ;

27. Nor 'naked' persons ;

28. Nor those who quarrel with their father ;

29. Nor those who have forsaken their father, mother, Guru, holy fire, or sacred study.

30. All those persons are said to defile a company, because they have been expelled from the community of Brâhma*n*as. Let a wise man avoid carefully, therefore, to entertain them at a *S*râddha.

LXXXIII.

1. The following persons sanctify a company :

2. A Tri*n*â*k*iketa ;

---

27. See LXIV, 5, note.

29. The particle *k*a here refers to the following further persons mentioned in a Sm*ri*ti : a shepherd, one who lives by the prostitution of his own wife, the husband of a woman who had another husband before, and one employed to carry out dead bodies. (Nand.)

LXXXIII. 1-19. M. III, 128-148, 183-186 ; Y. I, 219-221 ; Âpast. II, 7, 17, 22 ; Gaut. XV, 28.

2. Nand. has two explanations of the term Tri*n*â*k*iketa : 1. One who has thrice kindled the Nâ*k*iketa fire. 2. One who has studied,

3. One who keeps five fires;

4. One who can sing the Sâmans called *Gye-shtha*;

5. One who has studied the whole Veda;

6. One who has studied one Vedânga;

7. One who has studied either the Purâ*n*as (Legends), or the Itihâsas (Epics), or grammar;

8. One who has studied one of the Dharma*s*âstras (Institutes of the Sacred Law);

9. One purified by visiting sacred places of pilgrimage;

10. One purified by offering sacrifices;

11. One purified by austere devotion;

12. One purified by veracity;

13. One purified by (constantly muttering) Mantras;

14. One intent upon muttering the Gâyatrî;

15. One in whose family the study and teaching of the Veda are hereditary.

16. One who knows the Trisupar*n*a (the text which thrice contains the word Supar*n*a).

---

in consequence of a vow, the portion of the Yagur-veda called Tri*nâki*keta. See Âpast. II, 7, 17, 22, with Dr. Bühler's note, and the Petersburg Dictionary.

4. Sâma-veda II, 209–211, &c.

7. Grammar is again mentioned here, although it forms part of the Vedângas mentioned in Sûtra 6. But there the Prâti*s*âkhyas are meant. (Nand.)

8. The number of the Smr*i*tis or Dharma*s*âstras, according to Nand., amounts to fifty-seven. The now current tradition gives thirty-six as their number; but upwards of a hundred works of this description must have been actually in existence. See Dr. Bühler's Introduction to the Bombay Digest, p. xii seq.

16. See above, LVI, 23, and Dr. Bühler's note on Âpast. loc. cit. Nand. proposes another interpretation also of the term Trisupar*n*a, ' one who has thrice kindled a fire in honour of Supar*n*a.'

17. A son-in-law;

18. And a grandson. All these persons are worthy (to be fed at a *S*râddha);

19. And, particularly, devotees.

20. There is a stanza recited by the manes, which refers to this subject:

21. 'May that man be born to our race, who feeds a Brâhma*n*a devotee assiduously at a *S*râddha, by which repast we are satisfied ourselves.'

LXXXIV.

1. He must not offer a *S*râddha in a country inhabited by barbarians.

2. He must not visit a country inhabited by barbarians (excepting on a pilgrimage).

3. By (constantly) drinking water from (or bathing in) a pool situated in a foreign (barbarous) country, he becomes equal to its inhabitants.

4. Those countries are called barbarous (mle*k*-*kh*a) where the system of the four castes does not exist; the others are denoted Âryâvarta (the abode of the Âryans).

---

18. According to Nand., the particles *k*a and iti refer to the sister's son and other relatives, as enumerated by Yâ*g*ñavalkya I, 220, 221.

19. Nand. thinks that *k*a here refers to ascetics.

LXXXIV. 2. Nand. quotes a stanza of Devala to the effect that one who has visited the countries of Sindh, of the Sauvîras, Surât, and the adjacent parts, Bengal proper, Kali*n*ga, South Bihâr, and Malwa requires to be initiated a second time.

3. '*K*a refers to pools belonging to *K*and*â*las or other degraded castes.' (Nand.)

4. Âryâvarta is the name of the whole tract of land which extends from the eastern to the western ocean, and is bounded by the Himâlayas and by the Vindhya mountains in the north and south. See Manu II, 21, 22.

LXXXV.

1. A *Srâddha* offered at the (Tîrtha or place of pilgrimage called) Pushkaras confers eternal bliss upon the giver;

2. And so does the muttering of prayers, the offering of burnt-oblations, and the practice of austerities in that place.

3. Even by merely bathing at Pushkara he is purified from all his sins.

4. The same effect may ·be produced at *Gayâ-sîrsha*;

5. And near Va*t*a (Akshayava*t*a);

6. And on the Amaraka*nt*aka mountain;

7. And on the Varâha mountain;

LXXXV. 1. Pushkara, according to the common acceptation of the term, is the name of a celebrated place of pilgrimage near Ag*m*îr, the modern Pokur. See Lassen, Indian Antiquities, I, 113. Nand. quotes a Sm*ri*ti passage to the effect that there are three Pushkaras, and a passage of the Mahâbhârata, in which it is stated that one Pushkara is sacred to Brahman, another to Vish*n*u, and a third to Rudra.

3. Nand. asserts with regard to the use of the name Pushkara in the singular number in this Sûtra, that it means even a single bath has the consequence here mentioned.

4. Gayâ*s*îrsha is the name of a mountain near Gayâ in Bihâr, a celebrated place of pilgrimage. Compare Yâg*ñ*avalkya I, 260.

5. There exists one Akshayava*t*a in Bihâr (Nand.) and another in Prayâga (Allahabad). The 'undecaying banyan-tree' (Akshay Ba*t*) is an object of worship at Allahabad even now, and was so already in the times of Hwen Thsang. See Cunningham, Ancient Geography of India, p. 389; St. Julien, Voyages des Pèlerins Bouddhistes, II, 278.

6. Nand. states that both the Tîrtha called Amaraka*nt*aka on the Mekalâ mountain in the Vindhya range and the whole mountain of that name are meant.

7. 'This is a certain boar-shaped mountain.' (Nand.) It seems very probable that the Tîrtha of Bâramûla, the ancient Varâha-

8. And anywhere on the bank of the Narmadâ (Nerbudda) river;

9. And on the bank of the Yamunâ (Jumna);

10. And, particularly, on the Gangâ;

11. And at Ku*s*âvarta;

12. And at Binduka; 13. And upon the Nîlgiri hills; 14. And at Kanakhala; 15. And at Kub-*g*âmra; 16. And on the Bh*r*igutunga (mountain); 17. And at Kedâra; 18. And on the Mahâlaya (mountain); 19. And on the Na*d*antikâ (river); 20. And on the Sugandhâ (river); 21. And at *S*âkam-bharî; 22. And at Phalgutîrtha; 23. And on the

---

mûla in Ka*s*mîr, is meant. See Bühler, Ka*s*mîr Report, p. 12, where a 'Varâha hill' is mentioned as adjacent to that town.

11. This Tîrtha 'is situated upon the mountain called Tryam-baka, where the Godâvarî river takes its rise.' (Nand.) Tryambaka is the modern Trimbak (the name of a place of pilgrimage situated near Nâsik).

12. 'Binduka is the name of a Tîrtha in the Dekhan. Bilvaka, as other texts read (the MS. on which the two Calcutta editions are based among the number), is the name of another Tîrtha in the Dekhan.' (Nand.)

14. There is one Kanakhala in the Himâlayas, and another near Trimbak. (Nand.)

15. There is one plain of that name in Orissa, and another in Haridvâr. (Nand.)

16. This is the name of a sacred mountain near the Amara-ka*nt*aka range, according to Nand.; in the Himâlayas, according to others. See the Petersburg Dictionary.

17. Kedâra (the Kedâr mountains?) is in the Himâlayas. (Nand.)

18, 19. These two names are not defined by Nand.

20. This is a river in the vicinity of the Saugandhika mountain. (Nand.)

21. *S*âkambharî is the modern Shâmbar, which lies 'in the desert of Marude*s*a, on the salt lake.' (Nand.)

22. 'Phalgutîrtha is a Tîrtha in Gayâ.' (Nand.)

23. Mahâgangâ, 'the great Gangâ,' is the Alakânandâ river

Mahâgangâ;   24. And at Trihalikâgrâma;   25.
And at Kumâradhârâ; 26. And at Prabhâsa; 27.
And particularly anywhere on (the bank of) the
Sarasvatî;

28. At Gangâdvâra (Haridvâr), at Prayâga (Allahabad), where the Gangâ falls into the ocean,
constantly in the Naimisha forest, and especially
at Benares;

29. And at Agastyâsrama;

30. And at Kanvâsrama (on the Mâlinî river);

31. And on the Kausikî (Kosi river);

32. And on the bank of the Sarayû (Surju river
in Oudh);

33. And on the confluence of the Sona (Sone)
and Gyotishâ rivers;

34. And on the Srîparvata (mountain);

(Nand.), which takes its rise in the Himâlayas and falls into the
Ganges.

24. 'Trihalikâgrâma means Sâlagrâma.   There is another
reading, Tandulikâsrama.' (Nand.)

25. This is the name of a lake in Kasmîr, which the god Ku-
mâra by a mighty stroke caused to stream forth from the Kraunka
mountain (see Vâyu-purâna); or Kumâradhârâ is situated near the
southern ocean in the plain of Ishupâta. (Nand.)

26. Prabhâsa is the name of a Tîrtha near Dvârakâ, on the
western point of Kattivar. (Nand.)

27. Regarding the river Sarasvatî and its reputed holiness, see
particularly Cunningham, Ancient Geography of India, I, 331 seq.,
and Manu II, 17.

28. The Naimisha forest is in the northern country. (Nand.)

29. 'Agastyâsrama is situated near Pushkara (Sûtra 1), on the
bank of the Sarasvatî.   There is another Agastyâsrama in the
south, near Svâmisthâna.' (Nand.)

33. The confluence of those two rivers is in the centre of the
Vindhya range.   For the name of the second, another reading is
Gyotîratha. (Nand.)

34. The Srîparvata or Srîsaila, where the Mallikârguna (symbol
of Siva) is worshipped, is in the Dekhan. (Nand.)

35. And at (the Tîrtha situated on the Yamunâ, which is called) Kâlodaka.

36. And at Uttaramânasa (in the Kedâr mountains, in the Himâlayas).

37. And at Vadavâ (in the Dekhan).

38. And at Matangavâpî (in the southern part of Gayâ);

39. And at Saptârsha; 40. And at Vishnupada;

41. And at Svargamârgapada (or Rathamârga);

42. And on the Godâvarî river (in the Dekhan);

43. And on the Gomatî (river);

44. And on the Vetravatî (river);

45. And on the Vipâsâ (river);

46. And on the Vitastâ (river);

47. And on the banks of the Satadru (river);

48. And on the Kandrabhâgâ (river);

49. And on the Irâvatî (river);

50. And on the banks of the Indus;

51. And on the southern Pañkanada;

52. And at Ausaga (?);

53. And at other such Tîrthas;

---

39. Saptârsha, 'the Tîrtha of the seven Rishis' (Nand.), is perhaps the present Satara, in the country of the Mahrattas.

40. Nand. places this Tîrtha in the centre of Gayâ. There is another of the same name, which is placed on the Kailâsa mountain.

43. The Gomatî (the Gunti, near Lucknow) rises in the Naimisha forest. (Nand.) See 28.

44. The Vetravatî (the modern Betwah, near Bhilsah) is situated in Ahikkhattra. (Nand.)

45–49. The Vipâsâ (Beas), Vitastâ (Jhelum or Behut), Satadru (Sutlej), Kandrabhâgâ (Chenâb), and Irâvatî (Ravee) are the five rivers of the Pañgâb (Pañkanada in Sanskrit).

51. This is the name of the confluence of five rivers in the Dekhan : the Krishnâ, Venâ, Tunga, Bhadrâ, and Kona. (Nand.)

52. 'Ausaga (v. l. Augasa; read Ausiga ?) means Sûrpâraka' (Nand.), which was situated probably on the mouth of the Krishnâ (Kistna).

54. And on the banks of (other) holy rivers;

55. And anywhere at the birth-place of a deity, (such as Râma, Krishna, and others);

56. And on sand-banks; 57. And near water-falls; 58. And on mountains; 59. And in arbours (the sporting-places of Krishna); 60. And in woods; 61. And in groves; 62. And in houses smeared with cow-dung; 63. And in 'pleasant spots.'

64. There are some stanzas recited by the manes, which refer to this subject:

65. 'May that person be born to our race, who will give us libations of water, taken from streams abounding with water, especially if their floods (coming from the Himâlayas) are cool.

66. 'May that excellent man be born to our race, who offers us a Srâddha attentively at Gayâsîrsha or at Vata.'

67. A man must wish to have many sons, be-cause if only one of them goes to Gayâ (and offers a Srâddha to him after his death), or if he performs a horse-sacrifice, or if he sets a dark-coloured bull at liberty [1], (he will acquire final emancipation through him.)

LXXXVI.

1. Now follows the ceremony of setting a bull at liberty, (which should take place)

2. On the days of full moon in Kârttika or Âsvina.

3. When performing this rite, he must first ex-amine the bull.

---

63. The term manogña, 'a pleasant spot,' means 'a place close by the house, where sacred basil is planted,' or other such places. (Nand.)

67. [1] See the next chapter.

LXXXVI. 1–18. Pâr. III, 9; Sânkh. III, 11. Regarding the cor-responding section of the Kâthaka Grihya-sûtra, see Introduction.

4. (The bull must be) the offspring of a milch cow having young ones living.

5. He must have all marks.

6. He must be dark-coloured;

7. Or red, but having a white mouth, a white tail, and white feet and horns.

8. He must be one who protects the herd.

9. Then, after having (kindled) a blazing fire among the cows (in the cow-pen) and strewed Kusa grass around it, let him boil with milk a dish sacred to Pûshan, and offer (two oblations) in the fire with the Mantras, 'May Pûshan follow our cows[1],' and 'Here is pleasure[2].' And let a blacksmith mark the bull :

10. On the one flank (the right), with a discus; on the other flank (the left), with a trident.

11. After he has been marked, let him wash the bull with the four Mantras, (beginning with the words), 'The golden-coloured[1],' and with (the five Mantras, beginning with the words), 'May the divine (waters help and propitiate us')[2].

12. Having washed and adorned the bull, he must bring him near, together with four young cows,

---

5. 'I. e. the bull must not be deficient in any limb.' (Nand.) This interpretation is supported by the Grihya-sûtras.

6. Nand. mentions two interpretations of the term nîla, 'dark-coloured :' 1. a bull who is all white, and is therefore said to be of the 'Brâhmana kind;' 2. one whose body is white, whereas his tail, his hoofs, and his face are black, and his horns blue. Cf. L, 25.

8. Nand. interprets yûthasyâkhâdakam by nishektâram, 'one who covers the cows.' My rendering is based upon Devapâla's comment on the corresponding passage of the Kâthaka Grihya-sûtra. See also Pâr. and Sânkh. loc. cit.

9. [1] Rig-veda VI, 54, 5, &c. — [2] Vagas. Samh. VIII, 51; Kâth. Âsv. IV, 6, &c.

11. [1] Taitt. Samh. V, 6, 1, 1, 2, &c. — [2] Rig-veda X, 9, 4–8, &c.

which must also have been washed and decorated, and he must mutter the Rudras [1], the Purushasûkta, and the Kûshmân*d*îs [2].

13. Then let him pronounce in the bull's right ear the Mantra, 'The father of calves;'

14. And the following (Mantras):

15. 'Holy law is a bull and is declared to have four feet [1]: him I choose for the object of my worship; may he protect me wholly.

16. 'This young (bull) I give you as husband (O ye calves), roam about sportingly with him for your lover. May we not be deficient in progeny, O king Soma, and may we live long, and may we not be oppressed by our enemies.'

17. He must drive away the bull together with the calves in a north-eastern direction and give a pair of garments, gold, and a vessel made of white copper to the officiating priest.

18. The blacksmith shall receive as wages as much as he claims, and food prepared with a great deal of butter, and (three) Brâhma*n*as shall be fed.

19. Any pool from which the bull drinks after

---

12. [1] Taitt. Sa*m*h. IV, 5, 1–11. — [2] See LVI, 7.

13. Nand. states expressly that this Mantra is from the Kâ*th*aka. It is found Kâ*th*. XIII, 9; Taitt. Sa*m*h. III, 3, 9, 2; Kâ*th*. Gr*i*hya-sûtra XLVII.

15. [1] This term refers perhaps to the 'four feet of a judicial proceeding.' See Nârada 1, 11; 2, 9.

16. Taitt. Sa*m*h. III, 3, 9, 1, &c. The second half of this Mantra is found in the Kâ*th*aka Gr*i*hya-sûtra only.

18. The clause regarding the 'food,' which has been rendered in accordance with Nand.'s Commentary, might also be construed with 'fed,' which would bring the whole into accordance with the precepts of the Kâ*th*aka Gr*i*hya-sûtra and of the two other Gr*i*hya-sûtras.

having been set at liberty, that entire pool will refresh the manes of him who has set the bull at liberty.

20. The earth which is anywhere dug up by the bull exulting in his strength, is converted into delicious food and drink to satisfy the manes.

LXXXVII.

1. Now on the day of full moon in the month Vaisâkha he must spread out upon a woollen blanket the skin of a black antelope (together with the horns and hoofs), after having adorned the former with gold and the latter with silver, and after having ornamented the tail with a string of pearls.

2. After that, he must cover (that part of the blanket which is not covered by the skin) with sesamum.

3. And he must adorn the navel with gold.

4. He must cover (the skin) with a couple of new garments.

5. He must place all sorts of perfumes and jewels upon it.

LXXXVII. 1. The particle atha, 'now,' indicates the beginning of a new section, treating of gifts. It comprises Chapters LXXXVII–XCIII. (Nand.) The commentator infers from a corresponding passage of the Matsya-purâ*n*a, that the following further rules are implied in this Sûtra. The ceremony may also take place on the full moon days in the months Mâgha, Kârttika, and Âshâ*dh*a, on the twelfth day after the summer solstice, and during an eclipse of the sun or moon. The silver on the hoofs must weigh five Palas, and the gold on the horns ten Suvar*n*as (or two Palas and a half). The place must be pure, smeared with cow-dung, and covered with Ku*s*a grass.

3. 'The Skânda-purâ*n*a states that the eyes must be adorned with jewels.' (Nand.)

5. 'And garlands of flowers and other objects must be placed upon it, as *k*a indicates.' (Nand.)

6. After having placed on its four sides (beginning with the eastern side) four metallic dishes (of copper, silver, white copper, and gold respectively) filled with milk, sour milk, honey, and clarified butter respectively, (and having poured out water) he must give (the skin, seizing it by the tail), to a Brâhmana, who is an Agnihotrin [1], decked with ornaments, and clad in two garments.

7. There are (the following) stanzas in regard to this subject:

8. 'He who bestows (upon a pious Brâhmana) the skin of a black antelope, together with the hoofs and horns, after having covered it with seeds of sesamum and garments, and adorned it with all sorts of jewels:

9. 'That man doubtless obtains the same reward as if he were to bestow the whole earth on him, bordered as it is on every side (by the oceans), together with the oceans and caverns, and with rocks, groves, and forests.

10. 'He who places sesamum, gold, honey, and butter on the skin of a black antelope and gives the whole to a Brâhmana, annihilates the consequences of all his own evil actions.'

LXXXVIII.

1. A cow in the act of bringing forth a young one is (comparable to) the earth.

2. By bestowing such a cow upon a Brâhmana, after having decked her with ornaments, he obtains the same reward as if he were to bestow the earth (upon him).

---

6. [1] See LXVIII, 6, note.
LXXXVIII. 1. Y. I, 207. — 4. Y. I, 206.

3. There is a stanza in regard to this subject:

4. 'One who full of faith and with intense application of mind gives away a pregnant cow, enters heaven for as many Yugas (or ages of the world) as that cow and her calf together have hairs on their bodies.'

LXXXIX.

1. The month Kârttika is sacred to the god Agni.

2. Agni is the first of all gods.

3. Therefore is that man purified from every sin committed during the past year, who persists during the month Kârttika in bathing (daily) out of the village, in muttering the Gâyatrî, and in taking a single meal each day, consisting of food fit for oblations.

4. He who bathes (at the prescribed time, early in the morning) constantly, during the whole month Kârttika, who keeps his organs of sense under control, who mutters (the Gâyatrî), who eats food fit for oblations only, and who governs his passions, is purified from every sin.

XC.

1. If on the fifteenth of the bright half of the month Mârgasîrsha the moon enters the lunar asterism Mrigasiras, he must give at the time when the moon rises (a vessel with) a golden centre, containing a Prastha of ground salt, to a Brâhmana.

2. By (performing) this rite he obtains beauty and good fortune in a future birth.

XC. 3, 5. Âpast. II, 8, 18, 19; II, 8, 19, 1.—7. M. IV, 232.
1. One Prastha = sixteen Palas. (Nand.)

3. If on the full moon day of the month Pausha the moon enters the lunar asterism Pushya, he must rub over his body with a dough prepared with white mustard-seeds, anoint himself with a kumbha [1] of clarified butter made of cow-milk, wash himself with (water and with) all sorts of medicinal herbs, all sorts of perfumes, and all sorts of seeds, wash (an image of) Bhagavat Vâsudeva (Vishnu) with clarified butter, and worship him with perfumes, flowers, incense, with a lamp, with eatables, and the like [2], offer an oblation in the fire with Mantras tending to the praise of Vishnu (such as Rig-veda I, 22, 17, and others), Mantras tending to the praise of Indra (such as Rig-veda VI, 47, 11, and others), Mantras tending to the praise of Brihaspati (such as Rig-veda II, 23, 15, and others, and with one Mantra tending to the praise of Agni Svishtakrit), and cause three Brâhmanas to pronounce the benediction, after having bestowed clarified butter and gold upon them [3].

4. To the priest (who has performed the burnt-oblation for him) he must give a pair of garments.

5. By (performing) this rite he obtains prosperity (pushyate) [1].

6. If on the full moon day in the month Mâgha the moon enters the lunar asterism Maghâ and he performs a *Srâddha* with sesamum on that day, he is purified.

---

3. [1] See V, 12, note. — [2] 'And the like' means 'betel.' (Nand.) — [3] The rite described in this Sûtra appears to be identical with the ceremony called Yugâdya, 'the beginning of the present age of the world,' in later works. See Wilson, On the Religious Festivals of the Hindus, in the Royal Asiatic Society's Journal, IX, 89.

5. [1] This is a play upon words. See LXXVIII, 8, note, and below, Sûtra 9 ; XCII, 14, &c.

7. If on the full moon day in the month Phâlguna the moon enters the lunar asterism Uttaraphâlgunî, and he gives on that day a bedstead, quite complete and covered with good rugs, to a Brâhmana, he obtains an amiable, handsome, and wealthy wife.

8. A woman who does the same, (obtains) a husband (possessing those qualities).

9. If on the full moon day of the month *K*aitra the moon enters the lunar asterism *K*itrâ, and he gives a variegated (*k*itra) garment (to a Brâhmana) on that day, he obtains good fortune.

10. If on the full moon day of the month Vai*s*âkha the moon enters the lunar asterism Vi*s*âkhâ, and he feeds on that day seven Brâhmanas with sesamum mixed with honey, in order to please king Dharma, he is purified from his sins.

11. If on the full moon day of the month *G*yaish*th*a the moon enters the lunar asterism *G*yesh*th*â and he gives on that day an umbrella and a pair of shoes (to a Brâhmana), he becomes possessed of many cows.

12. If on the full moon day of the month Âshâ*dh*a the moon is seen in conjunction with the lunar asterism Uttarâshâ*dh*â and he gives food and drink (to a Brâhmana) on that day, he renders (the satisfaction effected by) them imperishable.

13. If on the full moon day of the month *S*râva*n*a the moon is seen in conjunction with the lunar asterism *S*rava*n*a and he gives a milch cow covered with two garments, together with food (to a Brâhmana), he attains heaven.

14. If on the full moon day of the month Praush-

---

7. Susa*m*skr*i*ta, 'quite complete,' means 'provided with curtains and the like.' (Nand.)

*th*apada (or Bhâdrapada) the moon is seen in conjunction with the lunar asterism Uttaraprosh*th*apadâ (or Uttarabhâdrapadâ), and he gives a cow (to a Brâhma*n*a) on that day, he is cleansed from every sin.

15. If on the full moon day of the month Âsvayu*g*a (or Âsvina) the moon is seen in conjunction with the lunar asterism A*s*vinî, and he gives a vessel filled with clarified butter, and gold (to a Brâhma*n*a) on that day, he obtains an excellent digestive faculty.

16. If on the full moon day of the month Kârttika the moon enters the lunar asterism K*ri*ttikâ, and he bestows on that day, at the time of moonrise, upon a Brâhma*n*a, a white bull, or one of a different colour, together with all sorts of grains, all sorts of jewels, and all sorts of perfumes, after having lighted lamps on both sides (of the bull), he will meet with no danger on perilous roads.

17. If on the third day of the bright half of the month Vai*s*âkha he worships, after having fasted, Vâsudeva (Vish*n*u) with (one thousand and eight, or one hundred) unbroken grains (of barley, while muttering the Mantra, Om namo bhagavate vâsudevâya [1]), and offers up the same in fire, and gives them (to a Brâhma*n*a), he is purified from every sin.

18. And whatever he gives on that day becomes imperishable.

19. If on the twelfth day of the dark half following on the full moon day of the month Pausha, he washes himself, after having kept a fast, with sesamum-seeds, gives water mixed with sesamum

---

17. [1] See XLIX, 1, note.
19. This is evidently the ceremony which is called Sha*t*tiladâna

(to the manes), worships Vâsudeva with sesamum, offers up (part of) the same in fire, gives to Brâhmanas of it, and eats (the remainder himself) he is purified from his sins.

20. (If) on the twelfth day of the dark half following on the full moon day of the month Mâgha, (the moon enters Sravana), he must keep a fast till the moon has entered that asterism, and place two lamps with two large wicks near (an image of) Vâsudeva ;

21. Placing on the right hand (of the image of Vâsudeva, and kindling, a lamp) containing one hundred and eight Palas of clarified butter, with an entire piece of cloth (together with the fringes) dyed with saffron (as wick) in it ;

22. (And placing) on its left, (and kindling, a lamp) containing one hundred and eight Palas of sesamum oil, with an entire piece of white cloth (as wick) in it.

23. He who has performed this rite obtains exquisite happiness, in whatever kingdom, in whatever province, and in whatever race he may be born again.

24. He who gives daily during the whole month Âsvina clarified butter to Brâhmanas, in order to please the two Asvins, obtains beauty.

25. He who feeds daily during that month (three) Brâhmanas with (milk and other) bovine productions, obtains a kingdom.

26. He who feeds on the Revatî day of every month (three) Brâhmanas with rice boiled in milk

---

in later works ; see Wilson loc. cit. The name of the latter is derived from the fact that it consists, precisely like the ceremony described in the present Sûtra, of six acts, in all of which Tila, i. e. sesamum-seeds, forms an essential ingredient.

with sugar and mixed with honey and clarified butter, in order to please (the goddess) Revatî, obtains beauty.

27. He who daily throughout the month Mâgha offers sesamum-seeds in fire and feeds (three) Brâh-ma*n*as with sour rice-gruel mixed with clarified butter, obtains an excellent digestive power.

28. He who bathes in a river and worships king Dharma on the fourteenth of both halves of every month, is purified from every sin.

29. One desirous of obtaining the manifold advantages attending an eclipse of the sun or moon must constantly bathe in the mornings during the two months Mâgha and Phâlguna.

XCI.

1. The digger of a well has (the consequences of) the half of his evil acts taken from him as soon as the water comes forth from it.

2. A digger of pools is for ever freed from thirst, and attains the world of Varu*n*a.

3. A giver of water shall never suffer from thirst (in heaven, for a hundred Yugas or ages of the world).

4. He who plants trees will have those trees for his sons in a future existence.

5. A giver of trees gladdens the gods by (offering up) their blossoms to them.

6. (He gladdens) his guests by (giving) their fruits to them;

7. (He gladdens) travellers with their shade;

XCI. 14. Y. I, 211. — 15, 16. M. IV, 229. — 17, 18. Y. I, 209.

8. (He gladdens) the manes with the water (trickling down from their leaves) when it rains.

9. A maker of dikes attains heaven.

10. A builder of temples enters the dwelling-place of that deity to whom he has erected a temple.

11. He who causes (a temple erected by another) to be whitewashed acquires brilliant fame.

12. He who causes (such a temple) to be painted with (a different) colour (such as blue, yellow, and others) attains the world of the Gandharvas.

13. By giving flowers he becomes fortunate.

14. By giving ointments he acquires renown.

15. By giving a lamp he obtains an excellent eye-sight and exquisite happiness.

16. By giving food he obtains strength.

17. By removing the remains of an offering to a deity he obtains the same reward as for giving a cow.

18. The same reward is also obtained by scouring a temple, by smearing it (with cow-dung and the like), by removing the leavings of the food of a Brâhmana, by washing his feet, and by nursing him when sick.

19. He who consecrates anew a well, or a park, or a pool, or a temple (when they have been soiled) obtains the same reward as he who first made them.

XCII.

1. Protecting (one attacked by robbers, or by tigers, or otherwise in danger) is more meritorious than any (other) gift.

2. By doing so he obtains that place of abode (after death) which he desires himself.

3. By giving land he obtains the same (heavenly reward).

4. By giving land to the extent of a bull's hide only he is purified from every sin.

5. By giving a cow he attains heaven.

6. A giver of ten milch cows (obtains) the mansion of cows (after death).

7. A giver of a hundred milch cows enters the mansions of Brahman (after death).

8. He who gives (a milch cow) with gilt horns, with hoofs covered with silver, with a tail wound with a string of pearls, with a milk-pail of white copper, and with a cover of cloth, shall reside in heaven for as many years as the cow has hairs on her body;

9. Particularly, if it is a brown cow.

10. He who has given a tamed bull is (equal in virtue to) a giver of ten milch cows.

IV, 231; Y. I, 208. — 8, 9. Y. I, 204. 205. — 10. Y. I, 210. — 10–12. M. IV, 231. — 12, 13. Y. I, 210. — 13, 14. M. IV, 230. — 19, 20. M. IV, 232; Y. I, 211. — 21–23. M. IV, 229, 232. — 21. Y. I, 210. — 27. M. IV, 232; Y. I, 211. — 28–32. Y. I, 211. — 31. M. IV, 230.

4. Nand. defines 'a bull's hide' as a measure of surface 300 Hastas (see X, 2, note) long by ten Hastas broad. See, however, V, 183.

8. According to a Smriti quoted by Nand., the gold upon the horns of the cow shall weigh ten Suvarnas, the silver on her hoofs ten Palas, the white copper of which the milk-pail is made fifty Palas, and she shall have copper on her back, which must also weigh fifty Palas.

9. 'The meaning is, that a brown cow sends even his ancestors as far as the seventh degree to heaven, as Yâgñavalkya (I, 205) says.' (Nand.)

11. The giver of a horse attains the mansion of Sûrya (the sun-god).

12. The giver of a garment (attains) the mansion of *K*andra (the god of the moon).

13. By giving gold (he attains) the mansion of Agni (the god of fire).

14. By giving silver (rûpya, he obtains) beauty (rûpa).

15. By giving dishes (pâtra) made of (gold or silver or other) metal he renders himself worthy (pâtra) to obtain everything he may desire.

16. By giving clarified butter, honey, or oil (he acquires) freedom from disease;

17. The same by giving (boiled or otherwise dressed) drugs.

18. By giving salt (lava*n*a, he obtains) personal charms (lâva*n*ya).

19. By giving grain (produced in the rainy season, such as *S*yâmâka grain, he acquires) satiation;

20. The same (effect is obtained) by giving grain (produced in winter or spring, such as wild turmeric or wheat).

21. A giver of food (obtains) all the rewards (enumerated above).

22. By giving grain (of any of the kinds not mentioned before, such as Kulattha or Kodrava grain, he obtains) good fortune.

23. A giver of sesamum (obtains) such offspring as he desires.

24. A giver of fuel (obtains) an excellent digestive power;

25. And he obtains victory in every fight.

26. By giving a seat (he obtains) high rank.

27. By giving a bed (of the kind declared above.

XC, 7, he procures) a wife (possessed of the qualities mentioned above).

28. By giving a pair of shoes (he obtains) a carriage yoked with mules.

29. By giving an umbrella (he attains) heaven.

30. By giving a fan or a chowrie (he obtains) prosperity in travelling.

31. By giving a house (he receives) the post of governor of a town.

32. Whatever a man is most fond of in this world (himself) and what his family like best, all that he must bestow upon a virtuous (Brâhma*n*a), if he wishes it to become imperishable.

XCIII.

1. What is given to another than a Brâhma*n*a produces the same fruit in the world to come.

2. (What is given) to one who calls himself a Brâhma*n*a (because he was born and initiated as such, but who does not perform his daily duties) produces twice the same fruit.

3. (What is given) to one who has studied the main portions of the Veda produces a thousand times the same fruit.

XCIII. 1–4. M. VII, 85 ; Gaut. V, 20. — 7. M. IV, 192. — 8. M. IV, 195. — 9–13. M. IV, 196–200.

1. 'The term abrâhma*n*a (one not a Brâhma*n*a) refers to Kshatriyas and the like.' Kullûka on M. VII, 85. Dr. Bühler's rendering of Gautama V, 20 agrees with this interpretation. Nand., on the other hand, refers the term abrâhma*n*a to six kinds of Brâhma*n*as enumerated by *S*âtâtapa, who have infringed the rule of their caste by taking their substance from a king, or by selling or buying forbidden articles, or by sacrificing for a multitude of persons, &c. The term 'the same fruit' means that a person shall receive in a future world what he has given in this. (Nand.)

4. (What is given) to one who has mastered the whole Veda, produces infinite fruit.

5. A domestic priest may claim gifts from his own employer (but from no one else).

6. And so may a sister, a daughter and sons-in-law (or other connections claim gifts from their brother, father, &c., but not from a stranger).

7. One who knows his duty must not give even water to a twice-born man who acts like a cat, or to a Brâhmana who acts like a crane, or to one who has not studied the Veda.

8. One who constantly hoists the flag of religion, and who is avaricious, crafty, deceitful, pitiless, and a calumniator of everybody, such a man is said to act like a cat.

9. One who hangs his head, who is bent upon injuring others and upon his own gain, artful, and falsely demure, such a man is said to act like a crane.

10. Those who act like cranes in this world, and those who act like cats, fall into (the hell called) Andhatâmisra[1] on account of their wickedness.

11. If a man has committed an offence and does penance for it, he must not do so under pretext of performing an act of piety, covering his crime under a (fictitious) vow, and imposing on women and Sûdras.

12. A Brâhmana who acts thus, is despised in the next life and in this by those who know the Veda, and the penance performed by him under such false pretence goes to the (demons called) Râkshasas.

---

10. [1] See XLIII, 3.

13. One who gains his subsistence by wearing (a lock on the crown of the head or other) distinguishing marks of a caste or religious order, to which he does not belong, takes upon himself the (consequences of the) sins committed by those who have a right to those marks, and enters in a future birth the womb of an animal.

14. He must not give (to a panegyrist) from vain-glory, or from fear, or to a friend (from whom he hopes to obtain benefit), nor (must he bestow gifts), with a view to acquire religious merit, upon dancers or singers : that is a fixed rule.

XCIV.

1. A householder, when he sees his skin has become wrinkled and his hair turned grey, must go to live in a forest.

2. Or (he must do so) when he sees the son of his son.

3. Let him (before going into the forest) entrust the care of his wife to his sons, or let her accompany him.

4. Let him keep the sacred fires in his new abode as before.

5. He must not omit to perform the five sacri-

XCIV. 1, 2. M. VI, 2. — 3, 4. M. VI, 3, 4 ; Y. III, 45 ; Âpast. II, 9, 22, 8, 9. — 5. M. VI, 5, 16 ; Y. III, 46 ; Gaut. III, 29. — 6. M. VI, 8 ; Y. III, 48. — 7. M. VI, 26 ; Y. III, 45 ; Âpast. II, 9, 21, 19. — 8. M. VI, 6 ; Âpast. II, 9, 22, 1 ; Gaut. VI, 34. — 9, 10. M. VI, 6 ; Y. III, 46, 48. — 9, 11. Gaut. III, 34, 35. — 11. M. VI, 18 ; Y. III, 47. — 12. M. VI, 15 ; Y. III, 47 ; Âpast. II, 9, 22, 24. — 13. M. VI, 28 ; Y. III, 55. 'The duties of a householder having been declared, he now goes on to expound the duties of an hermit.' (Nand.)

5. See LIX, 20 seq.

fices, but (he must perform them) with (fruits, herbs, or roots) growing wild.

6. He must not relinquish the private recitation of the Veda.

7. He must preserve his chastity.

8. He must wear a dress made of skins or bark.

9. He must suffer the hairs of his head, of his beard, and of his body, and his nails to grow.

10. He must bathe at morning, noon, and evening.

11. He must either collect provisions, after the manner of the pigeon, for a month, or he must collect them for a year.

12. He who has collected provisions for a year, must throw away what he has collected on the day of full moon in the month Âsvina.

13. Or an hermit may bring food from a village, placing it in a dish made of leaves, or in a single leaf, or in his hand, or in a potsherd, and eat eight mouthfuls of it.

XCV.

1. An hermit must dry up his frame by the practice of austerities.

2. In summer he must expose himself to five fires.

---

6. The use of the particle *ka* implies, according to Nand., that the practice of distributing gifts should likewise be continued.

11. The particle vâ here refers, according to Nand., to a third alternative mentioned by Manu (VI, 18), that he should gather provisions sufficient for six months.

XCV, 1. M. VI, 24. — 2–4. M. VI, 23; Y. III, 52. — 5, 6. M. VI, 19; Y. III, 50. — 7–11. M. VI, 5, 21; Y. III, 46; Âpast. II, 9, 22, 2; Gaut. III, 26. — 12, 13. M. VI, 20; Y. III, 50. — 14, 15. M. VI, 17; Y. III, 49. — 16, 17. M. XI, 235, 239.

3. During the season of the rains he must sleep in the open air.

4. In winter he must wear wet clothes.

5. He must eat at night.

6. He may eat after having fasted entirely for one day, or for two days, or for three days.

7. He may eat flowers.   8. He may eat fruits.

9. He may eat vegetables.

10. He may eat leaves.   11. He may eat roots.

12. Or he may eat boiled barley once at the close of a half-month.

13. Or he may eat according to the rules of the *K*ândrâya*n*a.

14. He shall break his food with stones.

15. Or he shall use his teeth as a pestle.

16. This whole world of deities and of men has devotion for its root, devotion for its middle, devotion for its end, and is supported by devotion.

17. What is hard to follow [1], hard to reach, remote, or hard to do, all that may be accomplished by devotion; since there is nothing that may not be effected by devotion.

---

6. Nand. considers the particle vâ to refer to the precept of Yâg*ñ*avalkya (III, 50), that the fast may also extend over a half-month or an entire month.

13. The particle vâ, according to Nand., implies that he may also perform K*rikkh*ras, as ordained by Yâg*ñ*avalkya (III, 50). Regarding the *K*ândrâya*n*a, see XLVII.

17. [1] Du*s*kara has been translated according to the usual acceptation of this term.   Nand. interprets it by 'hard to understand.'   This proverb is also found Subhâshitâr*n*ava 109, V*ri*ddha*k*ânakya's Proverbs XVII, 3.   See Böhtlingk, Ind. Sprüche, 5265.

XCVI.

1. After having passed through the first three orders and annihilated passion, he must offer an oblation to Pragâpati, in which he bestows all his wealth (upon priests) as fee for the performance of the sacrifice, and enter the order of ascetics.

2. Having reposited the fires in his own mind, he must enter the village, in order to collect alms, (but never for any other purpose).

3. He must beg food at seven houses.

4. If he does not get food (at one house), he must not grieve.

5. He must not beg of another ascetic.

6. When the servants have had their meal, when the dishes have been removed, let him beg food (consisting of the leavings).

7. (He must receive the food) in an earthen vessel, or in a wooden bowl, or in a vessel made of the bottle-gourd.

8. He must cleanse those vessels with water.

9. He must shun food obtained by humble salutation.

XCVI. 1. M. VI, 38; Y. III, 56. — 2. M. VI, 38, 43; Y. III, 56, 58. — 4. M. VI, 57. — 6. M. VI, 56; Y. III, 59; Gaut. III, 15. — 7, 8. M. VI, 54, 53; Y. III, 60. — 9. M. VI, 58. — 11. M. VI, 44. — 12. Gaut. III, 21. — 13. Gaut. III, 18. — 14–17. M. VI, 46. — 18. M. VI, 45. — 19, 20. M. VI, 47. — 23. Y. III, 53; Mahâbhârata I, 4605. — 24. M. VI, 49; Y. III, 201. — 25–42. M. VI, 61–64; Y. III, 63, 64. — 43. Y. III, 72. — 45–50. M. VI, 76, 77. — 51, 54–79. Y. III, 70, 84–90. — 80–88. Y. III, 100–104. — 89, 91. Y. III, 93–95. — 92. Y. III, 96–99. — 93–95. Y. III, 91, 92. — 96. Y. III, 179. — 97. M. XII, 12; Y. III, 178. — 97, 98. Bhagavad-gîtâ XIII, 1, 2.　　This chapter treats of ascetics. (Nand.)

4. 'This implies that he must not rejoice if he does get it, as Manu (VI, 57) says.' (Nand.)

10. He must live in an empty house.

11. Or (he must) live at the root of a tree.

12. He must not stay for more than one night in one village (except during the rainy season).

13. His only dress must be a small piece of cloth worn over the privities.

14. He must set down his feet purified by looking down.

15. He must drink water purified (by straining it) with a cloth.

16. He must utter speeches purified by truth.

17. He must perform acts purified by his mind.

18. He must neither wish for death nor for (a long) life.

19. He must bear abuse patiently.

20. He must treat no one with contempt.

21. He must not pronounce a benediction.

22. He must not salute any one reverentially.

---

10. 'Empty' means 'inhabited by no one else,' and implies that the house in question should be situated in a dark place, difficult of access. (Nand.)

11. 'The article vâ implies that he must live there alone.' (Nand.)

14, 15. Nand. assigns as the reason of both these rules, 'lest he should not kill some insect.' Kullûka (on M. VI, 46) gives the same reason for the second rule, but the looking down, according to him, is ordained in order that he may not accidentally tread upon a hair or other impure substance.

17. The sense of this Sûtra is, that in doubtful cases he must act as his mind prompts him to do. (Nand.)

21. 'The meaning is, that he must not utter a benediction when he has been reverentially saluted by any one. He must confine himself to saying, "O Nârâya*n*a." Others explain, that he must not utter a benediction in begging food.' (Nand.)

22. 'The sense is, that he must not salute any one reverentially who has reverentially saluted him, nor return his greeting other-

23. Should one man chop his one arm with an axe, and another sprinkle his other arm with sandal, he must neither curse the one in his mind, nor bless the other.

24. He must constantly be intent upon stopping his breath, upon retention of the image formed in his mind, and upon meditation.

25. He must reflect upon the transitoriness of the passage through mundane existence;

26. And upon the impure nature of the body;

27. And upon the destruction of beauty by old age;

28. And upon the pain arising from diseases bodily, mental, or due to an excess (of the bile,.&c.)

29. And upon (the pain arising from) the (five) naturally inherent (affections).

30. On his having to dwell in an embryo, covered with everlasting darkness;

---

wise than by saying, "O Nârâyana."   Others explain, that he must not make an obeisance in begging food.' (Nand.)

24. Nand. quotes a passage of the Yogasâstra, which states that one Dhâranâ = three Prânâyâmas (stoppings or regulations of the breath).   A passage of the Gâruda-purâna (quoted in the Petersburg Dictionary) states that one Dhâranâ = sixteen Prânâyâmas. I have taken the term dhâranâ in its ordinary acceptation of ' retention of an idea' (cf. Wilson, Vishnu-purâna V, 237) with regard to an analogous passage of Yâgñavalkya (III, 201), which is also quoted by Nand.

28. According to Nand., the particle *ka* is used to include other diseases, love, anxiety or wrath, caused by enemies, and other mental pangs.

29. They are, ignorance, egotism, love, wrath, and dread of temporal suffering (Nand., according to Patañgali).   The particle *ka*, according to Nand., is used in order to imply meditation upon the thousand births which man has to pass through, as stated by Yâgñavalkya (III, 64).

31. And on (his having to dwell) between urine and fæces;

32. On his having to suffer, (as an embryo,) pain from the cold and hot (food and drink, which his mother happens to have taken);

33. On the dreadful pain which he has to suffer, at the time of his birth, while the embryo is coming forth from the narrowness of the womb;

34. On his ignorance and his dependency upon his (parents and other) Gurus in childhood;

35. On the manifold anxieties arising from the study of the Veda (and from the other obligations of a student);

36. And (on the anxieties arising) in youth from not obtaining the objects of pleasure, and upon the abode in hell (ordained as punishment) for enjoying them, after they have been obtained unlawfully;

37. On the union with those whom we hate, and the separation from those whom we love;

38. On the fearful agonies of hell;

39. And (on the agonies) that have to be suffered in the passage of the soul through the bodies of animals (and of plants).

40. (And let him reflect thus that) there is no pleasure to be met with in this never-ceasing passage of the soul through mundane existence;

41. (And that) even what is called pleasure, on account of the absence of pain, is of a transient nature;

42. (And that) he who is unable to enjoy such pleasures (from sickness or some such cause), or who is unable to procure them (from poverty), suffers severe pangs.

43. He must recognise this human frame to consist of seven elements.

44. Those elements are, adeps, blood, flesh, serum of flesh, bone, marrow, and semen.

45. It is covered with skin.

46. And it has a nasty smell.

47. It is the receptacle of (the above-named) impure substances (adeps and the rest).

48. Though surrounded by a hundred pleasures, it is subject to change.

49. Though carefully supported (by elixirs and the like), it is subject to destruction.

50. It is the stay of carnal desire, wrath, greed, folly, pride, and selfishness.

51. It consists of earth, water, fire, air, and ether.

52. It is provided with bone, tubular vessels (carrying bile and phlegm through the body), tubes (conducting the vital airs), and sinews.

53. It is endowed with the quality of ra*g*as (passion).

54. It is covered with six skins.

55. It is kept together by three hundred and sixty bones.

56. They are distributed (as follows):

57. The teeth together with their receptacles are sixty-four in number.

---

46. The particle *k*a, according to Nand., refers to the fact that the human body is defiled by the touch of impure objects.

48. 'The meaning is that, though food and drink and other sensual enjoyments abound, they may cause pain as well as pleasure by producing phlegm, &c.' (Nand.)

51. 'Earth,' i. e. the flesh and bone, &c. ; 'water,' i. e. the blood ; 'fire,' i. e. the digestive faculty, the eyesight, &c. ; 'air,' i.e. the five vital airs ; 'ether,' i. e. the space enclosed by the airs, in the mouth, in the belly, &c. (Nand.)

58. There are twenty nails.

59. There are as many bones to the hands and feet (one at the root of each finger and toe).

60. There are sixty joints to the fingers and toes.

61. There are two (bones) to the two heels.

62. There are four to the ancles.

63. There are four to the elbows.

64. There are two to the shanks.

65. There are two to the knees and two to the cheeks.

66. (There are two) to the thighs and (two) to the shoulders.

67. (There are two) to the lower part of the temples, (two) to the palate, and (two) to the hips.

68. There is one bone to the organs of generation.

69. The backbone consists of forty-five (bones).

70. The neck consists of fifteen (bones).

71. The collar-bone consists of one (bone on each side).

72. The jaw likewise.

73. There are two (bones) at its root.

74. There are two (bones) to the forehead, (two) to the eyes, and (two) to the cheeks.

75. The nose has one bone, the nose-bone.

76. The ribs together with the joints called 'arbuda,' and with the joints called ' sthânaka,' consist of seventy-two (bones).

77. The breast contains seventeen bones.

---

76. 'There are thirteen ribs to each flank, which makes in all twenty-six ribs. There are twenty joints to them in the breast, called " arbuda," and twenty-six joints in the back, called " sthânaka," which makes a total of seventy-two bones.' (Nand.)

78. There are two temporal bones.

79. The head has four skull-bones. Thus (the bones have been enumerated).

80. There are in this human frame seven hundred tubular vessels (carrying bile and phlegm through the body, or arteries).

81. Of sinews, there are nine hundred.

82. Of tubes (conducting the vital airs, or nerves), there are two hundred.

83. Of muscles, there are five hundred.

84. Of tubular vessels (or arteries), the branches of the smaller tubular vessels, there are twenty-nine Lakshas (two millions nine hundred thousand) and nine hundred and fifty-six.

85. Of hair-holes, of the hair of the beard and of the head, there are three hundred thousand.

86. Of sensitive parts of the body, there are one hundred and seven.

87. Of joints, there are two hundred.

88. Of (atoms of) hairs (of the body), there are fifty-four Ko*t*is (or five hundred and forty millions) and sixty-seven Lakshas (making in all five hundred and forty-six millions and seven hundred thousand).

89. The navel, the principle of vital action (which dwells in the heart), the anus, semen, blood, the temples, the head, the throat, and the heart are the seats of the vital airs.

90. The two arms, the two legs, the belly, and the head are the six limbs.

91. Adeps, marrow, the left lung, the navel, the right lung, the liver, the spleen, the small cavity of the heart, the kidneys, the bladder, the rectum, the stomach, the heart, the large cavity (intestine), the

anus, the belly, and the two bowels in it (are the inner parts of the body).

92. The pupils of the eye, the eyelashes[1], the outer parts of the ears, the ears themselves, the tragus of each ear, the cheeks, the eyebrows, the temples, the gums, the lips, the cavities of the loins, the two groins, the scrotum, the two kidneys and breasts of females, which are composed of phlegm, the uvula, the hindparts, the arms, the shanks, the thighs, the fleshy parts of the shanks and thighs, the palate, the two bones (or muscles) at the upper end of the bladder, the chin, the soft palate, and[2] the nape of the neck: these are the 'places' (of vital energy) in the body.

93. Sound, tangibility, form or colour, savour, and odour are the (five) objects of sense.

94. Nose, eye, skin, tongue, and ear are the (five) organs of perception.

95. Hands, feet, anus, parts of generation, and tongue are the (five) organs of action.

96. Mind, intellect, the individual Self, and the indiscrete[1] are 'that which exceeds the senses.'

97. This human frame, O Earth, is called 'field.' He who knows (how to enter and how to leave) it is denominated, by those conversant with the

---

92. [1] Others interpret akshikû/e, 'the eyelashes,' by 'the joints between the eyes and the nose.' (Nand.) See also Böhtlingk's new Dictionary. — [2] The use of the particle *ka* implies, according to Nand., that the feet, hands, and other limbs mentioned in an analogous passage of Yâgñavalkya (III, 99) have also to be included in this enumeration.

96. [1] Nand. interprets avyaktam, 'the indiscrete,' by pradhânam, 'the chief one.' Both terms are in the Sânkhya system of philosophy synonyms of prak*ri*ti, 'that which evolves or produces everything else.'

subject, 'the knower of the field' (i. e. Self or Soul).

98. Know me, O illustrious one, to be the Self of all fields (whether born from the womb, or arisen from an egg, or from sweat, or from a germ or shoot). Those striving after final emancipation must constantly seek to understand the 'field' and to obtain a knowledge of the knower of the field.

XCVII.

1. Sitting with the feet stretched out and crossed so as to touch the thighs, with the right hand (stretched out and) resting upon the left, with the tongue fixed in the palate, and without bringing the one row of teeth in contact with the other, with the eyes directed to the tip of the nose, and without glancing at any of the (four) quarters of the sky, free from fear, and with composure, let him meditate upon (Purusha), who is separate from the twenty-four entities,

---

XCVII. 1. Y. III, 198–200. — 9. Y. III, 111, 201. This chapter treats of the means for obtaining that knowledge of the Âtman or Self, which has been declared at the end of the last chapter to be the road to final emancipation. (Nand.)

1. ' The twenty-four (it should be twenty-five) entities are stated in the Sânkhya to consist of the root-principle (mûlaprak*ri*ti), the seven productions evolved from it (vik*ri*taya*h*), the sixteen productions evolved from these, and Purusha (the soul), who is neither producer nor produced. (1) The " root-principle " is composed of the three qualities in equipoise : sattva, ra*g*as, and tamas (the most accurate rendering of these terms is perhaps that proposed by Elliot, " pure unimpassioned virtue," " passion," and " depravity inclining to evil." See Fitz-Edward Hall, Preface to Sânkhyaprava*k*anabhâshya, p. 44). (2) The " great entity " (Mahat) is the cause of apprehension. (3) The " self-consciousness " (aha*m*kâra) is the cause of refer-

2. He who is eternal, beyond the cognisance of the senses, destitute of qualities, not concerned with sound, tangibility, form, savour, or odour, knowing everything, of immense size,

3. He who pervades everything, and who is devoid of form,

4. Whose hands and feet are everywhere, whose eyes, head, and face are everywhere, and who is able to apprehend everything with all the senses.

5. Thus let him meditate.

6. If he remains absorbed in such meditation for a year, he obtains the accomplishment of Yoga (concentration of the thought and union with the Supreme).

7. If he is unable to fix his mind upon the being

---

ring all objects to self. (4–8) The "subtile elementary particles" (tan-mâtras) are identical with sound, tangibility, form, taste, and odour. (9–19) The eleven senses (i. e. the organs of perception and action enumerated in CXVI, 94, 95, and manas, "the mind"), and (20–24) the five "grosser elements" (ether, air, fire, water, and earth) are productions (from the former entities). Purusha, who is neither producer nor produced, is the twenty-fifth entity.' (Nand.)

2, 3. According to Nand., all the properties of Purusha mentioned in this Sûtra are such as distinguish him from the rest of the entities, the first two distinguishing him from 'self-consciousness' (ahamkâra), the voidness of quality distinguishing him from the 'root-principle' (mûlaprakriti), which is composed of three qualities, &c.

4. The properties of Pûrusha here mentioned are faculties only, so that there is no contradiction to the 'voidness of form' and the other properties enumerated in the preceding Sûtras. (Nand.)

6. The external signs of the accomplishment of Yoga, as stated by Yâgñavalkya (III, 202 seq.), are, the faculty of entering another body and of creating anything at will, and other miraculous powers and qualities. (Nand.)

destitute of form [1], he must meditate successively on earth, water, fire, air, ether, mind, intellect, self [2], the indiscrete [3], and Purusha [4] : having fully apprehended one, he must dismiss it from his thoughts and fix his mind upon the next one in order.

8. In this way let him arrive at meditation upon Purusha.

9. If unable to follow this method also, he must meditate on Purusha [1] shining like a lamp in his heart, as in a lotus turned upside down.

10. If he cannot do that either, he must meditate upon Bhagavat Vâsudeva (Vishnu), who is adorned with a diadem, with ear-rings, and with bracelets, who has the (mystic mark) Srîvatsa and a garland of wood-flowers on his breast, whose aspect is pleasing, who has four arms, who holds the shell, the discus, the mace, and the lotus-flower, and whose feet are supported (and worshipped) by the earth.

11. Whatever he meditates upon, that is obtained by a man (in a future existence): such is the mysterious power of meditation.

12. Therefore must he dismiss everything perish-

---

7. [1] The term nirâkâra, 'the being destitute of form,' evidently refers to Purusha here (cf. Sûtra 3), though Nand. interprets it as an epithet of 'Brahman.' — [2] 'Intellect' (buddhi) and 'self' (âtman), according to Nand., mean 'the great entity' (mahat) and 'self-consciousness' (ahamkâra), cf. note on Sûtra 1. — [3] 'The indiscrete' (avyaktam) means 'the chief one' (pradhânam), i. e. the Sânkhya 'root-principle' (see XCVI, 96). — [4] Nand. takes Purusha in this Sûtra and in 13. 15 to mean 'the twenty-sixth entity;' but it appears clearly from Sûtra 1, as from 16 also, that the Vishnu-sûtra, like the Sânkhya system, assumes twenty-five entities only, not twenty-six, like Yama, upon whose authority Nand.'s statement is based.

9. [1] Nand. interprets the term Purusha here by âtman, 'self.'

[7]   U

able from his thoughts and meditate upon what is imperishable only.

13. There is nothing imperishable except Purusha.

14. Having become united with him (through constant meditation), he obtains final liberation.

15. Because the great lord pervades the whole universe (pura), as he is lying there (sete), therefore is he denominated Puru-sha by those who reflect upon the real nature (of the Supreme Spirit).

16. In the first part and the latter part of the night must a man bent on contemplation constantly and with fixed attention meditate upon Purusha Vish*n*u, who is destitute of (the three) qualities (sattva, ra*g*as, and tamas[1]) and the twenty-fifth entity.

17. He (or it) is composed of the entities, beyond the cognisance of the senses, distinct from all the (other) entities, free from attachment (to the producer, &c.), supporting everything, devoid of qualities and yet enjoying (or witnessing the effect of) qualities.

18. It exists without and within created beings (as being enjoyed and as enjoyer), and in the shape both of immovable things (such as trees or stones) and of movable things (such as water or fire); it is undistinguishable on account of its subtlety; it is out of reach (imperceptible), and yet is found in the heart.

---

16. [1] See Sûtra 1, note.

17. Thus according to the reading asaktam, which is mentioned and explained as a var. lect. by Nand. He himself reads a*s*aktam, 'independent of *S*akti, power, i. e. the producer, the power of creation (prak*ri*ti), or illusion (mâyâ).' Mâyâ and prak*ri*ti are occasionally used as synonymous terms in the Sânkhya.

19. It is not distinct from creation, and yet distinct from it in outward appearance; it annihilates and produces by turns (the world), which consists of everything that has been, that will be, and that is.

20. It is termed the light of the sidereal bodies and the enemy of darkness (ignorance), it is knowledge, it should be known, it may be understood (by meditation), it dwells in every man's heart.

21. Thus the 'field,' knowledge (or meditation), and what should be known [1] have been concisely declared; that faithful adherent of mine who makes himself acquainted therewith, becomes united to me in spirit.

XCVIII.

1. When Vishnu had finished his speech [1], the goddess of the earth inclined her knees and her head before him and said:

2. 'O Bhagavat! Four (out of the five) grosser elements [1] are receiving their support from thee, and are constantly about thee: the ether, in the form of the shell; the air, in the form of the discus; the fire, in the form of the mace; and the water, in the form of the lotus. Now I also desire to attend upon thee, in my own shape, as the ground which Bhagavat's feet tread upon.'

---

21. [1] The 'field' has been discussed in XCVI, 43–97, 'knowledge' in XCVII, 1, and 'what should be known' in XCVII, 2–20. (Nand.)

XCVIII. 1. [1] Vishnu's speech is contained in Chapters II–XCVII. (Nand.)

2. [1] The fifth grosser element is the earth. See XCVII, 1, note.

3. Having been addressed thus by the goddess of the earth, Bhagavat answered, 'So be it.'

4. And the goddess of the earth, her desire having been gratified, did as she had said.

5. And she praised the god of the gods (as follows):

6. 'Om.   Adoration be to thee.

7. 'Thou art the god of the gods.

8. 'Thou art Vâsudeva.

9. 'Thou art the creator.

10. 'Thou art the god (who creates, preserves, and destroys) at will.

11. 'Thou art the gratifier of human desires.

12. 'Thou art the guardian of the earth.

13. 'There is neither beginning, nor middle, nor end in thee.

14. 'Thou art the lord (protector) of creatures.

15. 'Thou art the strong lord of creatures.

16. 'Thou art the exalted lord of creatures.

17. 'Thou art the lord of strength.

18. 'Thou art the lord of holy speech.

19. 'Thou art the lord (creator and preserver) of the world.

20. 'Thou art the lord of heaven.

21. 'Thou art the lord of woods (who makes the trees grow).

---

10. 'Or Kâmadeva means the god (or brilliant one) who is sought by those striving for religious merit, gain, love, or final liberation.' (Nand.)   The same interpretation is given by Sankara in his Commentary on the Vishnu-sahasranâma.   The ordinary meaning of Kâmadeva is 'the god of love.'

15, 16. Nand. renders the terms supragâpati and mahâpragâpati by 'the protector of those who have a splendid progeny (such as Kasyapa)' and 'the lord of him who has a large progeny (Brahman).'

22. 'Thou art the lord (producer) of (mother's) milk.

23. 'Thou art the lord of the earth (and causest it to yield its produce)

24. 'Thou art the lord of the waters.

25. 'Thou art the lord of the (eight) quarters of the sky.

26. 'Thou art the lord of (the principle) Mahat.

27. 'Thou art the lord of the wind.

28. 'Thou art the lord of happiness.

29. 'Thou art Brahman personified.

30. 'Thou art dear to Brâhma*n*as.

31. 'Thou pervadest everything.

32. 'Thou surpassest all conception.

33. 'Thou art attainable by knowledge (meditation).

34. 'Thou art invoked at many (offerings).

35. 'Thou art praised with many (hymns of the Veda).

36. 'Thou likest everything sacred.

37. 'Thou art fond of Brahman (the Veda).

38. 'Thou belongest to the (gods called) Brahmakâyas.

39. 'Thy size is immense.

40. 'Thou belongest to the Mahârâ*g*as.

---

26. See XCVII, 1, note.

28. Lakshmîpati has been translated according to Nand.'s interpretation. It usually denotes the husband of Lakshmî.

30. Or 'Brâhma*n*as are dear to thee.' Both explanations of the term brâhma*n*apriya are admissible, and mentioned by Nand. and by *S*ankara.

40, 41. Nand. interprets the two terms mahârâ*g*ika and *k*aturmahârâ*g*ika by 'he whose series of transmigrations is immense,' and 'he whose immense series of transmigrations is fourfold,' and

41. 'Thou belongest to the four Mahârâ*g*as.

42. 'Thou art brilliant.

43. 'Thou art most brilliant.

44. 'Thou art the seven (parts of a Sâman, or the seven divisions of the universe).

45. 'Thou art most blessed.

46. 'Thou art tone.

47. 'Thou art Tushita (or "satisfied with the honours shown to thee by faithful attendants").

48. 'Thou art Mahâtushita (or "highly satisfied even without being worshipped").

49. 'Thou art the tormentor (destroyer of the world).

50. 'Thou art wholly created.

51. 'Thou art uncreated.

52. 'Thou art obsequious (to thy followers).

53. 'Thou art sacrifice.

54. 'Thou art the (recipient of the) great sacrifice.

55. 'Thou art connected with sacrifices.

56. 'Thou art the fit recipient of offerings.

57. 'Thou art the consummation of offerings.

58. 'Thou art invincible.

---

he refers the latter epithet to the four parts, of which Purusha is said to consist. He quotes Rig-veda X, 90, 4, where it is said that Purusha ascended to the sky with three of his constituent parts, and that the fourth remained in this world. But both terms cannot be separated etymologically from Mahârâ*g*a, the name of a certain class of deities in the Buddhistic system of religion.

44. Thus Nand. Compare I, 56, note.

46. Nand.'s interpretation of the epithet svara, 'tone' (or 'air breathed through the nostrils'), as being a compound of the prefix su and the root *ri* in the sense of 'acquisition, insight,' and meaning 'most wise,' is inadmissible.

54. This epithet, according to Nand., refers to the sacrifice mentioned in a text of the Vâ*g*asan. Sa*m*hitâ (XIX, 12), which begins with the words 'The gods prepared a sacrifice.'

59. 'Thou art Vaiku*nth*a.

60. 'Thou art unbounded (both in time and space).

61. 'Thou surpassest (the organs of sense, mind, and intelligence).

62. 'Thou art of old.

63. 'Thou art friendly to the gods.

64. 'Thou art the protector of living beings.

65. 'Thou wearest radiant locks of hair.

66. 'Thou takest thy share of acts of worship.

67. 'Thou takest thy sacrificial cake.

68. 'Thou art lord over everything.

69. 'Thou art the support of all.

70. 'Thy ears are pure.

71. 'Never ceasing homage is paid to thee.

72. 'Thou art blazing fire (or " Thou art shining with clarified butter offered up to thee ").

73. 'Thou cuttest (foes) to pieces with thy axe.

74. 'Thou hast a lotus springing from thy navel.

75. 'Thou holdest a lotus (in thy hand).

76. 'Thou wearest a garland of lotus-flowers.

77. 'Thou art the lord of the senses.

78. 'Thou hast one horn.

---

59. Nand. proposes two interpretations of this epithet: 1. the producer of Mâyâ (the power of illusion); 2. the son of Viku*nth*â, the mother of Vish*n*u in one of his Avatâras. Vaiku*nth*a is also the name of Vish*n*u's paradise.

70. 'I.e. "thou hearest the sacred revelation." Or *sukisravah* = "he whose names are pure." ' (Nand.) The same interpretation is given by *S*ankara. See also Mahâbhârata XII, 13250.

73. 'The epithet kha*nd*aparu*s*u refers either to Vish*n*u's slaying the Daityas in the form of *S*iva, or to his wearing an axe as the slayer of the Kshatriyas in the form of Para*s*urâma.' (Nand.) The latter interpretation is proposed by *S*ankara also, and kha*nd*aparasu is a very common epithet of Para*s*urâma.

78. The one horn is meant, by which Vish*n*u, in his descent as

79. 'Thou art the great boar.

80. 'Thou art the tormentor (of the Asuras, or of the righteous and the unrighteous).

81. 'Thou art eternal.

82. 'Thou art infinite. 83. Thou art Purusha. 84. Thou art the great (unbounded) Purusha. 85. Thou art (the sage) Kapila. 86. Thou art the teacher of the Sânkhya. 87. Thy powers are everywhere. 88. Thou art virtue. 89. Thou art the giver of virtue. 90. Thy body is virtue (law). 91. Thou art the giver of both virtue and wealth. 92. Desires are gratified by thee. 93. Thou art Vish*n*u. 94. Thou art triumphant everywhere. 95. Thou art capable of bearing (the extremities of heat and cold and any others). 96. Thou art K*ri*sh*na*. 97. Thou art the lotus-eyed god. 98. Thou art Nârâya*n*a (the son of Nara). 99. Thou art the final aim. 100. Thou art the resort of all beings. 101. Adoration, adoration (be to thee)!'

102. The goddess of the earth, after her desire had been gratified, and after she had thus praised

---

a fish, is said to have dragged the ship of Manu behind him. (Nand.)

79. This epithet refers to Vish*n*u's boar-incarnation. See I, 1 seq.

85, 86. See Introduction.

101. Nand. observes that the divers epithets which are given to Vish*n*u in this chapter are precisely equal in number to the ninety-six chapters, of which the law part of the Vish*n*u-sûtra is composed. This coincidence is curious enough, though it is not quite perfect. For it is by a highly artificial interpretation only that Nand. makes out Sûtra 101 to contain an epithet of Vish*n*u, viz. by interpreting the two separate words namo nama as a compound, meaning 'he who is worshipped by the worshipful, i.e. by Brahman and the other gods;' and Sûtra 6 contains no epithet at all.

(Vish*n*u) with a cheerful mind, addressed herself to the goddess (Lakshmî).

XCIX.

1. After having seen *Srî* (Lakshmî), the goddess of the earth, highly pleased, questioned (in the following manner) that goddess, who was stroking the feet of Vish*n*u, the god of the gods, who was shining with the splendour of her austerities, and whose face was radiant like melted gold.

2. 'O charming lady! Thy hands are as beautiful as the expanded red lotus. Thou art holding the feet of him whose navel resembles the expanded red lotus. Thou art constantly residing in an abode resembling the expanded red lotus. Thy waist has the colour of the expanded red lotus.

3. 'Thy eyes resemble blue lotus-flowers; thy hue is radiant like gold; thy robe is white; thy body is adorned with gems; thy face is radiant like the moon; thou art resplendent like the sun; thy power is immense; thou art the sovereign (or producer) of the world.

4. 'Thou art repose (final liberation), the highest among the (four) objects of human pursuit; thou art Lakshmî; thou art a support (in danger); thou art *Srî*; thou art indifference (the freedom from all worldly pursuits and appetites, which is the consequence of final emancipation); thou art victory;

---

4. The 'four objects of human pursuit' are, kâma, 'desire' (and its gratification), artha, 'gain,' dharma, 'religious merit,' and moksha, 'final emancipation.' The goddess is called Lakshmî, because she is the aim (lakshyate) of all beings. She is called Srî, because she serves Purushottama (Vish*n*u), or because she is the resort of all. (Nand.)

thou art beauty; thou art the splendour (of the sun and moon personified); thou art renown; thou art prosperity; thou art wisdom; thou art the power of expression; thou art the purifier.

5. 'Thou art the food of the manes; thou art forbearance; thou art the earth (or the repository of wealth); thou art fixity; thou art the basis (or stability); thou art the source of the benefit derived from sacrifices; thou art highest prudence; thou art wide-spread renown; thou art freedom from envy; thou art the food given to the gods; thou art mental power; thou art intelligence.

6. 'As the first of the gods (Vishnu) pervades the whole aggregate of the three worlds (sky, atmosphere, and earth), even so doest thou, O black-eyed bestower of gifts. Yet I inquire for the dwelling, in which thy superhuman power is residing.'

7. The goddess of the earth having thus spoken to her, Lakshmî, standing by the side of the chief of the gods, enunciated the following answer: 'I am constantly at the side of the brilliant destroyer of Madhu, O goddess, who shinest like gold.

8. 'But learn from me, where I reside (besides), O support of the world, from the instruction of him, whom I am constantly reflecting upon in my mind, and whom the virtuous call the husband of *Srî*, and from my own recollection.

9. 'I reside in the sun, in the moon, and in the cloudless atmosphere in which the flock of the stars is spread out. (I reside) in that cloud, from which the waters of the rain pour down, in that cloud

---

6. Lakshmî is said to pervade everything, like Vishnu himself, because she is his *Sakti*, i.e. his energy or active power personified as his wife. (Nand.)

which is adorned with Indra's bow, and in that cloud from which the rays of lightning flash forth.

10. '(I reside) in bright gold and silver, and in spotless gems and clothes, O goddess of the earth. (I reside) in rows of whitewashed palaces and in temples decorated with the attributes of deities.

11. '(I reside) in fresh cow-dung, in a noble elephant in rut, in a horse exulting in his vigour, in a proud bull, and in a Brâhma*n*a who studies the Veda.

12. 'I reside in a throne, in an Âmalaka (Dhâtrî) shrub, in a Bèl tree, in an umbrella, in a shell (trumpet), in a lotus-flower, in blazing fire, and in a polished sword or mirror.

13. 'I reside in jars filled with water and in painted (halls), in which there are chowries and fans; in splendid golden vessels, and in earth recently thrown up.

14. '(I reside) in milk, butter, fresh grass, honey, and sour milk; in the body of a married woman, in the frame of an unmarried damsel, and in the frame of (images of) gods, of ascetics, and of officiating priests.

15. '(I reside) in an arrow, in one who has returned (victorious) from battle, and in one who has fallen on the field of honour and proceeded to a seat in heaven; in the sound of (repeating) the Veda, in the flourish of the shell (trumpet), in the sacrificial exclamations addressed to the gods and to the manes, and in the sound of musical instruments.

16. '(I reside) in the consecration of a king, in the marriage ceremony, in a sacrifice, in a bride-groom, in one who has washed his head, in white flowers, in mountains, in fruits, in (islets in the

middle of a river and other) pleasant spots, and in large streams.

17. '(I reside) in lakes filled with water, in (pure) waters, and in ground covered with fresh grass, in a wood abounding in lotuses (and fruits), in a new-born infant, in a suckling, in one exulting in joy, in a virtuous man, and in one wholly bent upon practising the law.

18. '(I reside) in a man who observes approved usages, in one who constantly acts up to the sacred law, in one modestly, and in one splendidly attired, in one who keeps his organs of sense and his mind under control, in one free from sin, in one whose food is pure, and in one who honours his guests.

19. '(I reside) in one who is satisfied with his own wife (and does not covet other men's wives), in one bent upon doing his duty, in one eminently virtuous, in one who refrains from eating too often (i.e. three or four times a day), in one constantly adorned with flowers, in one who associates with such as anoint their limbs with fragrant unguents, in one who is scented with perfumes (himself), and in one adorned (with bracelets and ear-rings).

20. '(I reside) in one habitually veracious, in one friendly towards all creatures, in a married householder, in one forbearing, in one free from wrath, in one skilled in his own business, and in one skilled in other men's business, in one who never thinks of any but propitious things, and in one constantly humble.

21. '(I reside) in women who wear proper ornaments always, who are devoted to their husbands, whose speeches are kind, who keep up saving habits, who have sons, who keep their household utensils in

good order, and who are fond of offering domestic oblations.

22. '(I reside) in women who keep the house clean (by scouring it, plastering it with cow-dung, and the like), who keep their organs of sense under control, who are not quarrelsome, contented, strictly observing the law, and charitable; and I always reside in the destroyer of Madhu.

23. 'I do not remain separated from Purushottama[1] for a single moment.'

C.

1. Those among the twice-born who will act according to (the precepts promulgated in) this excellent law-code, which has been proclaimed by the god himself, shall obtain a most excellent abode in heaven.

2. It purifies from sin, it is auspicious, it leads to heaven, procures long life, knowledge (of the four objects of human pursuit) and renown, and increases wealth and prosperity.

3. It must be studied, it must be borne in mind, it must be recited, it must be listened too, and. it must be constantly repeated at Srâddhas by persons desirous of prosperity.

[4. This most sublime, mysterious collection of doctrines has been proclaimed to thee, O goddess of the earth. In a kindly spirit and for the best of the world (have I promulgated) this body of eternal

23. [1] See I, 51.

C. 2. See XCIX, 4, note.

4. This last clause I consider, for divers reasons, to be an addition made by a modern copyist. 1. It is not commented upon in

laws, which is conducive to happiness, the best means of purification, destructive of bad dreams, productive of a great deal of religious merit, and the source of prosperity.]

Dr. Bühler's copy of the Vai*g*ayantî. 2. It takes up, without any purpose, the speech of Vish*n*u, which had been concluded in XCVII, 21. 3. Recommendations to study and recite the laws just promulgated, like those contained in C, 1–3, form the conclusion of several other Dharma*s*âstras. 4. The substantive saubhâgyam is used like an adjective. 5. The first part of the whole passage is a detached hemistich.

GENERAL INDEX.

p. refers to the pages in the Introduction and Notes.

X

SANSKRIT INDEX.

p. refers to the pages in the Introduction and Notes.

ADDITIONS AND CORRECTIONS.

I, 17 (p. 4) *read* Râkshasas — I, 22 (p. 5) *for* bow *read* shaft — V, 48 (p. 29) *and* V, 77 (p. 31) *for* or one *read* and one — VIII, 9 (p. 49) *before* one *add* and approved by both (parties) — XIV, 4 (p. 61) *close before* an — XVIII, 19, 22 (p. 72) *for* Sûdra *read* Vai*s*ya — XVIII, 38 (p. 73) *for* two parts *read* eight parts — XXI, 1 (p. 83) *read* clothes, ornaments, and — XXI, 5 (p. 84) *for* added fuel to *read* strewed grass round — XXII, 68 (p. 94) *for* head *read* beard — XXIII, 22 (p. 100) *for* sesamum *read* mustard — XXIII, 36 (p. 101) *read* grain exceeding — XXIII, 38 (p. 102) *read* cow, trodden or sneezed — XXIV, 7 (p. 106) *for* whip *read* goad — XXX, 3 (p. 123) *invert the position of* Upâkarman *and* Utsarga — XLIX, 8 (p. 156) *ditto of* full *and* new — LI, 57, 58 (p. 169) *for* left *read* given.

Notes: page 12, *after* –4-9 *add* (14) *and after* –16, 17. *add* M. X, 63; Y. I, 122 — p. 14, note 1, *before* –79, 80. *add* 77, 78. Y. I, 308, 313. – 78. M. VII, 79. — p. 25, note 1, *read* 140-146 . . . XLV, L. *Add at the end of this note* –196. M. VIII, 386 — p. 30 *add* 52. I have translated the reading pañ*ka*sata*m*, which however is hardly so appropriate as the reading pañ*kâ*sata*m*, 'fifty' kârshâpa*n*as. See M. VIII, 2, 97 — p. 32 *add* 88. It is perhaps more advisable to translate '(shall pay) . . . (as a fine),' than to supply the above parentheses. The reading of Nand.'s gloss is doubtful — p. 42, l. 7 from below, *after* 45 *add* ; Colebrooke, Dig. I, 5, CLXXXV. – 37. Y. II, 48. — p. 54 *add* 20, 22. The translation of *s*îrsha by 'fine' rests upon Nand.'s comment — p. 62 *add* Gautama (XVIII, 6) speaks of the appointment of 'one who belongs to the same caste' (Bühler); but the term yonimâtra is ambiguous, and may be referred to 'relatives on the mother's side' as well. — p. 123, note 1, *read* 34-38 *and* 43-47 — p. 131, 17, *read* The next proverb (18) — p. 132, 3, *read* XXXIII — p. 138, 35, *read* XLVII and XLVI, 18. — p. 162 *add* 5. Thus Nand. Taken as part of a Dvandva compound, vratâni would mean 'and the Vratas.' See M. XI, 152 — p. 185, 3 *and* p. 186, 26 *read* X, 190 *and* X, 90. — p. 190 *read* LIX, 1. M. III, 67 — p. 198, 5 *add* 'ekakara, "one who has one hand only" (Nand.), may also mean "with one hand." ' See Âpast. I, 1, 4, 21 ; Gaut. IX, 11. — p. 202, 36.[1] Professor Max Müller points out to me, that the Buddhist Bhikshus do 'wear the marks of an order to which they do not belong' – na vidhivat pravraganti. Viewed in this light, Nand.'s interpretation tends to confirm my own. Cf. Âpast. I, 6, 18, 31.

Transliteration of Oriental Alphabets adopted for the Translations of the Sacred Books of the East.

CONSONANTS.	MISSIONARY ALPHABET. I Class.	II Class.	III Class.	Sanskrit.	Zend.	Pehlevi.	Persian.	Arabic.	Hebrew.	Chinese.
Gutturales.										
1 Tenuis	k	...	....	क	𐬐	[illegible]	ك	ك	כּ	k
2 " aspirata	kh	...	....	ख	𐬑	[illegible]	...	...	כ	kh
3 Media	g	...	....	ग	𐬔	[illegible]	گ	...	גּ	...
4 " aspirata	gh	...	....	घ	𐬖	[illegible]	...	...	ג	...
5 Gutturo-labialis	q	...	....	...	....	...	ق	ق	ק	...
6 Nasalis	ṅ (ng)	...	....	ङ	{ 𐬢 (ng) / 𐬣 (N) }	...	...	...	...	...
7 Spiritus asper	h	...	....	ह	𐬵 (𐬶 *hv*)	[illegible]	ه	ه	ה	h, hs
8 " lenis	'	...	....	...	....	...	ا	ا	א	...
9 " asper faucalis	ʻh	...	....	...	....	...	ح	ح	ח	...
10 " lenis faucalis	ʼh	...	....	...	....	...	ع	ع	ע	...
11 " asper fricatus	...	*ʻh*	....	...	....	...	خ	خ	ח	...
12 " lenis fricatus	...	*ʼh*	....	...	....	...	...	...	...	...
Gutturales modificatae (palatales, &c.)										
13 Tenuis	...	*k*	....	च	𐬗	[illegible]	چ	...	...	*k*
14 " aspirata	...	*kh*	....	छ	....	...	...	...	...	*kh*
15 Media	...	*g*	....	ज	𐬘	[illegible]	ج	ج	...	...
16 " aspirata	...	*gh*	....	झ	....	...	غ	غ	...	...
17 " Nasalis	ñ	...	....	ञ	....	...	...	...	...	...

CONSONANTS (continued).	MISSIONARY ALPHABET.			Sanskrit.	Zend.	Pehlevi.	Persian.	Arabic.	Hebrew.	Chinese.
	I Class.	II Class.	III Class.							
18 Semivocalis	y			य	दद [init. ऌष्]	و	ي	ي	׳	y
19 Spiritus asper		(ẏ)								
20 „ lenis		(ẏ)								
21 „ asper assibilatus		s		श			ش	ش		
22 „ lenis assibilatus		z		ष			ژ			z
Dentales.										
23 Tenuis	t			त			ت	ت	ת	t
24 „ aspirata	th			थ					ת	th
25 „ assibilata			TH				ث	ث		
26 Media	d			द			د	د	ד	
27 „ aspirata	dh			ध					ד	
28 „ assibilata			DH				ذ	ذ		
29 Nasalis	n			न			ن	ن	נ	n
30 Semivocalis	l			ल			ل	ل	ל	l
31 „ mollis 1		l		ळ						
32 „ mollis 2			L							
33 Spiritus asper 1	s			स			(ث)س	س	שׁ	s
34 „ asper 2			s (ʃ)						ס	
35 „ lenis	z						(ذ)ز	ز	ז	z
36 „ asperrimus 1			z (ʒ)				ص	ص	צ	ʒ, ʒh
37 „ asperrimus 2			ẓ (ʒ̇)				ض			

Dentales modificatae (linguales, &c.)										
38 Tenuis		*t*		ट			ط	ط	ט	
39 „ aspirata		*th*		ठ			ظ	ظ		
40 Media		*d*		ड	[illegible]	[illegible]				
41 „ aspirata		*dh*		ढ				ض		
42 Nasalis		*n*		ण	[illegible]	[illegible]				
43 Semivocalis	r			र			ر	ر	ר	
44 „ fricata		*r*								r
45 „ diacritica			R							
46 Spiritus asper	sh			ष	[illegible]	[illegible]				sh
47 „ lenis	zh								ע	
Labiales.										
48 Tenuis	p			प	[illegible]	[illegible]	پ		פ	p
49 „ aspirata	ph			फ					פ	ph
50 Media	b			ब	[illegible]	[illegible]	ب	ب	ב	
51 „ aspirata	bh			भ					ב	
52 Tenuissima		*p*								
53 Nasalis	m			म	[illegible]	[illegible]	م	م	מ	m
54 Semivocalis	w				[illegible]					w
55 „ aspirata	hw									
56 Spiritus asper	f						ف	ف		f
57 „ lenis	v			व	[illegible]	[illegible]	و	و	ו	
58 Anusvâra		*m*		ं	[illegible]					
59 Visarga		*h*		ः						

III Class.

No.	Name	Transl.		(Pāli)		Devanāgarī	Script	Arabic	Arabic	Arabic	Hebrew	Transl.
1	Neutralis	ə̆										ă
2	Laryngo-palatalis	ĕ										
3	„ labialis	ŏ						ا (fin.)				
4	Gutturalis brevis	a				अ		ا (init.)	ـَ	ـَ	ַ	a
5	„ longa	â		(a)		आ		ا	ـَا	ـَا	ָ	â
6	Palatalis brevis	i				इ			ـِ	ـِ	ִ	i
7	„ longa	î		(i)		ई		ى	ـِي	ـِي	ִי	î
8	Dentalis brevis	*li*				ऌ						
9	„ longa	*lí*				ॡ						
10	Lingualis brevis	*ri*				ऋ						
11	„ longa	*rí*				ॠ						
12	Labialis brevis	u				उ			ـُ	ـُ	ֻ	u
13	„ longa	û		(u)		ऊ		ا	ـُو	ـُو	וּ	û
14	Gutturo-palatalis brevis	e					ε (e) ζ (e)					e
15	„ longa	ê (ai)		(e)		ए	ʒ, ʒ	ا			ֵ	ê
16	Diphthongus gutturo-palatalis	âi		(ai)		ऐ			ـَي	ـَي		âi
17	„ „	ei (ĕi)										ei, êi
18	„ „	oi (ŏu)										
19	Gutturo-labialis brevis	o									ֹ	o
20	„ longa	ô (au)		(o)		ओ		ا	ـُ	ـُ	וֹ	
21	Diphthongus gutturo-labialis	âu		(au)		औ	(au)		ـَُو	ـَُو		âu
22	„ „	eu (ĕu)										
23	„ „	ou (ŏu)										
24	Gutturalis fracta	ä										
25	Palatalis fracta	ï										
26	Labialis fracta	ü						ء				ü
27	Gutturo-labialis fracta	ö										